T0312123

Mastering Executive Coaching

This book aims to enrich the knowledge and toolkit of executive coaches and help them on their development path towards mastery. Edited by three leading practitioners, it brings together the expertise of an international range of Master Coaches, and provides evidence-based practical chapters across a broad range of topics, including contracting, ethical dilemmas, coaching board members and non-executive directors, and the use of psychometrics.

Mastering Executive Coaching will be essential reading for executive coaches, consultants and trainers who are looking to develop their practice. It will also be highly relevant for Masters-level students of coaching and coaching psychology.

Jonathan Passmore is an internationally recognized chartered psychologist and multi-award-winning coach. He has held board level roles in public, private and not-for-profit organizations, and has worked for PWC, IBM and was managing director of Embrion, a psychology consulting company working in the oil and gas sector. He is professor of psychology at the University of Evora, Portugal and director of the Henley Centre for Coaching, Henley Business School.

Brian O. Underhill is an industry-recognized expert in the design and management of worldwide executive coaching implementations. He is the author of *Executive Coaching for Results: The Definitive Guide to Developing Organizational Leaders* and founder of CoachSource, the world's largest executive coaching provider, with over 1,100 coaches in 100 countries. Brian's executive coaching work has successfully focused on helping clients achieve positive, measurable, long-term change in leadership behavior.

Marshall Goldsmith is a world-renowned business educator and coach. He has been recognized every year for the past four years as one of the "Top 10 Business Thinkers in the World" and a top-rated executive coach by Thinkers50. He is the author or editor of 35 books, which have sold more than two million copies, been translated into 30 languages, and become bestsellers in 12 countries.

To Victor Passmore, a WW2 veteran,
father and an inspiration. – JP

To my beautiful wife, Julie, with all my love.
Prov 31:30. – BU

To Alan Mulally – The former CEO of Boeing
Commercial Aircraft and Ford. I view him as
the greatest corporate leader of this century.
Although, in theory, I was his coach, I have
learned more about leadership from him than
anyone I have ever met! – MG

Mastering Executive Coaching

Edited by Jonathan Passmore,
Brian O. Underhill and
Marshall Goldsmith

Routledge
Taylor & Francis Group

LONDON AND NEW YORK

First published 2019
by Routledge
2 Park Square, Milton Park, Abingdon, Oxon OX14 4RN

and by Routledge
52 Vanderbilt Avenue, New York, NY 10017

Routledge is an imprint of the Taylor & Francis Group, an informa business

British Library Cataloguing-in-Publication Data
A catalogue record for this book is available from the British Library

Library of Congress Cataloging-in-Publication Data
Names: Passmore, Jonathan, editor. | Underhill, Brian O.,
    1969– editor. | Goldsmith, Marshall, editor.
Title: Mastering executive coaching / edited by Jonathan
    Passmore, Brian Underhill and Marshall Goldsmith.
Description: Abingdon, Oxon ; New York, NY : Routledge,
    2019. | Includes bibliographical references and index.
Identifiers: LCCN 2018035720 | ISBN 9780815372929
    (hardback) | ISBN 9780815372912 (pbk.) | ISBN
    9781351244671 (ebook)
Subjects: LCSH: Executive coaching.
Classification: LCC HD30.4 .M3726 2019 | DDC
    658.4/07124—dc23
LC record available at https://lccn.loc.gov/2018035720

ISBN: 978-0-8153-7292-9 (hbk)
ISBN: 978-0-8153-7291-2 (pbk)
ISBN: 978-1-351-24467-1 (ebk)

Typeset in Bembo
by Apex CoVantage, LLC

Contents

Figures

Tables

Contributors

Tim Anstiss MD

Tim is a medical doctor and tutor at Henley Business School. He has written widely on coaching, positive psychology, and well-being and runs a private coaching and consulting practice.

John L. Bennett PhD

John is the Wayland H. Cato Jr. Chair in Leadership, Professor of Business & Behavioral Science, and Director of the Graduate Programs with the McColl School of Business at Queens University of Charlotte. He is author of numerous articles and three books, including *Coaching for Change* (Routledge, 2014), and serves on the editorial board of *International Coaching Psychology Review*.

Paul Brown PhD

Paul is a clinical and organizational psychologist, executive coach, and supervisor. The first Professor of Organisational Neuroscience in the UK, he is now Faculty Professor – Applied Neuroscience, Monarch Business School, Switzerland. Living in Laos, Southeast Asia, he consults and teaches worldwide.

Mary Wayne Bush EdD

Mary Wayne is an internationally recognized coach researcher, speaker, and writer. She has authored original research on executive coaching and is the co-author of *Coaching for Change* (Routledge, 2014). Mary Wayne served on the faculty of the doctoral program in Organization Development and Change at Colorado Technical University and is on the editorial board of *Coaching: An International Journal of Theory, Research and Practice*.

David Clutterbuck

David is Visiting Professor at Henley Business School and Co-founder of the European Mentoring and Coaching Council. He is now one of two EMCC special ambassadors, tasked with spreading good practice internationally. Author, co-author, or editor of some 70 books, he is practice lead for Coaching and Mentoring International, a network of trainer-consultants in 40 countries.

Damian Goldvarg PhD

Damian has 30 years of experience providing executive coaching, leadership training, and facilitation in over 50 countries. He is a Master Certified Coach, is an accredited coach supervisor (ESIA), and received his PhD in Organizational Psychology from Alliant University. He was the 2013–2014 ICF Global President.

Suzy Green PhD

Suzy is a clinical and organizational psychologist, the founder of The Positivity Institute, and an Honorary Fellow for the Centre for Positive Psychology, Melbourne Graduate School of Education, University of Melbourne, Australia.

Peter Hawkins PhD

Peter is Visiting Professor at Henley Business School and an internationally renowned consultant. He has published widely and his previous books include *Leadership Team Coaching* and *Coaching, Mentoring and Organizational Consultancy*.

Rebecca J. Jones PhD

Rebecca is Associate Professor and MSc Coaching program director at Henley Business School, UK. Her research interests lie in examining factors that influence coaching effectiveness and utilizing quantitative research methodology to explore the efficacy of coaching.

Manfred F. R. Kets de Vries PhD

Manfred is the Distinguished Clinical Professor of Leadership Development and Organizational Change and the Raoul de Vitry d'Avaucourt Chaired Professor of Leadership Development, Emeritus, at INSEAD. He is the founder of the INSEAD Global Leadership Centre.

Andrew Ktoris

Andrew is the assistant director of HR People and Organizational Development, at the University of Birmingham, UK. He leads the University's Coaching Academy.

Kate Lanz

Kate has had a successful career in international business, notably with Diageo, before training in psychology and establishing her thriving global practice as an executive coach and supervisor. Kate is currently completing a doctorate based in her research into applied neuroscience in business with a focus on gender. She is based in London.

Anja Lindberg

Anja is a PCC-certified Coach by ICF, CBT-therapist, author and holds an MA in organizational psychology. She is CEO of Coachutbildning Sverige AB, the first Swedish coach-training company with a training accredited by ICF. Anja has worked for many years on developing, training and supervising managers, coaches, teams and organizations internationally.

Kimcee McAnally PhD

Kimcee is the Chief Coaching Officer (CCO) for CoachSource and co-authored *Executive Coaching for Results: The Definitive Guide to Developing Organizational Leaders*. She is a PCC (professional certified coach) with ICF and a certified coach supervisor.

Margaret Moore

Margaret is a 17-year veteran of the biotechnology industry, founded the Wellcoaches School of Coaching for health professionals in 2000, which has trained more than 11,000 coaches in 50 countries. Margaret is co-founder and co-director of the Institute of Coaching at McLean Hospital and co-author of the *Coaching Psychology Manual*.

Howard Morgan

Howard was named one of the 50 top coaches globally, has been recognized as one of five coaches with "a proven track record of success," and has published several books. As an executive coach, Howard has led major organizational change initiatives in partnership with senior executives across all levels and industries.

Colm Murphy

Colm is an executive and team coach and the founder of Dublin based Dynamic Leadership Development. He is also Head of Coaching Programmes at Smurfit UCD Executive Development. Colm is completing a doctorate in Team Coaching at Portsmouth Business School, UK.

Chris Pollino

Chris is a member of the People Development Group at Genentech, where he manages executive assessment, coaching, and succession and talent management. Chris holds a BS degree from Babson College, an MBA from Northeastern

University, an MA in Counseling Psychology from USF, and coaching certification from Columbia's Coaching Program.

Doug Riddle PhD

Doug led the coaching practice at the Center for Creative Leadership with a global team ensuring the best professional coaching and coaching education available to clients worldwide. Doug is the lead editor on the widely praised *CCL Handbook of Coaching in Organizations* (2015) and has written multiple articles. He holds doctorates in psychology and theology and is a licensed psychologist and Fellow of the American Psychological Association.

Josh Rogers MA ACC

Josh is the global executive practice leader for Walmart, Inc., where he is responsible for coaching strategy and operations, cadre management, and internal coach development. Josh also serves as lead internal coach.

Caroline Rook PhD

Caroline is a lecturer at Henley Business School. Her research relates to creating healthy workplaces. She has been involved in research and practice related to leadership, well-being, and coaching at Lord Ashcroft International Business School, INSEAD, and University of Exeter.

Philippe Rosinski

Philippe is Professor at the Kenichi Ohmae Graduate School of Business in Tokyo, an author, and a coaching pioneer. He has written widely, including two books: *Coaching across Cultures* and *Global Coaching*. He was the first European to have been designated Master Certified Coach by the ICF. Based in Belgium, Philippe enjoys serving clients and cooperating with partners internationally.

Ryan Sharman

Ryan is a People and Organization Development Consultant at the University of Birmingham. He is one of the internal executive level coaches of the Coaching Academy.

Ole Michael Spaten PhD

Ole is a licensed psychologist, accredited supervisor, and director of the Coaching Psychology Unit, Aalborg University. He is a leading pioneer in Danish coaching and conducted the first randomized control trial in Scandinavia evaluating the effectiveness of brief cognitive behavioral coaching. Ole is the founding editor-in-chief of the *Danish Journal of Coaching Psychology*.

Charles I. Story

Charles is President of ECS Group, Inc. He has more than 35 years' experience in the leadership development arena and is certified as an executive coach by the Behavioral Coaching Institute. He provides coaching solutions to organizations that want to develop and retain a strong base of executive talent. Clients have included Microsoft, EY, Deloitte, and many others.

Eve Turner

Eve is a Fellow at Henley Business School and the University of Southampton, and an award-winning coach and coach supervisor with Master Executive Coach and Supervision accreditation. Eve has co-edited one book on supervision and has two more co-authored books in the pipeline. She set up and leads the Global Supervisors' Network for qualified, experienced supervisors to continue learning through monthly, virtual sessions.

Rebecca Turner PhD

Rebecca founded San Francisco–based Turner Consulting Group, supporting executives and teams for leadership excellence and developing a winning culture. She is known for her approach to challenging conflicts in organizations, including healthcare, finance, and technology. She is a former professor of Organizational Psychology, California School of Professional Psychology.

Christian van Nieuwerburgh PhD

Christian is Professor of Coaching and Positive Psychology at the University of East London and the Executive Director of Growth Coaching International, a leading provider of coach training for the education sector. He is the editor-in-chief of the academic journal, Coaching: An International Journal of Theory, Research and Practice.

Part I

Mastering themes

Chapter 1

Mastering executive coaching

Jonathan Passmore, Brian O. Underhill, and Marshall Goldsmith

Imagine my surprise (Underhill) as I walked into Marshall Goldsmith's office in the mid-1990s to find him on speakerphone with a client of a cell phone service provider. Many of us worked for Marshall, conducting thousands of 360 debrief sessions up until that point – generally one session by phone or in person to review a leader's multi-source feedback from their key stakeholders.

This client – the VP Marketing – was saying, "Marshall, I loved that one feedback session you did with me. But I want more! Can we do many more of those, perhaps for 1 entire year?" Marshall quickly agreed. And she went on, "And can some of your consultants coach other members of my team?" Marshall agreed again.

Soon I found myself assigned to two leaders, armed with their feedback report and a mandate to coach them for one year. But there was just one problem; I wondered to myself: "What were we supposed to do with these people for one entire year?"

Our 360 debrief work morphed into full-year executive coaching, literally overnight based on client demand, and we had to figure it out as we were going along. This, and a score of other similar conversations around the same time, and the coaching industry was underway.

Origins of coaching

Coaching as a profession has a fairly recent history compared to other professions (Brock, 2015). The years 1995–1996 are identified as critical in the life of the coaching profession, according to industry historian Vikki Brock (Brock, 2015; Brock, 2018). During these years, Thomas Leonard formed the International Coach Federation (ICF) as an alumni association for graduations of his own Coach U academy; graduates of Coaches Training Institute (formed by Laura Whitworth) would join the Professional and Personal Coaches Association (PPCA) in northern California. At this point, there were already eight professional coaching schools. A 1996 *Newsweek* article may have been one of the first mass media acknowledgements of the arrival of coaching (Hamilton, 1996). A special issue of *Consulting Psychology Journal* devoted entirely to coaching also appeared in 1996. And coincidentally (and somewhat comically), 1996 is the year I (Underhill) began working for Marshall Goldsmith, who had just put out his first of what would become over 30 books (Hesselbein, Goldsmith, & Beckhard, 1996).

In the UK, John Whitmore, Graham Alexander, and Alan Fine had been working with clients, helping them reflect on their performance. From these conversations, starting in the 1980s the GROW model emerged. Others joined the wagon train spurred on by John's book *Coaching for Performance* (Whitmore, 1992). This led to the development of several coaching programs in the UK, including one of the most popular, a distance learning course, from Newcastle College. I (Passmore) and many other UK coaches started here in the late 1990s, with this first step into coaching, applying these skills inside my organizations to help develop individual and team performance. In parallel with this, the EMCC (European Coaching and Mentoring Council) was being formed by David Megginson, David Clutterbuck, and others, and by the early 2000s the UK saw the formation of the Special Group in Coaching Psychology – a group within the British Psychological Society – by Stephen Palmer, Alison Whybrow, and Jonathan Passmore, and the formation of the Association of Coaching by Katherine Tulpa and Alex Szabo.

This process of coach development was being played out in a dozen or more countries across the world, each with its own unique pathway.

Since 2000, the pace of growth has continued in the coaching industry (e.g., Abel & Nair, 2012; Dunlop, 2017; Passmore, Brown, & Csigas, 2017). The number of coaches in the marketplace has exploded. The International Coach Federation boasted 400 subscribers in 1996, 7,900 in 2004, and 25,000 members in 2014 (International Coach Federation, n.d.). ICF estimates a total industry of 53,300 coaches in 2016 (up from 47,500 in 2012), with 1,500 new coaches per year in the past four years (International Coach Federation, 2012; International Coach Federation, 2016). An "executive coaching" search in the PsycINFO database produced 238 citations between 2012 and 2017, compared to just 32 between 1995 and 2000 (Dunlop, 2017). Twenty-three coaching associations were identified in 2014 (Maltbia, Marsick, & Ghosh, 2014), which rose to 37 professional coaching associations just four years later (Peer Resources, 2018). As early as 2007, universities were establishing coaching degree programs, with 19 such programs emerging in Australia, UK, US, and Canada (Grant, 2008) at institutions such as Columbia, Queens University of Charlotte, Sydney, East London, Oxford Brookes, and Henley Business School. In its 10-year study on the profession, the Conference Board noted, "the story of executive coaching in organizations over the past 10 years is one of remarkable growth" (Abel, Ray, & Nair, 2016, p. 7).

This has brought on immediate concerns regarding widely varying coaching methodologies, practitioner backgrounds/training, uncertain results, and disparate costs. Anyone could hang out a business card and declare, "I am an executive coach." A 2004 *Harvard Business Review* article dubbed the new profession 'the Wild West.' The authors noted, "like the Wild West of yesteryear, this frontier is chaotic, largely unexplored, and fraught with risk, yet immensely promising" (Sherman & Freas, 2004).

Indeed, this promise has been materializing over the past two decades with the massive adoption of corporate-wide executive coaching programs, the rise of internal coaches, increased recognition of international accreditation standards, and a slow but gradual shift from 'magic' and 'art' towards 'science' and 'evidence-based practice,' as coaching has followed the development pathway of many other emerging professions from case study towards meta-analysis (Passmore & Fillery Travis, 2011). The early days of coaching's focus on poor performers has largely been replaced with a focus on coaching the brightest and the best. Executives increasingly view working with a coach as a status symbol. A US study found the use of coaching for performance problems has decreased by 10% during the five years from 2013 to 2018 (Underhill et al., 2013; Coach-Source, 2018).

Why coaching – why now?

Many industries have emerged with the advent of new technologies, which when built upon themselves further expanded multiple applications of that technology.

But given that coaching is not particularly reliant on the advent of any new technology, why would now be the time for coaching to reach full stride?

We believe that there is now a good evidence base (Bozer & Jones, 2018; Jones, Woods, & Guillaume, 2016) and that there is increasing collaboration between professional bodies around ethics and coach training. Clearly more needs to be done in both camps of science and practice.

Alongside this, the challenges of a global economy, increasing migration, and technological change all make for a world of work that is more dynamic and in which there is a blurring of home and work. Coaching has a role to play in helping people to navigate these boundaries and make the right choices for them, their families, and their organizations, while in other domains – from safety to driver development, prisons to healthcare – coaching can play a role in helping individuals to take greater personal responsibility and become more 'choiceful.'

Towards mastery

In 2016, we (Underhill) made special arrangements for seasoned senior coaches in our network to finally get their ICF Professional Certified Coach (PCC) training. Many had been coaching for 10–20 years, often with doctorate degrees and other relevant trainings, but simply had not pursued (or even needed) an official credential in the field. ICF rules were changing in the fall, so if there was ever a time to get this training, it would be now.

Worried that no one would sign up, we negotiated a liberal cancellation policy with our PCC trainer. Though our clients were beginning to favor certified coaches, it was still a minority view. Most of these coaches were quite successful already and really had little need for additional training of this nature. We put out the announcement with fingers crossed.

The class sold out in seven days. We quickly added a second class, which sold out in four days.

Perhaps this is as great an example as any of the openness toward a senior coach furthering their own growth and development. Practitioners in this field often speak of "continuous learning," "self-development," etc. Coaching conferences have been increasing in frequency, with increasing numbers of practitioners in attendance. Much like our desire to assist clients toward greater mastery of their craft, we as coaches also desire to further our own growth and development – our mastery.

Towards the future

As we have noted above, various forms of coaching are emerging, with coaching being used for driver development (Passmore & Mortimer, 2011), on offshore oil rigs (Passmore, 2013), in prisons (McGregor, 2015), and in the armed forces (Passmore & Rehman, 2012). In reality, coaching can be used in any situation where there are opportunities for learning and time pressures are not critical. The evidence is that coaching is a far more powerful style, than instruction. It enables individuals to make choices about what would work best for them and how to vary principles to individual circumstances. It thus may be of little surprise that it has become the tool of choice for development in organizations.

The journey to mastery

As three active authors in the field, we were conscious of the proliferation of coaching titles. Each has something to offer the reader, but most books remain focused on the new or emerging coach. We wanted to offer a titled aimed at more the more experienced practitioners, helping them on their journey towards mastery, and at those working at the senior leader or c-suite level in organizations. To do this, we have invited a range of voices, with different experiences and with different perspectives, to contribute their insights. In addition to the normal chapter and references, we have asked our contributors to also include a series of resources. These are designed as a resource for those wanting to take their knowledge deeper. They typically include YouTube video clips and links to articles or books.

In Chapter 2, Eve Turner and Peter Hawkins discuss the issue of contracting and how master coaches can enhance the way they contract to improve client outcomes for individuals and organizations through the use of tripartite and multi-party contracts.

In Chapter 3, Eve Turner and Jonathan Passmore discuss the issue of coaching ethics. They note how ethics is central to everyday thinking, as well as coaching. They discuss the emergence of ethics in professional bodies and offer an ethical decision-making framework to complement the professional ethics codes for use by professional coaches.

In Chapter 4, Rebecca J. Jones and Brian O. Underhill provide an overview of the training evaluation theory and evidence and translate how this can be applied to evaluating coaching. Using a framework of coaching outcomes, they show how coaching can be evaluated at multiple levels.

In Chapter 5, Rebecca Turner, Howard Morgan, and Charles I. Story explore behavioral change. This chapter introduces executive coaching approaches and techniques for working with senior leaders who exhibit 'unhelpful' and 'negative' behaviors that can lead to dissatisfaction or unhealthy relationships at work.

In Chapter 6, Mary Wayne Bush and John Bennett explore how coaches can contribute towards wider organizational change. Their chapter focuses on how coaching supports those who lead change and can contribute toward more successful change outcomes and includes key approaches and tools for working with change managers.

Ole Michael Spaten and Suzy Green focus on the role of meaning, purpose, values, and strengths in Chapter 7. They argue that by providing senior leaders the opportunities to engage in executive coaching, not only can they increase their own levels of meaning but they may, through their influential roles, also assist their organizations to create greater levels of meaning for others in their organizations.

In Chapter 8, Doug Riddle explores what coaches can do to make the value to the organization more obvious and direct rather than depend on anecdotal evidence from their clients' expressing satisfaction with the quality of their work.

In Chapter 9, Philippe Rosinski discussed how senior teams can benefit from cross-cultural team coaching. In the chapter, Philippe introduces the 10 co-steps process for coaching intercultural executive teams and discusses the application of his cultural orientations framework (COF) for use with more senior clients.

In Chapter 10, David Clutterbuck and Colm Murphy explore 'internally resourced coaching.' The contributors note the growth of line managers adopting a coaching style of management and the use of internal accredited coaches within organizations. These new internal coaches can be both highly effective and financially prudent, driving both improved performance and financial savings by reducing the need for external coaches.

In Chapter 11, Brian O. Underhill discusses an emerging trend in executive coaching of centralizing coaching provision. This involves bringing the provision of coaching services under one external provider. The aim is to improve the coordination of coaching and to improve the overall quality control of coaching provision by setting minimum standards for the external provider. As a way forward, Underhill offers the 4C coaching maturity model, where coaching moves from a casual activity to an integrated practice across the organization at five levels, from how it's marketed to what's on offer (menu), how it's overseen (management), how it's measured (metrics), and who delivers it (members).

In Chapter 12, Tim Anstiss and Margaret Moore explore the potential benefits of health and well-being coaching for senior leaders, whose health challenges, such as obesity and lack of exercise, can have significant and serious implications for themselves as well as creating risk factors for their organizations.

In Chapter 13, Manfred F. R. Kets de Vries and Caroline Rook explore clinical issues facing experienced coaches working in the c-suite: how to identify these conditions and what coaches should do to help their clients move forward, if that's possible. Specifically, they look at four different clinical issues: the narcissistic personality, bipolar personality, anti-social personality (commonly known as psychopathic personality), and the obsessive-compulsive personality, and how these can manifest themselves in c-suite leaders.

In Chapter 14, Paul Brown and Kate Lanz argue that evidenced-based and specifically neuroscience-informed coaching is the way forward in our work with leaders. They acknowledge that while our knowledge of brain science is still in its infancy, they claim that coaching is fundamentally about helping individuals make changes to their brain and also to help leaders better understand this tool.

In the final four chapters, we present a series of case studies focusing on the application in a number of diverse organizations, including IKEA, Walmart, a university (University of Birmingham, UK), and a biotech company.

We hope the book provides a useful tool for your continued developmental journey as a coach, supported by the additional materials offered by each contributor.

References

Abel, A. L., & Nair, S. (2012). *Executive coaching survey: 2012 edition*. New York, NY: The Conference Board.

Abel, A. L., Ray, R. L., & Nair, S. (2016). *Global executive coaching survey 2016: Developing leaders and leadership capabilities at all levels*. New York, NY: The Conference Board.

Bozer, G., & Jones, R. J. (2018). Understanding the factors that determine workplace coaching effectiveness: A systematic literature review. *European Journal of Work and Organizational Psychology.* 27(3), 342–361.

doi:10.1080/1359432X.2018.1446946

Brock, V. (2015). *The history of Coaching*. Retrieved June 25, from www.vikkibrock.com/wp-content/uploads/2015/09/History-of-Coaching-by-Vikki-Brock-Management-Article.pdf

Brock, V. (2018). Personal communication with Brian Underhill, July 7, 2018.

CoachSource. (2018). *Executive coaching for results: Industry research*. San Jose, CA: CoachSource, LLC.

Dunlop, C. W. (2017). *The success and failure of the coaching industry*. Retrieved July 1, 2018, from www.forbes.com/sites/forbescoachescouncil/2017/10/05/the-success-and-failure-of-the-coaching-industry/#91977d66765f

Grant, A. (2008). Past, present and future: The evolution of professional coaching and coaching psychology. In S. Palmer & A. Whybrow (Eds.), *Handbook of coaching psychology: A guide for practitioners* (pp. 43–59). Sussex, UK: Routledge.

Hesselbein, F., Goldsmith, M., & Beckhard, R. (1996). *The leader of the future*. San Francisco, CA: Jossey-Bass.

International Coach Federation. (n.d.). *History of ICF*. Retrieved July 3, from https://coachfederation.org/history

International Coach Federation. (2012). *2012 ICF global coaching study: Executive summary*. Retrieved July 7, from https://coachfederation.org/app/uploads/2017/12/2012ICFGlobalCoachingStudy-ExecutiveSummary.pdf

International Coach Federation. (2016). *2016 ICF global coaching study: Executive summary*. Retrieved June 26, 2018, from http://researchportal.coachfederation.org/MediaStream/PartialView?documentId=2779

Jones, R. J., Woods, S. A., & Guillaume, Y. R. F. (2016). The effectiveness of workplace coaching: A meta-analysis of learning and performance outcomes from coaching. *Journal of Occupational and Organizational Psychology, 89*(2), 249–277 doi:10.1111/joop.12119

Maltbia, T. E., Marsick, V. J., & Ghosh, R. (2014). Executive and organizational coaching: A review of insights drawn from literature to inform HRD practice. *Advances in Developing Human Resources, 16*(2), 161–183.

McGregor, C. (2015). *Coaching behind bars: Facing challenges and creating hope in a women's prison*. Maidenhead: Open University Press.

Hamilton, K. (1996). Need a life? get a coach. *Newsweek*, February 5, 1996, p48 Retrieved August 21, 2018, from https://coachesconsole.com/v3/uploads/supplements/needalifegetacoach_032c1ef00b345.pdf

Passmore, J. (2013). Coaching in safety critical environments. *The Coaching Psychologist, 9*(1), 27–30.

Passmore, J., Brown, H., & Csigas, Z. (2017). *The State if Play in European Coaching and Mentoring*. Henley Business School-EMCC: Henley on Thames. Retrieved August 21, from www.henley.ac.uk/articles/european-coaching-mentoring-research-project

Passmore, J., & Fillery-Travis, A. (2011). A critical review of executive coaching research: A decade of progress and what's to come. *Coaching: An International Journal of Theory, Practice & Research, 4*(2), 70–88.

Passmore, J., & Mortimer, L. (2011). The experience of using coaching as a learning technique in learner driver development: An IPA study of adult learning. *International Coaching Psychology Review, 6*(1), 33–45.

Passmore, J., & Rehman, H. (2012). Coaching as a learning methodology – a mixed methods study in driver development using a Randomized Controlled Trial and thematic analysis. *International Coaching Psychology Review, 7*(2), 166–184.

Peer Resources. (2018). *Professional associations*. Retrieved July 1, 2018, from www.peer.ca/coachorgs.html#profs

Sherman, S., & Freas, A. (2004, November). The wild west of executive coaching. *Harvard Business Review, 82*(11), 82–90.

Underhill, B. O., McAnally, K., Bastian, C., Desrosiers, M., Golay, l., & Tuller, M. (2013). *Executive coaching industry research: 2013 final report*. San Jose, CA: CoachSource, LLC.

Whitmore, J. (1992). *Coaching for Performance*. London: Nicholas Breadley.

Chapter 2

Mastering contracting

Eve Turner and Peter Hawkins

Introduction

Contracting for coaching, mentoring, or supervising is growing as the profession grows. Much of this growth is in organizations, for coaches, mentors, and supervisors, working both internally and externally, and the need for rigorous contracting has never been greater. Organizations are under pressure to deliver strong results, with often decreasing finances, and they need to prove the value of investment in this area. Coaches, mentors, and supervisors are balancing the need to provide added value, for example providing organizational themes from coaching, while maintaining trust and confidentiality with their individual clients.

The Ridler Report, an annual review of corporate purchasers of coaching (Mann, 2016), suggests that three-quarters of organizations encourage line managers to review coachee's objectives in a three-way meeting (2016, p 61), underpinning how prevalent this form of contracting is. Organizations rate the areas of "increase in coachee's business performance" (92%), "coachee develops greater self-awareness," (92%) and "coachee develops their leadership" (91%) as the most relevant to their definition of coaching, with "coach makes suggestions/gives advice for action to coachee" (30%) as rated bottom (Mann, 2016, p. 14). As coaches, mentors, and supervisors, how does this fit with our purpose for coaching? It is through contracting that we will establish aligned goals and then be able to evaluate accordingly.

In this chapter, we consider what we mean by tripartite and multi-stakeholder contracting, why contracting is important to all parties, and how we ensure it works in the best interests of all those involved and to the wider benefit of society.

Theory and evidence

All forms of coaching relationships need to begin with a clear contract, co-created between the coach, the coachee (whether an individual or a group or team), and the joint purpose or work they are undertaking together. This we refer to as the coaching triangle – the coach, the coachee, and the work. This is similar to English's "The Three-Cornered Contract" in relation to work-shops that she had been contracted to run by a third party (1975, p. 383). The theme has been developed by researchers and authors (Hay, 2007; Rogers, 2008; Eriksson, 2011; Passmore & Fillery-Travis, 2011; Ogilvy & Ellam-Dyson, 2012; Cowan, 2013; Lee, 2016; Turner & Hawkins, 2016). Hay uses the three corners to represent the client, the practitioner, and the organization, often represented by HR (2007, p. 113). English also refers to a four-cornered contract, adding the line manager because they "can provide valuable developmental support to your clients provided they understand the nature of the coaching" (2007, p. 115). Hay further refers to multi-party contracting where there may be a variety of stakeholders, such as a consultancy employing the coach an organiza-tion uses, or professional bodies, which may be 'silent' but will have an influence (2007, pp. 117–118).

Many authors and researchers have advocated the benefits of involving mul-tiple stakeholders in the coaching contract. Stewart, Palmer, Wilkin, and Ker-rin (2008) show that coaches, coaches, and stakeholders agree that positive coaching transfer is related to a pro-development organizational climate, access to development, and procedural support for development (2008, p. 99). Rog-ers believes, "The more you and your client can include the whole system, the more effective the coaching is likely to be" (2008, p. 123). Passmore and Fillery-Travis point to the relevance of a wider support network for coaching (2011, p. 77).

There is some evidence that management support can have a positive impact on coaching outcomes (e.g., Goldsmith & Morgan, 2004; Knights & Poppleton, 2007; Stewart et al., 2008; Ogilvy & Ellam-Dyson, 2012; Carter & Miller, 2009; Mann, 2016; Turner & Hawkins, 2016). However, there has been little published research about the means to achieve this. Kilburg (2000) provided a "Model Agreement for Coaching Services" (2000, pp. 235–236). However, while there are references to confidentiality, the provision of resources, and a signature from the 'Client's sponsor/supervisor (if appropriate),' it is unclear how active a role the organization plays. Elsewhere he states that the "initial agreement may need to include other parties, such as the vice-president for human resources, and the executive's manager or manager once removed as part of the negotiations and for accountability for outcomes and payment" (2000, p. 72).

Rostron (2013, pp. 264–266) provides a list of questions to use in contract-ing, crucially including whether the line manager and senior management are supportive of the coaching process. She notes the link between coaching and the overall working system and believes this has "huge implications for the coach's interventions with the executive" (2013, p. 266). She quotes O'Neill describing coaches needing "to hold a 'bifocal' view, being able to see their cli-ent in the system as well as seeing oneself in the system" (2013, p. 267). Rostron talks of "agreed meetings between coach, executive and line management"

(2013, p. 269) and of the potential for "conflict of interest between the goals and expectations of the individual being coached, and those of the company, as well as the issues of quality standards and confidentiality" (2013, p. 270).

Goldsmith and Morgan's research in eight major corporations demonstrates that coaching has considerably greater success when the organization is actively involved (2004, online). In discussing how to create a coaching culture, Hawkins warns of the danger of becoming too focused on the individual client and advocates that "good executive coaching always maintains a focus on all three clients: the individual, the organization and the relationship between the two" (2012, p. 56). He sees multi-stakeholder contracting as a way to achieve this and advocates the use of evaluation that also harvests the collective learning for the organization from all the different coaching that is going on.

The potential for lack of clarity around contracting on outcomes is discussed by Coutu and Kauffman describing "sketchy mechanisms for monitoring the effectiveness of a coaching engagement" (2009, online) in their research with 140 coaches. All but eight said the "focus shifted from what they were originally hired to do." While 3% said they were hired to address personal issues, 76% responded positively when asked if they had ever assisted executives with personal issues. We are not suggesting that there is a problem per se discussing personal issues; indeed, we firmly acknowledge that the person doesn't leave the rest of themselves at the workplace front door. It is more the challenge that Peterson raises: "The problem is when organizations ask for one thing and get something else. Often companies have no idea what the coaches are really doing." In part, he puts this down to coaches being "very lax in evaluating the impact of their work and communicating results to executives and stakeholders" (2009, online).

Eriksson's research in Sweden with 85 organizational representatives, including coaches, found that "there is no communication between the three parties (coachee, purchaser, and executive coach)" (2011, p. 24). She advocates a three-way meeting to "make necessary clarifications around the commission," monitor the quality and the outcome, and discuss evaluation.

Multi-stakeholder contracting is one way to ensure there is agreement on evaluation through shared responsibility and is highlighted in Turner and Hawkins' research. Drawing on 651 coaches, organizational representatives, and individual clients, they found that the vast majority (four-fifths) of coaches and organizational representatives believed multi-stakeholder contracting was good practice; nearly all the remainder, along with individual clients, did not have strong views (2016, p. 56). The areas highlighted by Ogilvy and Ellam-Dyson, Eriksson, and others were borne out with respondents believing that greater clarity was key to successful contracting and evaluation.

Lee emphasizes this, believing that "Contracting is a way of putting executive coaching into operational form so that ambiguity is replaced with predictability" (2016, p. 42). He differentiates five types of contracting as in Table 2.1.

Passmore (2016) talks of four types of coaching contracts, their purpose, and the relevant parties, as seen in Table 2.2.

Table 2.1 Lee's types of contracting

	Types of contracting
"1	Pre-contracting, the decisions that precede the formal contracting efforts
2	Change contracts, describing the ways the client (individual coachee) hopes to develop as an executive with the support of the coach and sponsoring organization.
3	Process contracts, which contain the methods and responsibilities of the coach, the client, and others that combine to make coaching happen
4	Business contracts, specifying the commercial and legal arrangements between the coach and the sponsor
5	Psychological contracts, the tacit but potentially powerful expectations among the parties."

Adapted from Lee (2016, pp. 40–41)

Table 2.2 Passmore's types of contracting

Type	Purpose	Parties
Coaching contract	To manage the main client relationship	Coaching provider and purchaser
Multi-party agreements	To establish focus of sessions and roles of respective parties	Key stakeholders
Session agreements	To establish an agreement for the duration of an individual client program	Coach and individual coachee
Homework agreements or contracts	To agree what respective parties might do between sessions	Coach and individual coachee

Passmore (2016)

A fundamental question in coaching, central to contracting and on which there has been no universal agreement, is "Who is the client?" In her research, St John-Brooks (2014) gets differing responses from internal coaches. One thought that employers' interest was so fraught with difficulty it was not worth considering, while another respondent thought the primary responsibility should be to the organization. Eriksson highlighted a contrast between the executive coach group who had a more personal and holistic individual "life as a whole" level and the purchasers' "more result-oriented focus with a task/result oriented focus tied to company development" (2011, pp. 4–5). Scoular describes the con- tractual situation as "tricky," believing the "real client is not the person sitting in front of you, it's the organization paying the bill" (2011, p. 64). She argues that:

usually former therapists . . . maintain that the 'client' to whom they have primary and sole responsibility is the person sitting in front of them. I feel quite passionately that this is wrong: ethically, and indeed legally, if the coach is contracted with the organization then the organization is the client.

(2011, p. 65)

Yet, as Passmore et al. (2017) note from their research, the majority of coaches still believe that the individual client is their primary or sole client, even in organizational client projects. Hawkins (2017) argues that this is a false dichotomy as for the individual or team to flourish they must be in dynamic co-creation with their environmental niche and thus in service of their stakeholders.

Contracting in team coaching is an even more complex process. Hawkins (2017) argues that team coaches must be clear between the initial engagement contract, which might be with the team leader or team gatekeeper, and the fuller contract after the completion of the initial inquiry process, which needs to be with the whole team. He also argues the need to get the multistakeholder voices into both the inquiry and second contracting processes.

There is also some evidence of varied comfort in working with organizations in multi-stakeholder contracting. In research with six coaches, Cowan aimed to understand "the experiences of external executive coaches working with coachees' assigned goals . . . to find out about the issues they face . . . and to explore with them how they manage that process" (2013, p. 14). She notes, "The process for contracting for, and managing, assigned goals, presents opportunities but also pitfalls to which a less experienced or reflective coach may be vulnerable. This has implications for the profession in terms of standards and training" (2013, p. 23).

Aims and processes in contracting

The contracting process in coaching is to establish the fundamental three pillars of the 'Why, What, and How' that this particular coaching relationship must build their work upon. To establish the 'Why,' or purpose of the coaching, we engage the coachee in three simple inquiries:

1   "Tell me about you and what has brought you here?"
2   "Tell me about who your work is in service of? What do those stakeholders currently value and what do they need you to develop and step up to in the future?"
3   "What is the work we need to do together, that you cannot do by yourself or elsewhere? How will that create value for you, your work, and your stakeholders?"

Only when we have discovered together the purpose of our coaching partnership (the 'Why'), can we turn to exploring the 'What' – what the coaching will focus on. Here we take a broader, more nuanced view of goal setting as advocated by David, Clutterbuck, and Megginson (2013).

1   What is the work we need to do together? This looks at the two parties involved, the coach and coachee but this is in conjunction with the next point.
2   What is the work the stakeholders need us to do together so that benefits and impact from the coaching are maximized, whether that be for employees in the organization, shareholders, customers, or the wider world and its inhabitants? (We also recognize that benefits for family and friends are important and this is always relevant even though this chapter highlights organizational work.)
3   How can we 'future-proof' our outcomes so that the benefits are not just for now, but will also be for the future, the legacy?

We can then contract for the 'How' – how we will undertake this work together. Hawkins and Smith (2013, p. 175) describe how the contracting process needs to cover six key areas:

1   Practicalities – this includes areas such as the timing and frequency of sessions, payments, and agreements on postponements;
2   Boundaries – between coaching, counseling, and therapy; around what is and is not confidential;
3   Working Alliance – sharing expectations on both sides, covering areas like learning style, how trust is best built, hopes and fears;
4   The Session Format – how the time will be spent, processes that might be used;
5   The Organizational Context – critical stakeholders and their expectations, coaching policy, mutual responsibilities, support for the coachee within the workplace, how evaluation will be done and reported; and
6   The Professional Context – such as observing a professional body's codes of ethics and complaints procedures.

Our interest in contracting arose from coaching situations brought to us in supervision, traceable to the contracting stage. Drawing on our learning, we suggest that the key aims of contracting are ensuring clarity and ensuring value for all the stakeholders as follows:

1   to the individual and their development, now and in the future; so, this emphasizes the legacy for coaching;
2   to all the stakeholders, internal and external to the organization; this could include customers, direct reports, peers, shareholders, the board, contractors, etc.; and
3   the impact on global stakeholders and the wider eco-systems within which the organization forms a part. An example taken from supervision was a coach who discovered that the organization's aims for coaching had the potential to reduce health outcomes in a non-Western country (see Chapter 3 on ethics, p. 26).

To achieve value, we are sharing responsibility and not taking it upon ourselves alone. This quote (Turner & Hawkins, 2016, p. 55) from a UK coach with more than 10 years' experience highlights the dichotomy that some coaches feel:

> I do have an underlying belief that if the coachee works on things that are important to them, then this will have a ripple effect on their performance ... but I also think that they may have blind-spots that the business needs to help them to identify as goals for the coaching.

In multi-stakeholder meetings, coaches who were working both internally and externally primarily identify their role as being that of a facilitator (Turner & Hawkins, 2016, p. 58), to "ensure each party is clear about the agreement and expected results" as described by a North American coach with more than 10 years' experience (2016, p. 56). This is mirrored by an organizational representative who believes the aim is to enable "clear expectation awareness and agreement – whether this is for personal, intrinsic outcome or a more organisational focus" (2014, internal manager responsible for learning and development, unpublished).

All the parties contributing to the research – coaches, organizations, and individual clients – agreed on the same top four outcomes for multi-stakeholder meetings (2016, p. 58):

1   greater clarity of outcomes;
2   agreement on what coaching can/cannot deliver;
3   better alignment of individual and organization objectives; and
4   ensuring support to apply the individual client's development back in the organization.

The need for clear aims and processes does not appear to differ between internal and external coaching. Seventy-seven percent of internal coaches in further education believed a "clear organizational purpose" was one of the top 10 essentials in internal coaching (Turner, 2012, p. 8). This is underpinned by St. John-Brooks' research with internal coaches, setting out that providing strategic purpose is crucial (2014).

When contracting, we aim to get the stakeholders' voices in the room. One tool is using 360° feedback on behaviors, ensuring there are representatives of the wider system, internally and externally, at different hierarchical levels and across departments. It can also be insightful, in addition, to get feedback from family and friends.

There can be increased complexity where a coach is working with many people within the same organization, even within the same team, for example:

•   How do we contract when we are working with peers simultaneously, or with a senior leader and their direct reports?

- What does confidentiality mean and what are the implications for trust and openness?
- How do we retain a compassionate but detached perspective when different coachees may be contradicting each other and even criticizing each other and allocating blame?
- How do we ensure we don't 'buy into' any one story but retain a wider systemic perspective, and "wide-angled empathy" (Hawkins, 2019, p. 74) and thus add value to all the stakeholders?
- How do we adhere to the concept of equality between all the elements of the wider system, of which the coachees play a part, alongside the stakeholders, whether customers, direct report, board members, HR, etc.?

Some coaches are comfortable dealing with this complexity that can create challenges for confidentiality, such as remembering who said what. We can't unknow what we know, so if we are about to coach "Suzanne," and "Dimitri" has just accused her in your coaching session of belittling him in a meeting or of being incompetent, are we fully able to step back and ensure we are not affected? Is that realistic? Contracting is a tool that allows us to address such questions openly with our coachees. It is the exploration that counts, rather than having all the answers.

The research with coaches and organizational representatives summarizes the key challenges (Turner & Hawkins, 2016, p. 59) in multi-stakeholder contracting as:

1   coaching being used by the organization to deal with something a line manager has avoided;
2   boundary management between the three or more parties to the coaching (coach, client, and organizational representative(s));
3   maintaining confidentiality; this included the organization sometimes seeking updates on progress without the individual coachee's knowledge or agreement, for example in 'off-line' meetings or phone calls; and
4   setting outcomes that are agreed upon between the individual client and the line manager.

These findings mirror research done by Passmore (2016) with the company IKEA. When coaches were asked what got in the way of delivering successful multi-stakeholder contracting, the responses were:

- "Time – need to get on with the coaching assignment."
- "Reluctance from the coachee – concern about breaching confidentiality."
- "Reluctance from the manager – not signed up to coaching."
- "Reluctance from coach – concern about competence to manage the dynamic."

This also presumes that organizations, coaches, and coachees take part in multi-stakeholder meetings. Even those who do use them may not do so all the time. Around half of organizations and coaches surveyed had been involved in such meetings half the time in the previous year, while two-fifths had used this form of contracting one-quarter of the time or less. When it does take place, the majority lasted for one to two hours and involved an HR representative or, slightly less frequently, the line manager alongside the coach and coachee (Turner & Hawkins, 2016, pp. 56–57).

The Ridler reports, which survey organizations about coaching, have shown an increase over time in the numbers of organizations holding multi-stakeholder meetings, with three-quarters of organizations encouraging line managers to get involved in reviewing objectives in a three-way meeting (Mann, 2016). Their research also shows that it is not the norm for organizations to encourage HR or line managers to brief coaches, without the coachee present, prior to the coaching engagement beginning (Mann, 2016, p. 61). Nearly half (49%) said they encouraged coaches to get 360° feedback from the coachee's close colleagues (Mann, 2016, p. 61). It is important to recognize that 360° feedback on the coachee can be quite different from asking stakeholders, "How does this person currently provide value for you and your work, and how could they create more value for you?" which provides data on the relational engagement and performance.

Based on the research and our own practice, it is ideal if coaches can have individual conversations with all parties to the coaching prior to the first multi-stakeholder meeting. This will enable the coach to ensure that the coachee's and the organization's outcomes are broadly aligned and to use their intuition as to any ethical, cultural, or other challenges. This includes assessing whether there are covert aims, such as to sack the person if the coaching is seen to be unsuccessful, or even using coaching as a mask for a decision already taken (see point 5 below). One of us, Eve, then provides all parties with an overview in writing, prior to the meeting, of the aims of a multi-stakeholder meeting, covering areas addressed in the next section on tools and techniques.

Tools and techniques used in contracting

Turner and Hawkins's contracting research with 569 coaches provides guidance on effective contracting with stakeholders (Turner & Hawkins, 2016). We have also drawn on our own experience. The outcomes for contracting include:

1   Clarifying the aims for the coaching – ensuring alignment between the coachee and the organization.
2   A shared understanding of any organizational guidance that would influence contracting, such as procedures for handling bullying, harassment, or breaches of workplace confidentiality.
3   A shared understanding of the ongoing role of the sponsor in the coaching, such as ensuring any additional support is put in place.

4   A shared understanding of

    a   what will make the coaching successful;

    b   how this will be evaluated;

    c   when it will be evaluated; and

    d   by whom will it be evaluated.

5   A shared understanding of what could happen if the coaching:

    a   is successful – such as promotion, a new role, involvement in a project, a pay rise.

    b   is not successful – such as remaining in the same role, missing out on a financial bonus, being demoted, or even losing their job.

6   A share understanding of confidentiality and the circumstances in which it could be breached, taking into account: the law; health, safety, and well-being; having supervision; organizational requirements.

7   Copies of, or links to, the professional body code(s) of ethics to which we subscribe and the details of how a coachee or organization can complain about us to our professional body, should they feel this is necessary.

In Turner and Passmore's research into supervisors' roles in helping coaches deal with ethical dilemmas, the results indicate "that contracts are one of the key resources that individuals turn to when seeking to understand how to navigate a tricky dilemma" (2017, p. 39).

Bluckert provides 10 key questions related to contracting as part of good practice and suggests that if the contract is two-way, "You will want to satisfy yourself that not having a third-party organizational sponsor is appropriate" (2006, p. 13). Rostron's overview of the process includes a range of questions to ask when setting up the contract, starting with "What are the needs of the individual executive client versus those of the organisation?" and focuses on clarifying outcomes and their evaluation, checking the coachee's readiness for coaching, and considering feedback and monitoring mechanisms (2013, pp. 264–265). Engellau's lessons, alongside being specific about the terms of the coaching contract, include being up-front about what is non-negotiable and having a systemic point of view (2016). Bird and Gornall highlight the need for a checklist of things to consider and agree with corporate clients and sponsors as the coaching relationship is established (2016). Even more useful is the EMCC (2011) guidance for its members, which includes a Commercial Coaching Agreement, prepared with legal advice from an international law firm.

Turner and Hawkins' research project (2016) resulted in 10 "top tips," collated from coach themes offered in an open-ended question. These are outlined in Table 2.3 in order of priority. It is worth emphasizing theme 8, being brave. Being prepared to walk away is challenging, particularly when this is a coach's sole source of income and they may have a mortgage or rent to pay and a family

Table 2.3 Top 10 coach themes for successful multi-stakeholder contracting

Top Themes	Coaches
1 Clarity	Be clear on expectations (of stakeholder, client, and yourself), boundaries, confidentiality, and what coaching is and isn't.
2 Honesty and transparency	Ensure honesty and transparency in communication. Do not fear to challenge the line manager and/or ask the important questions. Coach the line manager so he/she is able to provide meaningful feedback.
3 Leading and planning	Take the lead in contracting. Plan ahead; provide a clear, concise contract.
4 Setting outcomes and measures	Establish clear desired outcomes and measures of success.
5 Impartiality	Be impartial. Listen. Be curious.
6 Engaging and encouraging	Engage with the client and stakeholder as partners. Encourage the individual client to lead the interim meetings. This supports the client in strengthening their interactions with their manager and HR.
7 Flexibility	Be flexible – respond to individual circumstances and stick with professional management practice and responsibilities.
8 Being brave	Be brave and firm. Do not fear to walk away if stakeholder expectations are unrealizable.
9 Understanding the problem	Aim to understand what really lies at the root of the problem.
10 Rapport and a safe space	Put effort into building a positive rapport and creating a safe space.

to support. Our own experience has been that organizations have often been 'testing' us, and this may be symptomatic of the culture. In the case of one of us, being prepared to walk away brought considerable further work through a senior leader whose respect for, and understanding of, both coaching and us as a professional increased. It can also increase the value to the organization, providing modeling for good boundary management.

To support this, more draft contracts, like that provided by the EMCC, could be made available by other coaching professional bodies and by training providers. Professional bodies could also play a role in doing, or supporting, further research in the field, developing from the ICF's 2013 study into organizational coaching. There is also evidence that coaches, mentors, and supervisors would welcome wider training in contracting; professional bodies and training organizations can play a role. Contracting training could include consideration of ethical challenges such as whether it is acceptable to discuss more personal agendas in the coaching or to discuss the individual leaving the organization. As coaches, if we model openness and transparency, these will be areas we can raise in contracting, ensuring that we can serve the interests of all stakeholders.

Case study

Peter Milligan is an experienced executive coach working with organizations since 1993 and is a supervisee of Eve's. He kindly agreed for his case, which is in his words, to be included along with his name.

Peter pays attention to the systemic aspects of organizations and has worked with some companies for many years, creating both opportunities and challenges. He builds trust with key players and over time develops ongoing knowledge that he can't 'unknow' and can even lead to mutual over-familiarity. The trust the organizations have in him means Peter is frequently asked to work with several peers within a senior team. This may also include the line manager and often the CEO or another board member. The complexities of multi-stakeholder contracting and re-contracting have been an ongoing part of our supervision together.

Peter writes:

> The key area of potential challenge for me has been around confidentiality, particularly when working with several people within an organization. For example, my work with a senior leader made me aware of concerns around the performance of one of her team who I was also coaching. At that point, the concerns had not been expressed to the team member, but a discussion about a change in his role was going on. In a subsequent session with that team member, I was put in a challenging position. He was aware that there might be changes coming but not any detail about the potential consequences for him. He asked me what I knew and while I didn't want to lie, I was not at liberty to answer this question fully. I was able to refer to our contracting and the agreement that I would keep all stakeholder conversations confidential (barring legal, and health or safety considerations), and it was also a powerful reminder of the need for clarity and alignment of outcomes and context from the start.
>
> Whether through conversation with a line manager, sponsor or another coachee, the coach can become aware of information pertaining to a coachee that they are not yet aware of. Sometimes there are organizational reasons for this (e.g., forthcoming structural changes yet to be announced), and sometimes it is simply avoidance of a conversation that the stakeholders perceive to be difficult. In the latter case, I have often been able to get the three stakeholders (coachee, line manager and me as coach) to sit down and have a conversation, a reminder that contracting is not a one-off.
>
> My advice is to be very clear about our role and to recognize we can be a catalyst for change through our presence. One of the reasons I enjoy this work is that it has great power for change, but it also comes with great

responsibility and potentially greater risks. We need to state from the out-set what our role is and understand that we are working within a system and not just with an individual. For me, the point of multi-stakeholder contracting is to encourage everyone to think of the system and what will enable that to work better, and not just think from an individual perspective.

I am also conscious that a mistake I can make is to believe that what I have said is heard, understood, agreed and that one iteration is sufficient. So, I now revisit multi-stakeholder contracting regularly, and am clearer about everyone's roles: coach, individual client, organization and other stakeholders.

The wider lesson for me is that as a coach we are part of the system and not part of the system – it is paradoxical. Our presence has an impact on the individuals and on the system and yet ultimately the measure of our good work is that we're not required for ever. We're walking on a path with them, a journey of discovery. We have the questions that heighten the awareness of the individual and those within the context, so they are all better equipped and can deal more effectively with the future.

Conclusion

Peter's story shows the importance of all parties understanding the value and impact of multi-stakeholder contracting. Clarity in contracting is essential to understanding what the outcomes are and how they will be delivered. It cannot be expected to cover every eventuality. However, it can provide a baseline, from agreement on the extent to which personal issues will be the focus of the coaching and whether it is acceptable for the coachee to discuss leaving the organization or even support them in doing so, regardless of the circumstances, to dealing with situations where more than one person is being coached and the resulting challenges to confidentiality. So, ethically it ensures that outcomes and their evaluation are done overtly, with the agreement of all parties. Contracting should also cover all the hygiene factors necessary for coaching: an approved timescale, number of sessions, and cost; it can also outline the support structure that will help the coachee take their learning back into the organization and make this a value-added initiative, for all stakeholders.

Developing yourself

The following resources are helpful in reflecting on how you grow your mastery in contracting, but the most helpful development is to keep experimenting in (a) how you can more clearly establish the clarity of the three pillars of the 'Why, What, and How' in every coaching relationship, and (b) how can you ensure the coaching creates benefits for a wider range of stakeholders, beyond the coachee, by bringing their voice into the contracting process.

Clutterbuck, D. (2015). *Managing the three-way contract in executive coaching and mentoring*. Retrieved September 25, 2018, from www.davidclutterbuckpartnership.com/managing-the-three-way-contract-in-executive-coaching-and-mentoring/

EMCC. (2011). Commercial Coaching Agreement. Retrieved January 14, 2018, from www.emccouncil.org/uk/

Goldsmith, M. (2005). *Changing leadership behavior*. Retrieved September 25, 2018, from www.marshallgoldsmith.com/articles/changing-leadership-behavior/

Goldsmith, M. (2013). *The pay for results approach*. Retrieved September 25, 2018, from www.marshallgoldsmith.com/articles/coaching-for-behavioral-change/

Hawkins, P. (2012). *Creating a coaching culture*. Maidenhead: Open University Press.

Hawkins, P. (2014c) The challenge for coaching in the 21st century. *e-Organisations and People*, 21(4), Winter.

Hodge, A. (2015). *Multi-stakeholder contracting*. Retrieved January 14, 2018, from http://alisonhodge.com/wp-content/uploads/2016/09/multi_stakeholder_contracting.pdf

ICF. (2013). *ICF organizational coaching study*. Retrieved September 25, 2018, from http://icf.files.cms-plus.com/FileDownloads/2013OrgCoachingStudy.pdf

Turner, E., & Hawkins, P. (2015). *Summary report on multi-stakeholder contracting for the ICF 2015*. Retrieved September 25, 2018, from http://researchportal.coachfederation.org/Document/Download?documentId=2714

Turner, E., & Hawkins, P. (2016). Multi-stakeholder contracting in executive/business coaching: An analysis of practice and recommendations for getting maximum value. *In the International Journal for Evidence-Based Coaching and Mentoring, 14*(2), 48–65. https://doi.org/10.24384/IJEBCM/14/2

References

Bird, J., & Gornall, S. (2016). *The art of coaching*. Abingdon: Routledge.

Bluckert, P. (2006). *Psychological dimensions of executive coaching*. Maidenhead: Open University Press.

Carter, A., & Miller, L. (2009). *Increasing business benefits from in-house coaching schemes*. Brighton: Institute for Employment Studies. Retrieved September 25, 2018, from www.employment-studies.co.uk/system/files/resources/files/mp85.pdf

Clutterbuck, D. (2015). Eight coaching myths and misconceptions. *Global Coaching Perspectives, 6*, 9–11. Retrieved September 25, 2018, from http://c.ymcdn.com/sites/associationforcoaching.site-ym.com/resource/resmgr/Coaching_Perspectives/GCP_JULY_2015.pdf

Coutu, D., & Kauffman, C. (2009). What can coaches do for you? *Harvard Business Review*. Retrieved September 25, 2018, from https://hbr.org/2009/01/what-can-coaches-do-for-you

Cowan, K. (2013). What are the experiences of external executive coaches working with coachees' assigned goals? *International Journal of Evidence Based Coaching and Mentoring Special* (7), 14–25.

David, S., Clutterbuck, D., & Megginson, D. (2013). *Beyond goals – effective strategies for coaching and mentoring*. Farnham: Gower Publishing Limited.

EMCC. (2011). *Commercial coaching agreement*. Retrieved January 14, 2018, from www.emccouncil.org/uk/

Engellau, E. (2016). The dos and don'ts of coaching: Key lessons I learned as an executive coach. In M. F. R. Kets de Vries, K. Korotov, E. Florent-Treacy, & C. Rook (Eds.), *Coach and couch the psychology of making better leaders* (2nd ed.). Basingstoke: Palgrave Macmillan.

English, F. (1975). The three-cornered contract. *Transactional Analysis Journal*, 5(4), 383.

Eriksson, K. (2011). *Executive coaching: Diverse stakeholder perspectives and a model for agreed procurement procedures* (abridged version). Submitted for the award of Doctor of Philosophy at the University of Derby (unpublished).

Goldsmith, M., & Morgan, H. (2004). Leadership is a contact sport. *Strategy and Business, 36*. Retrieved September 25, 2018, from https://www.strategy-business.com/article/04307

Hawkins, P. (2012). *Creating a coaching culture*. Maidenhead: Open University Press.

Hawkins, P. (2014). The Challenge for Coaching in the 21st Century. *e-Organisations and People, 21*(4), Winter.

Hawkins, P. (2017). *Leadership team coaching: Developing collective transformational leadership* (3rd ed.). London: Kogan Page.

Hawkins, P., & Smith, N. (2013). *Coaching, mentoring and organizational consultancy: Supervision and development*. Maidenhead: Open University Press/McGraw Hill.

Hawkins, P. (2019). Resourcing – The neglected third leg of supervision. In E. Turner and S. Palmer (Eds.), *The heart of coaching supervision – working with reflection and self-care*. Abingdon: Routledge.

Hay, J. (2007). *Reflective practice for supervision and coaches*. Maidenhead: Open University Press.

ICF. (2013). *ICF organizational coaching study*. Retrieved September 25, 2018, from http://icf.files.cms-plus.com/FileDownloads/2013OrgCoachingStudy.pdf

Kilburg, R. (2000). *Executive coaching – developing managerial wisdom in a world of chaos*. Washington, DC: American Psychological Association.

Knights, A., & Poppleton, A. (2007). *Research insight: Coaching in organisations*. London: Chartered Institute of Personnel and Development.

Lee, R. J. (2016). The role of contracting in coaching: Balancing individual client and organizational issues. In J. Passmore, D. Peterson, & M. Freire (Eds.), *The Wiley-Blackwell handbook of the psychology of coaching and mentoring*. Chichester: John Wiley & Sons.

Mann, C. (2016). *6th Ridler report: Strategic trends in the use of coaching*. London: Ridler & Co. Retrieved September 25, 2018, from www.ridlerandco.com/ridler-report/

Ogilvy, H., & Ellam-Dyson, V. (2012). Line management involvement in coaching: Help or hindrance? A content analysis study. *International Coaching Psychology Review*, 7(1), 39–54.

Passmore, J. (2016, December 9). *Organisational coaching and stakeholder contracting*. Presentation to the British Psychological Society Special Group in Coaching Psychology.

Passmore, J., Brown, H., Csigas, Z. et al. (2017). *The state of play in European coaching: Coaching and mentoring research project*. Henley-on-Thames: Henley & EMCC, from https://www.researchgate.net/publication/321361866_The_State_of_Play_in_European_Coaching_and_Mentoring

Passmore, J., & Fillery-Travis, A. (2011). A critical review of executive coaching research: A decade of progress and what's to come in *Coaching: An International Journal of Theory, Research and Practice*, 4(2), 70–88. Retrieved September 25, 2018, from http://dx.doi.org/10.1080/17521882.2011.596484

Peterson, D. B. (2009, 6). *Does your coach give you value for your money?* In D. Coutu and C. Kauffman (Eds.), 'What can coaches do for you?' *Harvard Business Review* (January). Retrieved September 25, 2018, from https://hbr.org/2009/01/what-can-coaches-do-for-you

Ridler Report: Mann, C. (2016). *Strategic trends in the use of coaching*. London: Ridler & Co. Retrieved January 16, 2018, from www.ridlerandco.com/ridler-report/

Rogers, J. (2008). *Coaching skills: A handbook* (2nd ed.). Maidenhead: Open University Press.

Rostron, S. S. (2013). *Business coaching: Wisdom and practice*. Knowres Publishing. Retrieved from ProQuest Ebook Central, January 16, 2018, from https://ebookcentral.proquest.com/lib/soton-ebooks/detail.action?docID=3544778.

Scoular, A. (2011). *Business coaching*. Harlow: Pearson Education Limited.

Stewart, L. J., Palmer, S., Wilkin, H., & Kerrin, M. (2008). Towards a model of coaching transfer: Operationalising coaching success and the facilitators and barriers to transfer. *International Coaching Psychology Review, 3*(2), 87–109.

St John-Brooks, K. (2014). *Internal coaching – the inside story*. London: Karnac Books Ltd.

Turner, E. (2012). Confidentiality and CPD opportunities top internal coaches' wishlist. *In Coaching at Work, 7*(4), 8.

Turner, E. & Hawkins, P. (2014). *2014 Coaches' survey – Research on multistakeholder contracting in coaching*. SurveyMonkey, unpublished data.

Turner, E., & Hawkins, P. (2016). Multi-stakeholder contracting in executive/business coaching: An analysis of practice and recommendations for getting maximum value. *In the International Journal for Evidence-Based Coaching and Mentoring, 14*(2), 48–65.

Turner, E., & Passmore, J. (2017). The trusting kind. *In Coaching at Work, 12*(6), 34–39.

Chapter 3

Mastering ethics

Eve Turner and Jonathan Passmore

Introduction

We are making ethical decisions all the time. Ethics, at its simplest, is how we make choices about our behavior based on what we consider to be 'right' or 'wrong.' These terms 'right' and 'wrong' carry with them historical, cultural, as well as personal values and a binary way of looking at the world. What might be consider 'wrong' 150 years ago, in most of Europe, homosexuality, is accepted or at least respected as a personal choice. In parts of the world, introduction or facilitation payments are common, while in other parts of the world these are considered bribes and likely to result in imprisonment. In this chapter, our working assumption is that ethical behavior demonstrates our moral values in action and is the basis of our daily lives and how we relate to others.

Dilemmas are one aspect of our ethical thinking, where we face difficult choices between two or more alternatives. We face ethical decisions constantly as coaches, mentors, supervisors, or leaders. Examples include concern that a work colleague is mentally unwell and could endanger himself; concern a coachee has been drinking alcohol and is about to drive home (see case study p. 35); concern a mentee has been forced into mentoring but faces losing her job if she doesn't comply; and hearing something that indicates a colleague is acting illegally. We will consider these in the wider context of our moral compass (Malik, 2014), providing ideas on how to manage ethical decision-making and explore the importance of developing and using a personal ethical decision-making framework to complement professional codes of ethics. The challenge for us is to be alert, in the here-and-now, to whatever we are presented with.

In this chapter, we will look briefly at the theory and evidence around ethics and how it impacts on our everyday thinking. The importance of ethics to the coaching and mentoring profession is highlighted, including the role of professional bodies and a brief review of the developing research and writing on this topic. We then consider tools and techniques, before providing a case study and some references for further reflection.

Theory and evidence underpinning ethics

The field of ethics has a long and rich history (Widdows, 2011; Carroll & Shaw, 2013; Malik, 2014). It formed part of the philosophies of the Greek writers Aristotle, Plato, and Socrates and has become a complex, ever-expanding field through the centuries. Latest traditions have included global ethics (Widdows, 2011), leadership ethics (Boaks & Levine, 2017; Heffernan, 2011), and ethics in the helping professions such as psychotherapy and counseling (Pope & Vasquez, 2016) and now coaching, mentoring, and supervision (Iordanou, Hawley, & Iordanou, 2017). Ethics is commonly divided into two parts: meta-ethics and normative ethics (Singer, 1994, p. 10). In this chapter, we are taking the stance of meta-ethics, reflecting on the practice of ethics from multiple perspectives, rather than taking a normative stance of seeking to influence how readers act through talking of good and bad, right or wrong.

Steare distinguishes three dominant philosophies that provide one way of considering the challenges we may face as coaches, mentors, supervisors, or leaders. He believes "Our Principled Conscience is guided by "moral principles" (this is not universally accepted, for example see Dancy, 2013); our Social Conscience focuses on what "is considered right or acceptable in a particular society"; and Rule Compliance is defined by our "legal rights and duties." (Steare, 2006, p. 22). Living within societies, practicing ethically can be seen as an intertwining of all three. What might that mean for us if, for example, a social requirement to do that which benefits the most people and harms the least leads to the adoption of a new way of working that will ensure a company survives but may mean a few people, including our coachee, lose their jobs, or a legal requirement to keep within the rules should lead to reporting anyone using drugs including smoking cannabis (would it be different if it was heroin or crack cocaine?). How might this mesh with our own moral values?

In a detailed examination of the history of ethical thinking, Malik concludes that

> it is comforting to imagine that notions of right and wrong, good and bad, come predefined by some external authority, that there already exists a moral map, and that our job is merely to work out how to navigate it, to find our way to the given moral north.
>
> (2014, p. 344)

He points instead to the responsibility we each have to make our own "moral map," which we can choose to see as "a highly disconcerting prospect . . . or a highly exhilarating one" (Malik, 2014, p. 344). Carroll and Shaw (2013, p. 19) also highlight how taxing it might be to practice ethically: "My mind is a moral maze where I end up continually facing yet another dead end. I long for the easy answer that removes any responsibility for having to go on an ethical journey where the destination is unclear." They note the challenges of contemporary living, such as when we might be colluding or when is it best to do nothing. In the coaching field, Iordanou et al. suggest, "the focus . . . should be cast not on solving ethical issues but, rather on creating those conditions and conversations that will bring them to the surface" (2017, p. 186).

Most of us would claim we want to live and practice ethically and to model this in our dealings with other people, but how easy is this? As practitioners, we make choices in our interactions with our clients, from the approaches we use and the way we ask questions to which questions we ask. "Even the use of explicit theoretical models is value-laden in practice, as the coach's choices are so intertwined with their personal values that it is not possible to say which interventions come from theories and which from personal beliefs" (Jackson & Bachkirova, 2019).

The issues of ethics in coaching was one of 10 topics prioritized by the Global Convention in Coaching (GCC) in 2008, which made several recommendations to establish a "rigorous evidence-based profession" (Rostron, 2009, p. 78) with a "common understanding of the profession" (2009, p. 80), including through creating 'a universal ethical code' from the diverse range of coaching ethical codes which exist today (for example in the English language ICF, EMCC-AC led Global Code of Ethics, WABC, and COMENSA). A lack of research was another of the 10 priorities. Since then, however, there has been relatively little written about ethics considering the importance of the topic to coaching practice, the wider professional development of coaching (Law 2005a and 2005b; Williams & Anderson, 2006; Passmore & Mortimer, 2011; Passmore, 2011; Lane, 2011; Bachkirova, Jackson & Clutterbuck, 2011; Lowman, 2012; Hodge, 2013; Hawkins & Smith, 2013; Carroll & Shaw, 2013; Iordanou & Williams, 2017; Iordanou et al., 2017), and the limited ethical research done (Armstrong & Geddes, 2009; Passmore, 2009; Duffy & Passmore, 2010; Moral & Lamy, 2017; Turner & Passmore, 2018). While this is a relatively short list, given a decade or more of coaching research and writing since the GCC and the centrality of this issue to practice, it still provides considerable material to draw on.

The different coaching professional bodies do provide codes of ethics and best practice (such as the Global Code of Ethics, APECS, APS, BPS, COMENSA, IAC, ICF, WABC codes etc.). These codes combine meta-ethics with normative ethics, providing both general principles that are not necessarily in complete alignment and some rules such as "Avoid any sexual or romantic relationship with current clients or sponsor(s) or students, mentees or supervisees" (ICF, 2018a: para 21). Such codes cannot be expected to be sufficient for all the complex situations practitioners may encounter.

The coaching bodies have increased their ethical activity in the last few years. In 2016, the AC and EMCC, picking up the GCC theme, together launched a Global Code of Ethics. This was reviewed in 2017–2018, and in 2018 three further bodies became signatories to the second version – APECS, AICP, and UNM; the hope remains that further professional bodies will become signatories. The ICF has required members applying for coach credentialing to complete an online ethics course since early 2016, runs an ethics hotline to support inquiries relating to its ethical code (2018b), and publishes an annual report on coaching complaints (ICF, 2017). Other professional bodies like the AC and EMCC also have complaints procedures, while the AC, APECS, and EMCC ask for responses to ethical questions for accreditation. A group is exploring the role of ethical guidelines in coaching supervision (AOCS and AC, 2017 onwards, including representatives from the EMCC and ICF) and the EMCC launched its own survey into ethics for an "EMCC International Provocations Report" (EMCC, 2017).

The authors of this chapter have been actively engaged in ethical research, exploring coach, coachee, professional body, and stakeholder attitudes. In the most recent series of studies, this has included: a large-scale European survey of coaches and organizational clients (Passmore, Brown, & Csigas, 2017); engagement with over 100 supervisors drawn mainly from the UK, North America, and Europe; a qualitative study with supervisors into the processes used in managing ethical dilemmas; and interviews with stakeholders, including professional coaching body chief executives, directors and chairs, police and insurers, on their attitudes to ethics. This collection of studies has highlighted significant inconsistencies in how coaching practitioners deal with ethical concerns. One example is the scenario of a coach or client breaking the law, and whether the coach or supervisor would report this action. The results suggest a lack of agreement about whether this should be reported, even where law breaking involves mandatory reporting of such matters (in some countries) or involves serious criminality. A second example of sexual relationships between coach and client received a similar level of mixed responses.

These responses of actual practice are at odds with the professional bodies, who advocate legal compliance. For example, the ICF is clear that breaches of ethics should be reported to them and has an Ethical Conduct Review process (2018c). It is also explicit about dos and don'ts, such as avoiding any sort of romantic relationship, as mentioned earlier. The need to discuss these areas more widely within the profession was a key theme among participants. The position of three largest professional coaching bodies is summarized in Table 3.1. This includes the ICF with approximately 30,000 members globally, Association for Coaching with more than 6,000 members mainly in the UK and Europe, and EMCC with 5,000 affiliated members across Europe, with the highest concentrations in the UK and Netherlands.

Aims and processes in ethics

Coaches and other practitioners can only achieve mastery in ethics through the way they operate in relation to others. Many of those reading this chapter will be working with executive clients in business, and the very nature of ethics in business is a field in itself. Boaks and Levine talk about ethical modes of leadership to achieve goals, ensuring "that the followers are not manipulated or

Table 3.1 Key ethical responsibilities by ICF and Global Ethical Code EMCC – AC

International Coach Federation (ICF)	Global Code of Ethics (AC and EMCC and v2 also APECS, AICP, UNM)
5 main sections	4 main sections
Professional Conduct at Large – covering all interactions in any professional capacity and including confidentiality, unlawful discrimination, contacting ICF for breaches in ethics, research protocols, storage of data, and impact of personal issues	Terminology – being aware of each signatory body's (at time of press AC and EMCC) definitions and terminology and precise meaning of words
Conflicts of Interest – including clarity for internal coaches, boundaries	Working with Clients – covering contracting, integrity, confidentiality, inappropriate interactions, conflict of interest and terminating professional relationships and on-going responsibilities
Professional Conduct with Clients – including ensuring clients know the nature of coaching; having clear agreements; being alert to cultural sensitivity; avoiding sexual or romantic relationships with current clients, sponsors or students, mentees, or supervisees; respecting the client's right of termination	Professional Conduct – maintaining the reputation of coaching and mentoring, recognizing equality and diversity, breaches of professional conduct, and legal and statutory obligations and duties
Confidentiality/Privacy – including clear agreements and abiding by the law	Excellent Practice – ability to perform, ongoing supervision, and continuing professional development and reflection
Continuing Development – of professional skills	Signatories to the Global Code of Ethics

deceived into acting this way and . . . are not prevented from exercising autonomy" (2017, p. 68). When we contract with our individual client and/or the organizational representative(s), how much is this in our minds? It is unlikely that we would be asked overtly to coach someone to do something illegal; however, a recent case brought to one of the authors in supervision highlights the personal challenges we may experience to our moral values. The supervisee was being asked to coach someone where the organization's aim was to support the individual to break into the developing world market. The company was a producer of goods that are linked to people's early death. We will all have a different reaction to that scenario, and it illustrates our moral values in action. Brooks advocates a leadership model, stakeholding, where all those that have a stake should have a say about its outcomes (Brooks, 2017, p. 208).

One of the aims of ethical mastery is for each of us to understand who we are, what drives us, and the influence that has on how we practice (Turner, 2012; Jackson & Bachkirova, 2019; Ryde, Seto & Goldvarg, 2019). An aim of ethical thinking is to consider what it is we believe about others and the world around us, what we consider the purpose of coaching to be, and then how we demonstrate congruence with that in the way we practice. Jackson and Bachkirova talk about the 3Ps, philosophy, purpose, and process. Considering those three areas, they write, "allows the practitioner to develop a coherence to their practice, both in terms of its internal consistency, and in terms of its alignment to the *self* of the practitioner" (Jackson & Bachkirova, 2019, p. 23).

This alignment of self reflects that none of us exists in a vacuum and among the influences on us will be our cultural background. Like Ryde et al. (2019, p. 42), we take this not just as "nationality or race but . . . geographical cultures such as countries and regions; social cultures such as race, class, sexual orientation and gender and organisational cultures." These cultures may influence the power between participants in a coaching relationship and therefore the potentiality for clients to be directed into certain actions, attitudes to those seen to be 'in authority' will differ, and it may be that the coach will feel intimidated in certain circumstances. For example, one of the authors, Eve, recalls a client who was facing a disciplinary procedure for bullying. This created two challenges related to her moral values: the first was that she finds bullying is a 'hot button' issue which may take her out of her compassionate and non-judgmental approach to clients; the other was dealing with behavior in the coaching session that appeared to reflect the organization's concerns.

Contracting is one process that can help us to maintain mastery in ethics (also see Chapter 2 by Turner & Hawkins, p. 21). It can, for example, help us decide if we are the correct coach for a client or their organization.

Pope and Vasquez argue that "the little-known club of ethically perfect therapists – those with errorless judgement and fallacy-free ethical reasoning – is so exclusive that no one ever qualifies for membership" (2016, p. 26). Our view is that we can safely replace the word therapist with coach, mentor, or leader. While membership of this club may be impossible, we believe that coaches need to make ethical thinking part of their everyday practice so that we develop more clarity. In short, the more we notice how we think about ethics, the more we can think critically about our own ethical judgment, reasoning, language, and justifications in our coaching and supervision practice.

Dryden has identified six themes in the dilemmas experienced by therapists (1997, pp 2–4). They resonate with coaching and mentoring themes:

1   Compromise dilemmas – for example, the tension between the 'ideal' and the 'pragmatic,' doing 'safe' work versus more 'risky' work, giving warmth or love to clients
2   Boundary dilemmas – such as how much personal information we reveal or around confidentiality when working in organizations

3   Dilemmas of allegiance – through membership of communities or bodies and trying to remain within a particular framework regardless of context
4   Role dilemmas – in internal practices this could be between leader and mentor or coach, or between colleague and coaching/mentoring manager
5   Dilemmas of responsibility – to what extent do we take responsibility for our clients' welfare?
6   Impasse dilemmas – what do we do when our work gets stuck?

Carroll and Shaw believe our history "feels like a story of two extremes. While there is no other species that can equal humans for altruism, care and compassion, there is also no other species that matches us for harm, cruelty and sadism" (2013, p. 44). They provide some strategies that might help us to "avoid the seduction to do wrong" (2013, p. 60):

- do not think *I*, think *we*;
- consider issues of power, domination, and privilege and how they can move over easily into abuse and harm of others who are less privileged;
- ask yourself if you would recommend what you are about to do to someone else;
- try to look at the behavior, not the intention – what am I actually doing? Too often we use our intention (which is almost always good) to evaluate our behavior (which is often not that good);
- ask yourself how this might be perceived from the other's point of view – use empathy to view actions from the recipient's point of view, which helps us to realize that to experience it from that other viewpoint can create a radical change in what we do;
- look for the truth in the opposite position to the one you hold – this can expose the error in your point of view;
- ask yourself: what are my ways and habits of denial?
- identify your Achilles heel;
- beware of the extremity of your ideals (fundamentalism)

(Carroll & Shaw, 2013, p. 60)

Tools and techniques in ethics

In considering tools and techniques, our starting point is to check our self-awareness and understanding of how and why we practice the way we do. To achieve this, we need to understand our personal philosophy (Jackson & Bachkirova, 2019), that is, what we believe about the world around us, including other people. Do we believe people are fundamentally good, well-intentioned, hard-working? To help hone this understanding, we can consider how we like to live: the sort of training we attend, books we like to read, films we like to watch, and holidays we prefer to go on. What do we see as the purpose of coaching? And finally, how do we practice in congruence with this? For example, if we believe people are well-intentioned and able and our aim is to help them unlock their own abilities, how would giving advice fit with this?

Underpinning this is power, which exists, whether acknowledged or unacknowledged, in all relationships. There will be many factors in how a coach is seen within a relationship; these will include the personality of the client, the reasons for the coaching, and the client's cultural background (including race, gender, sexuality, disability, age, religion). None of us comes 'neutral' to an assignment – we bring our histories and backgrounds with us. In Figure 3.1, three aspects of power are identified: personal, derived from who we are and how we relate to people; political, from the relationships we have developed; and positional, from the role we have (often in hierarchical terms). However, culture is a crucial factor in all of these.

COMENSA's ethical code includes a link to an ethical toolkit (2018) where there is an exercise "to provide you with an awareness of your ethical profile. With this tool you will feel more confident to make the choices that best reflect your core beliefs and values." Another exercise, on assumptions (Ryde et al., 2019, p. 45) is useful to determine views we might hold that we are not aware contain assumptions. Take, for example, time – if we consider the first thing that comes to our mind in relation to time and then ask a group of people to do the same, there will be a diversity of responses, especially if people come from a range of cultural backgrounds. What might any organization's assumption of time indicate – that staff can work at their own pace, that there is no pressure, that time is limited and we need to work long hours to be effective?

The use of ethical case studies can also support the development of mastery in ethics, and an ethical decision-making framework may be helpful (Duffy & Passmore, 2010; Passmore & Turner, 2018) – Figure 3.2. The key is to use a decision-making investigation that guides the coach in considering key questions, as opposed to coming up with specific right or wrong answers. In this model, we work broadly from left to right, bringing in external resources as appropriate. This is an aid to developing what Carroll and Shaw describe as

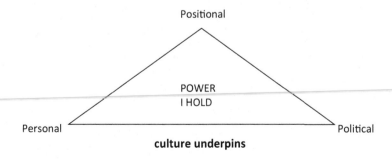

Figure 3.1 Culture and power model

Source: Turner, 2009, after French & Raven, 1959

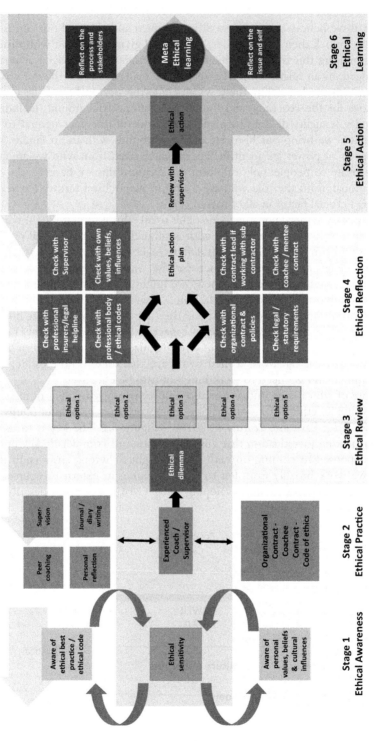

Figure 3.2 Passmore & Turner's Six Stage *APPEAR* Coaching Ethical Supervision Model

ethical maturity, developing confidence and ethical understanding. This places ethics at the heart of our everyday considerations, and this then becomes part of our "internal supervisor" (Casement, 1985), meaning our ethical thinking becomes routine and internalized, rather than being something special, in certain circumstances. When we then face a dilemma, we will have the resources to deal with it effectively.

A real situation in the UK, involving the police wanting to seize coaching notes, can be reviewed using this model (see Turner & Woods, 2015; Turner & Passmore, 2017). The coach involved brought this to supervision, and a number of options were generated and various external resources brought in to inform the decision-making, including the coach's professional insurers and professional body, before the final action was taken (Turner & Woods, 2015, p. 31). Turner and Passmore's research with supervisors (2018) highlighted additional resources, such as professional indemnity insurance and insurers' legal helplines.

Contracting is another crucial tool for ethical mastery, highlighted in stages 2 and 4 of our model. Coaching contracts vary widely across the coaching sector. While the EMCC publishes a Commercial Coaching Agreement, most coaches either have drafted their own contract, use less formal 'agreements,' or even use a verbal agreement that is discussed and agreed between the respective parties, either as a coach-coachee agreement or a tripartite agreement involving the sponsor.

What is important, however, is that coaches make conscious choices about what is included in their contract and how they might deal with ethical dilemmas that can arise. No contract can cover every situation. We believe that by providing examples of the types of illegality which could be disclosed and being explicit about the ethical code and complaints processes, both coachees and sponsors are empowered. Such actions help shift the relationship towards a more equitable and ethical relationship. This includes providing copies of, or links to, the professional code(s) of ethics to which we subscribe, and the details of how a coachee or organization can complain about us to our professional body, should they feel this is necessary.

Case study

Background/context

'Nazim' is a highly experienced coach who has been working for 10 years in the private and public sector and offers personal, executive, and business coaching. He has regular supervision, is a member of a coaching professional body, and has co-written this case study, albeit anonymously. Eve's own supervisor of supervision, Peter Hawkins, also provided support. The client in the case had come to coaching to focus on what was next in her professional life, as she had not worked for some time but wanted to.

Case study

In the second session, the client described herself as a "high functioning alcoholic"; during this session it emerged that the woman was driving afterwards to pick up her son and 6-month-old granddaughter, and 'Nazim' smelt alcohol strongly on her breath. As 'Nazim' saw it, the dilemma was two-fold. First, what use was he to an alcoholic? – the alcoholism became "the elephant in the room" as the client batted away any references to it. 'Nazim' decided he wasn't the right person to work with her because her issues were so complex and encouraged her to seek support elsewhere; was that the right call? Second, what was his role in the situation of her driving afterwards, potentially over the legal limit and knowing a young child would be a passenger (a 'hot button' for 'Nazim' as a father), and should he take any action, even call the police?

Reflection

In reflecting on this scenario, we will draw on the ethical decision-making model shown in Figure 3.2. Key, but not exhaustive, points include:

1   If a client turns up smelling of alcohol, they are telling us something. This may be an unconscious communication that they need our help, or it may be a sign that they do not place any value or show concern for how we might react.
2   As in many ethical situations, there is no 'easy' solution, and it is not our responsibility to find a solution with them.
3   We might share an anxiety but work to stay in a relational space, so we avoid becoming polarized, such as being parental or collusive.
4   We may be drawn into seeing the person as an 'ic.' In this case, an alcoholic. Our own values may play a part, driven by our own past experiences.
5   To stay in an adult space, we can develop a nuanced, coaching approach. Our aim is to avoid being directive unless the risk of harm to the person or others is likely and serious. We might start with 5a (below). It is only at 5d (below) that we might consider intervention, such as taking the car keys or, in extremis, calling the police.

    a   "I've smelled alcohol on your breath and you've told me you are drinking. How might that affect your driving on the way home with your child in the car?"
    b   "It sounds as if you have taken that risk before. What's the worst thing that could happen? . . . Right now, who is the most important person to you?"
    c   "I feel very uncomfortable with you driving home. I would really like you to leave your car keys here. I will get you a taxi and you can pop back to get your car tomorrow morning."

d   "I have explained I feel uncomfortable. I am offering to get a taxi to take you home. You may recall when we contracted at the start of our work I explained there may be times when I might need to break our confidentiality clause, if I felt there was a risk of harm to you or others. This is now one of those occasions. I care about you. You admit you are drunk. If you insist on driving, I will call the police. Please give me your car keys."

Conclusion

In this chapter, we have aimed to demonstrate that ethics is not something 'special.' It is an intrinsic part of our everyday life and happens moment-to-moment. We are making decisions based on our backgrounds, our history, the culture we have grown up in, and the norms of our society, as well as our personal values. Rather than taking what can be a simplistic stance around 'right' or 'wrong,' we have considered the nuances and looked at some of the writing to date in coaching and supervision and also drew on related fields. We have then provided some frames to use in thinking about ethical dilemmas, from considering our assumptions and the importance of contracting effectively to the possible use of models, such as a decision-making model and one around power. Finally, in the case study, we have highlighted a real-life situation and considered some staged steps to dealing with it. The chapter ends with some recommended readings, web resources, and references.

Developing yourself

Recommended readings

Jackson, P., & Bachkirova, T. (2019). The 3Ps of supervision and coaching – philosophy, purpose and process. In E. Turner & S. Palmer (Eds.), *The heart of coaching* supervision – *working with reflection and self-care*. Abingdon: Routledge.

Ryde, J., Seto, L. & Goldvarg, D. (2019). Diversity and inclusion in supervision. In E. Turner & S. Palmer (Eds.), *The heart of coaching supervision – working with reflection and self-care*. Abingdon: Routledge.

Iordanou, I., Hawley, R., & Iordanou, C. (2017). *Values and ethics in coaching*. London: Sage Publications Ltd.

Web resources

COMENSA ethical toolkit. Retrieved September 25, 2018 from www.comensa.org.za/content/images/the_ethics_toolkit_for_coaches_and_mentors.pdf

Global Code of Ethics. Retrieved September 25, 2018 from www.globalcodeofethics.org/

ICF Code of Ethics (2018a). Retrieved September 25, 2018 from https://coachfederation.org/code-of-ethics/

Turner, E., & Passmore, J. (2018). Ethical dilemmas and tricky decisions: A global perspective of coaching supervisors' practices in coach decision-making. In the International Journal of Evidence Based Coaching and Mentoring, 16(1), 126–142. Retrieved September 25, 2018, from https://radar.brookes.ac.uk/radar/items/da4e8785-60aa-4867-8aa7-caebf259a94f/1/

Journal of Business Ethics. Retrieved September 25, 2018 from www.springer.com/philosophy/ethics+and+moral+philosophy/journal/10551

Online courses such as Princeton and Stanford: retrieved September 25, 2018 from https://online.princeton.edu/course/practical-ethics and https://plato.stanford.edu/search/searcher.py?query=ethics

Turner, E., & Woods, D. When the police come knocking. In Coaching at Work, 10(6), 28–34. Retrieved September 25, 2018 from www.coaching-at-work.com/2015/10/30/when-the-police-come-knocking/

References

APECS. (2018). *Code of ethics.* Retrieved May 9, 2018, from www.apecs.org/ethical-guidelines

Armstrong, H., & Geddes, M. (2009). Developing coaching supervision practice: An Australian case study. *International Journal of Evidence Based Coaching and Mentoring*, 7(2), 1–15. Retrieved from http://ijebcm.brookes.ac.uk/documents/vol07issue2-paper-01.pdf

APS (Australian Psychological Society). (2018). *Code of ethics.* Retrieved September 25, 2018, from www.psychology.org.au/About-Us/What-we-do/ethics-and-practice-standards/APS-Code-of-Ethics

Association for Coaching. (2018). *AC complaints procedure.* Retrieved May 9, 2018, from www.associationforcoaching.com/general/custom.asp?page=ACComplaintsProc

Bachkirova, T., Jackson, P. & Clutterbuck, D. (2011). Coaching & Mentoring Supervision – Theory and Practice. Maidenhead: Oxford University Press.

Boaks, J., & Levine, M. P. (Eds.). (2017). *Leadership & ethics.* London: Bloomsbury Academic.

Brooks, T. (2017). Leadership and Stakeholding. In J. Boaks & M. Levine (Eds.), *Leadership & ethics.* London: Bloomsbury Academic.

Carroll, M., & Shaw, E. (2013). *Ethical maturity in the helping professions.* London: Jessica Kingsley Publishers.

Casement, P. (1985). *On learning from the patient.* London: Tavistock Publications.

COMENSA. (2018). *Code of ethics.* Retrieved September 25, 2018, from www.comensa.org.za/Information/EthicsRead

Dancy, J. (2013). An unprincipled morality. In R. Shafer-Landau (Ed.), *Ethical theory – an anthology* (2nd ed.). Chichester: Wiley-Blackwell.

Dryden, W. (1997). *Therapists' dilemmas.* London: Sage Publications Ltd.

Duffy, M., & Passmore, J. (2010). Ethics in coaching: An ethical decision making framework for coaching psychologists. *International Coaching Psychology Review*, 5(2), 140–151.

EMCC. (2012). *European mentoring and coaching council complaints and disciplinary procedure.* Retrieved February 22, 2018, from www.emccouncil.org/src/ultimo/models/Download/6.pdf

EMCC. (2017). *EMCC international ethics research survey.* Retrieved August 1, 2017, via individual author invitation.

French, J. R. P., & Raven, B. (1959). The bases of social power. In D. Cartwright and A. Zander (Eds), *Group dynamics.* New York: Harper & Row.

Global Code of Ethics for Coaches and Mentors. (2018). Retrieved September 25, 2018, from www.globalcodeofethics.org/

Hawkins, P., & Smith, N. (2013). *Coaching, mentoring and organizational consultancy – supervision, skills & development* (2nd ed.). Maidenhead: Open University Press.

Hawkins, P., & Turner, E. (2017). The rise of coaching supervision 2006–2014. *Coaching: An International Journal of Theory, Research and Practice*, 1–13. Retrieved from www.tandfonline.com/eprint/AxfVpA6637y9DYX2jg42/full or www.tandfonline.com/doi/full/10.1080/17521882.2016.1266002

Heffernan, M. (2011). *Wilful blindness*. London: Simon & Schuster UK Ltd.

Hodge, A. (2013). Coaching supervision – an ethical angle. In E. Murdoch & J. Arnold (Eds.), *Full spectrum supervision*. St Albans: Paloma Press.

IAC. (2018). *Ethics*. Retrieved September 25, from https://certifiedcoach.org/about/ethics/#code

ICF. (2017). *Ethical conduct and compliance report*. Lexington: ICF. Retrieved September 25, 2018, from https://coachfederation.org/app/uploads/2018/08/2017EthicalConductandComplianceReport.pdf

ICF. (2018a). *ICF code of ethics*. Retrieved September 25, 2018, from https://coachfederation.org/code-of-ethics/

ICF. (2018b). *ICF ethics hotline*. Retrieved September 25, 2018, from https://coachfederation.org/icf-ethics/

ICF. (2018c). *Ethical Conduct Review (ECR) process*. Retrieved September 25, 2018, from https://coachfederation.org/icf-ethics/

Iordanou, I., Hawley, R., & Iordanou, C. (2017). *Values and ethics in coaching*. London: Sage Publications.

Iordanou, I., & Williams, P. (2017). Developing ethical capabilities of coaches. In T. Bachkirova, G. Spence, & D. Drake (Eds.), *The Sage handbook of coaching*. London: Sage Publications.

Jackson, P., & Bachkirova, T. (2019). The 3 Ps of supervision and coaching: philosophy, purpose and process. In E. Turner & S. Palmer (Eds.), *The heart of coaching supervision – working with reflection and self-care*. Abingdon: Routledge.

Lane, D. (2011). Ethics and professional standards in supervision. In T. Bachkirova, P. Jackson, & D. Clutterbuck (Eds.), *Coaching and mentoring supervision*. Maidenhead: Open University Press.

Law, H. (2005a). The role of ethical principles in coaching psychology. *The Coaching Psychologist*, 1(1), 19–20.

Law, H. (2005b). The new code of ethics, human rights and its implications in relation to coaching psychology practice. *The Coaching Psychologist*, 1(1), 13–15.

Lowman, R. (2012). Coaching ethics. In J. Passmore, D. B. Peterson, & T. Freire (Eds.), *The Wiley Blackwell handbook of the psychology of coaching and mentoring*. Chichester: Wiley-Blackwell. doi:10.1002/9781118326459.ch5

Malik, K. (2014). *The quest for a moral compass*. London: Atlantic Books Ltd.

Moral, M., & Lamy, F. (2017). *Stretching ethical dilemmas – a creative tool for supervisors*. Presented at 7th International Conference on Coaching Supervision, Oxford Brookes University, Oxford and at 7th EMCC International Coaching and Mentoring Research Conference, Greenwich University, London.

Passmore, J. (2009). Coaching ethics: Making ethical decisions – novices and experts. *The Coaching Psychologist*, 5(1), 6–10.

Passmore, J. (2011). *Supervision in coaching: Supervision, ethics and continuous professional development*. London: Kogan Page.

Passmore, J., & Mortimer, L. (2011). Ethics: A balancing act. In L. Boyce & G. Hernez-Broome (Eds.), *Advancing executive coaching: Setting the course for successful leadership coaching.* San Francisco, CA: Jossey-Bass.

Passmore, J., Brown, H., & Csigas, Z. (2017). *The state of play of coaching and mentoring in Europe.* Henley-on Thames: Henley Business School and EMCC.

Passmore & Turner's Six Stage *APPEAR* Ethical decision-making model in Passmore, J., & Turner, E. (2018). Reflections on integrity – the *APPEAR* model. *In Coaching at Work, 13*(2), 42–46.

Pope, K. S., & Vasquez, M. J. T. (2016). *Ethics in psychotherapy and counselling* (5th ed.). Hoboken: John Wiley & Sons.

Rostron, S. S. (2009). The global initiatives in the coaching field. *In Coaching: An International Journal of Theory, Research and Practice, 2*(1), 76–85.

Ryde, J., Seto, L., & Goldvarg, D. (2019). Diversity and inclusion in supervision. In E. Turner & S. Palmer (Eds.), *The heart of coaching supervision – working with reflection and self-care.* Abingdon: Routledge.

Singer, P. (Ed.). (1994). *Ethics.* Oxford: Oxford University Press.

Steare, R. (2006). *Ethicability.* London: Roger Steare Consulting Limited.

Turner, E. (2009). Diagram of relationships and power v2. Unpublished.

Turner, E. (2012). The what, why and how of it. *In Coaching at Work, 7*(3), 15.

Turner, E., & Passmore, J. (2017). *Confidentiality, record keeping and ethical decision making: What to do when the police come calling?* Presentation, 23 Annual European Mentoring and Coaching Conference, Edinburgh. Retrieved from http://scotland2017.emccconference.org/speakers/eve-turner-jonathan-passmore

Turner, E., & Passmore, J. (2018). Ethical dilemmas and tricky decisions: A global perspective of coaching supervisors' practices in coach decision-making. *In the International Journal of Evidence Based Coaching and Mentoring, 16*(1), 126–142. Retrieved September 25, 2018, from https://radar.brookes.ac.uk/radar/items/da4e8785-60aa-4867-8aa7-caebf259a94f/1/

Turner, E., & Woods, D. (2015). When the police come knocking. *In Coaching at Work, 10*(6), 28–34.

Widdows, H. (2011). *Global ethics.* Durham: Acumen Publishing Limited.

Williams, P., & Anderson, K. S. (2006). *Law and ethics in coaching: How to solve – and avoid – difficult problems in your practice.* Hoboken, NJ: John Wiley & Sons.

WABC (Worldwide Association of Business Coaches). (2018). *Code of business coaching ethics and integrity.* Retrieved September 25, 2018, from www.wabccoaches.com/includes/popups/code_of_ethics_2nd_edition_december_17_2007.html

Chapter 4

Mastering evaluation

Rebecca J. Jones and Brian O. Underhill

Introduction

Evaluating coaching practice is a complex yet necessary task if we are to understand whether our coaching practice is effective in achieving the required results. However, the first step in evaluating coaching is to understand what the required results are; in other words, what outcomes we can expect to achieve from executive coaching. After that, we can then determine the tools and techniques we can use to measure these outcomes.

As the evaluation of coaching has only become a pertinent issue in recent years, the theory and evidence are somewhat underdeveloped. However, individuals seeking to evaluate coaching can benefit from the extensive theory and evidence in relation to evaluating other forms of learning and development, such as training, which has benefitted from many decades of scholarly attention.

Therefore, in this chapter, we provide an overview of the training evaluation theory and evidence and translate how this can be applied to evaluating coaching. This framework of coaching outcomes reports the multiple levels with which coaching can be evaluated. We provide recommendations regarding the tools and techniques that can be utilized in evaluating coaching at each of these levels. Finally, we present an illustrative case study of coaching evaluation in action.

Theory and evidence

The 'problem' with coaching evaluation

There is little consensus in the literature regarding the most appropriate outcome criteria for evaluating coaching (Grant, Passmore, Cavanagh, & Parker, 2010; MacKie, 2007; Smither, 2011). Whereas the overall objective of workplace coaching has been conceptualized as professional personal development that will ultimately lead to the achievement of organizational-level goals and objectives, the impact of coaching on outcomes remains unclear. Research conveys a mixed message as to the types and magnitude of outcomes one can expect from coaching. Although research and anecdotal reports of the impact of coaching from the coachees' perspective are plentiful, for many, these self-reported benefits of coaching are insufficient to build a strong business case for coaching. Rather, many stakeholders wish to see firm evidence for the impact of coaching. In this respect, a tried and tested framework to guide the evaluation of coaching is essential in order to collect consistent and reliable evidence that can be used by stakeholders, wishing to justify a return on investment from learning budgets spent on coaching, and practitioners, wishing to understand how their coaching has impacted their coachees' work and personal lives, in a more scientific manner.

However, the challenge of evaluating coaching in a consistent and reliable way is perhaps not surprising given that coaching is a one-to-one development tool that works with each coachee in a unique way, focusing on a unique set of outcomes for each coachee. Therefore, applying a standardized set of outcome criteria across all coachees may not necessarily capture the tailored focus of individual coaching sessions. This challenge is reflected in the inconsistency across coaching research with the types of outcome measures utilized. For example, several researchers have used measures that are recognized outcomes in the field of organizational behavior. This group of outcomes includes measures such as workplace well-being and resilience (Grant, Curtayne, & Burton, 2009), employee satisfaction (Luthans & Peterson, 2003), and depression and anxiety (Grant, Green, & Rynsaardt, 2010). A small number of researchers have attempted to tackle the challenging task of measuring the impact of coaching on actual results and performance, such as the work by Olivero, Bane, and Kopelman (1997), who examined objective measures of productivity. Also popular is the use of multi-source or 360-degree feedback ratings as an outcome measure in assessing coaching effectiveness (Smither, London, Flautt, Vargas, & Kucine, 2003) or even short "mini survey"–type metrics to capture 360-degree feedback (Goldsmith & Morgan, 2004; Underhill, Anderson, & Silva, 2005).

There are a number of reasons why the unsystematic evaluation of coaching as evidenced by the wide variety of outcome measures used by coaching scholars is problematic. First, knowledge builds through an accumulation of an understanding of a topic over time. An essential element of the scientific process is the replication of results in the same as well as different contexts and conditions. If results are not or cannot be replicated as different outcome measures are used in each study, then we can question whether the results of the original study were due to chance or perhaps some particular characteristic of that unique study. Furthermore, if studies use different outcomes, then outcomes cannot be grouped to establish a theme upon which coaching may impact. In relation to informing the practice of evaluating coaching, it is challenging to build a compelling case for the use of coaching without a guiding framework to categorize the different ways in which we can evaluate coaching that can aid our understanding of the impact of coaching at multiple levels, beyond the impact reported by coachees themselves. Therefore, to address the need to understand the levels at which we can evaluate coaching, we first turn to the literature around evaluating training. In particular, we review two key theories: Kirkpatrick's model of evaluation (1967, 1996) and Kraiger, Ford, and Salas's (1993) application of learning theory to training evaluation.

Kirkpatrick's (1967, 1996) model of training evaluation

Kirkpatrick's (1967) classic model of evaluation criteria proposes that the evaluation of training should be performed at four levels: reaction, learning, behavior, and results. Kirkpatrick (1996) states that the reaction level of evaluation can be viewed as a form of customer satisfaction: how satisfied were the trainees with the training that was delivered? Kirkpatrick specifies that this level of evaluation does not measure any actual learning that takes place; however, it is still important to evaluate training at this level, as trainees are unlikely to learn from a program they do not enjoy. Additionally, reaction-level information can be used to guide amendments or modifications to future training programs. Reaction to training are the most frequently collected form of evaluation in training, because they are extremely straightforward to measure and generally easy to collect.

Learning is described as the degree to which knowledge was acquired, skills were developed, or attitudes were changed as a result of the training. Kirkpatrick suggests that learning should be assessed in an experimental format by measuring the targeted outcome (i.e., the knowledge, skill, or attitude) before and after the training in order to compare any changes. Kirkpatrick recommends that the same data should also be collected from a control group to provide extra credibility to findings.

Kirkpatrick's third level of evaluation is behavior. This is described as the extent to which the trainee's behavior on the job changes as a result of the training: also known as transfer of training. Kirkpatrick specifies that evaluation at this level is challenging. As with the evaluation of learning, it requires a scientific approach; however, it is also important to consider the potential influence of a range of other factors. Kirkpatrick suggests evaluating behavior before and after training with data also collected from a control group, preferably by collecting appraisals of the trainee's behavior from a range of stakeholders.

Finally, evaluation should also be conducted at the results level. Kirkpatrick states that most training programs have desired results outlined as the main purpose or objective of the training. Examples of the types of results that a training program may aim to produce include reduced costs, higher quality, and increased production. Therefore, it is appropriate to measure the effectiveness of training in terms of the desired results that have been produced as a consequence of the training. However, as with measuring behavior, the assessment of the impact of training on results becomes complicated due to the range of other potential variables that may also contribute to these results.

Kirkpatrick's model is widely applied in research and practice (e.g., Alliger, Tannenbaum, Bennett, Traver, & Shotland, 1997; Arthur, Bennett, Edens, & Bell, 2003; Powell & Yalcin, 2010; Tharenou, Saks, & Moore, 2007) and represents a logical organization and progression of outcomes from the basic individual reaction to training through to training transfer and organizational results. The key feature of Kirkpatrick's model is the simplicity and practical applicability, which potentially explains its enduring success. However, Kirkpatrick's model has been criticized for oversimplifying learning from training and, as such, an alternative model was proposed by Kraiger et al. (1993).

Kraiger et al.'s (1993) application of learning theory to training evaluation

Kraiger et al. (1993) argue that when evaluating training, it is necessary to examine learning-based outcomes in a more sophisticated way, rather than combining learning and transfer outcomes as in the Kirkpatrick levels. They highlight the argument presented by Campbell (1988) that the most fundamental issues when evaluating training is whether the trainees have learned the material covered in the training. In response to the lack of a conceptual model that can guide researchers on how to evaluate learning, Kraiger et al. proposed a model of three classes of learning outcomes that can occur following training: cognitive, skill-based, and affective.

First, cognitive outcomes describe the quantity and type of knowledge learned and the relationships among these knowledge elements. Kraiger et al. propose that cognitive outcomes can be separated into verbal knowledge, the creation of suitable mental models for knowledge organization, and the ability to retrieve and apply knowledge via established cognitive strategies. They recommend that suitable evaluation methods of cognitive outcomes might include recognition and recall tests, free sort tasks (where trainees make judgments of the similarity or closeness among core elements of the course material), and probed protocol analysis (where trainees provide a step-by-step analysis of the necessary stages in successfully completing a task).

Next, Kraiger et al. suggest that learning should result in skill-based outcomes such as the development of technical or motor skills. Skill-based outcomes can be measured by the level of compilation the individual can demonstrate (i.e., a smooth, fast performance should be expected with advanced skills) and automaticity of performance (where the skill is demonstrated fluidly by automatic rather than controlled processing). Kraiger et al. suggest that some potential methods of assessing skill-based outcomes are behavioral observation and secondary task performance (where trainees perform the trained task while simultaneously performing a secondary task).

Finally, Kraiger et al. describe how learning should also result in affective outcomes. Based on Gagne's (1984) theory that attitudes about a learning outcome are important as they are determinants of behavior or performance, Gagne defines an attitude as an internal state that influences the individual's choice of personal action. Kraiger et al. expand this definition by including motivation and affect as training outcomes and suggest that affective outcomes can be evaluated by self-report measures.

Both the work of Kirkpatrick (1967, 1996) and Kraiger et al. (1993) have been hugely influential in guiding how training is evaluated in research and practice. As such, these theoretical models can provide an important guide to help us understand how we can evaluate coaching in a consistent and reliable manner.

Aims and processes in evaluating coaching

A solution to the coaching evaluation 'problem'

To address the gap in theory and practice on how to evaluate coaching, Jones, Woods, and Guillaume (2016) utilized the existing frameworks of training outcomes to propose that the outcomes of coaching be modeled in the following ways. With respect to Kraiger et al.'s (1993) three-component classification, Jones et al. (2016) proposed that the potential outcomes of coaching are similarly separated into cognitive, skill-based, and affective outcome criteria. Furthermore, Jones et al. suggest that in line with Kirkpatrick's (1996) theorizing, results outcomes are similarly important to coaching as for training (see Table 4.1), although Jones et al. argue that the nature of these outcomes in the

Table 4.1 Framework of coaching outcomes and summary of proposed coaching evaluation criteria

Outcome Criteria	Description	Measurement Methodology
Affective outcomes	Attitudes and motivational outcomes (e.g., self-efficacy, well-being, satisfaction)	Self-report questionnaires
Cognitive outcomes	Declarative knowledge, procedural knowledge, cognitive strategies (e.g., problem solving)	Recognition and recall tests, free sorts, probed protocol analysis
Skill-based outcomes	Compilation and automaticity of new skills (e.g., leadership skills, technical skills, competencies)	Behavioral observation in the workplace (e.g., multi-source feedback questionnaire) Skill assessment
Results	Individual, team, and organizational performance	Financial results, objective or goal achievement, productivity

(Jones et al., 2016)

context of coaching will be different from training. We now further expand on the theoretical underpinning of the Jones et al. framework for evaluating coaching in order to provide the reader with a strong understanding of why, how, and when coaching should be evaluated.

Cognitive outcomes from coaching

Referring to Kraiger et al.'s (1993) types of cognitive outcomes, Jones et al. propose that new verbal knowledge is the outcome least likely to be developed through coaching. Definitions of coaching generally agree that coaching does not involve providing instruction to the coachee (McAdam, 2005) and instead coaching is concerned with assisting the coachee in the process of making sense of existing knowledge (Swart & Harcup, 2013). Therefore, although the coaching process may involve the development of some new knowledge through discussion with the coach, the scope of new knowledge gained will be very different when compared to instructional training. Kraiger et al.'s second type of cognitive outcome is the creation of suitable mental models for knowledge organization. This type of cognitive outcome is potentially more likely than gaining new verbal knowledge in coaching, as the coach works with the coachee to help make sense of the information available to them. This process may involve the coachee making new associations between existing knowledge in order to address barriers or blockers to behavior change, therefore applying existing knowledge in new ways.

Finally, Kraiger et al. suggest that cognitive outcomes also include the ability to retrieve and apply knowledge via established cognitive strategies. This type of outcome may be particularly relevant when considering cognitive-behavioral coaching (CBC), where the focus is to change behavior by understanding the impact an individual's view on events has on the way they feel and act (Neenan & Dryden, 2010). During the course of CBC, the coach may work with the coachee to identify his or her view of the event or issue in question and, where necessary, challenge these views and realign them to a viewpoint that is more likely to bring about the results that the individual is looking for. The coachee would take away from the coaching session a new cognitive strategy to use in the situation being addressed.

The proposition that coaching can produce cognitive outcomes is potentially explained by Locke and Latham's (1990a, 1990b; Latham, Locke, & Fassina, 2002) high-performance cycle (a development of goal-setting theory). Latham et al. describe strategies as cognitive in nature and involving the development of skills and problem solving. Latham et al. proposed that goals activate the application of or search for strategies as part of an individual's goal-striving efforts. Therefore, goals motivate and guide the use of existing knowledge and strategies and, where necessary, promote the acquisition of new skills through problem solving and learning, leading to new strategies (Wood, Whelan, Sojo, & Wong, 2013).

A recent systematic review of the coaching literature conducted by Bozer and Jones (2018) demonstrated that cognitive outcomes are the least frequently evaluated outcome from coaching. This could be partially due to the challenging nature of accurately capturing the development of new mental models and problem-solving strategies following coaching. Despite the evaluation challenges at this level, some examples of the cognitive outcomes in the coaching literature include self-reported learning following coaching (Ammentorp, Jensen, & Uhrenfeldt, 2013); solution-focused thinking (Grant et al., 2017); problem solving (Gyllensten & Palmer, 2006); self-insight or self-awareness (Bozer, Sarros, & Santora, 2013); knowledge (Taie, 2011); and learning agility (Trathen, 2007).

Skill-based outcomes from coaching

Skill-based outcomes arguably have a similar level of importance in coaching compared to training. At the start of this chapter, it was described how the purpose of coaching is to achieve professional outcomes that are of value to the coachee. Examples of the types of skills that coaching may aim to develop include leadership, assertiveness, communication, decision-making, and delegation. Coaching is able to effectively promote skill acquisition and enhancement through the work-based application of improvement and development activities. For example, during the coaching process, the coach may discuss with the coachee potential opportunities in which they are able to practice the skills developed during coaching. These processes promote a focus on developing goal-related and job-specific skills (e.g., Grant et al., 2009).

Bozer and Jones (2018) identify in their review of the coaching literature that skill-based outcomes are one of the most frequently assessed types of outcomes following coaching. One of the reasons for the frequency in assessing outcomes at this level may be that coachees often set goals which revolve around the development of a new skill, and as such it is appropriate to evaluate whether that skill has been effectively developed following coaching. Some examples of skill-based outcomes from the coaching literature include self-rated performance (Jones, Woods, & Zhou, unpublished manuscript(a)); supervisor or other-rated performance (i.e., peer or direct report) (Bozer, Joo, & Santora, 2015); leadership skills (Williams, 2016); networking skills and career planning (Spurk, Kauffeld, Barthauer, & Heinemann, 2015); and safety-oriented communication skills (Kines et al., 2010).

Affective outcomes from coaching

Jones et al. (2016) argue that affective outcomes are relatively more important in coaching than training. Many of the valued outcomes of coaching represent affective outcomes (e.g., development of self-efficacy and confidence, reduction in stress, increase in satisfaction, and improved motivation). Therefore, the coaching intervention may focus on ways in which to directly develop and improve affective outcomes. However, there may also be an indirect impact from coaching on affective outcomes. In particular, goal setting (Latham et al., 2002) and the process of action planning for problem solving in experiential learning (Kolb & Kolb, 2008) are likely to exert influence on motivation and affective orientation to performance improvement. Furthermore, according to Locke and Latham's high-performance cycle (1990a), the process of working towards a challenging goal with a valued outcome (as occurs in coaching) creates a greater impact on affective reactions such as job satisfaction.

Bozer and Jones (2018) report that in the coaching literature, affective outcomes are the most frequently assessed outcome. This is likely to be for two key reasons: first, affective outcomes are very easily assessed utilizing self-report questionnaires, and second, due to the transient nature of many affective outcomes, coaching has the potential to have a positive impact at the affective level, even following a brief coaching intervention. Some examples of affective outcomes from the coaching literature include perceived coaching effectiveness (Jones, Woods, & Hutchinson, 2014); self-efficacy (Baron & Morin, 2010); work well-being (Jones, Woods, & Zhou, in press (b)); career satisfaction (Bozer et al., 2013); job satisfaction (Gyllensten & Palmer, 2005); stress (Bright & Crockett, 2012); intention to leave/quit (Ladegard & Gjerde, 2014); depression (Grant, 2014); resilience (Grant, 2014); anxiety (Grant et al., 2009); and organizational commitment (Luthans & Peterson, 2003).

Result outcomes from coaching

Finally, earlier in this chapter, it was noted that the aim of coaching is to contribute to achievement of organizational-level goals and objectives (Sonnentag & Frese, 2002). By aligning individual goal setting to these organizational-level goals and objectives, coaching may impact performance, making it sensible to include some measure of results, as per Kirkpatrick's model. Jones et al. (2016) propose that results might be measured in terms of impact on individual-, team-, and organizational-level performance.

As with training, most coaching has a results-based outcome as the desired objective of the coaching. In order to achieve this individual-level results objective, outcomes may also be produced at the cognitive, skill-based, and affective levels. For example, a coachee who wishes to develop leadership skills may have a results-based objective for wanting to develop this skill set. The coachee may anticipate that by improving his or her leadership skills, they may be able to take a more strategic lead in their role, consequently increasing the long-term profitability of their unit. The targeted change at the skill-based level is in order to generate a change at the individual results level.

Continuing this theme, an equally valid objective of coaching may be to produce results at the team level. Again, using the leadership skills example, the coachee may want to improve his or her leadership and communication skills in order to effectively bring their team together to work more collaboratively. An increased collaborative approach within the team may then lead to the team fulfilling more of the team-level objectives: a team-level results outcome.

Finally, it seems logical that if individual-level and team-level results objectives are aligned with organizational-level results objectives, then changes at either the individual or team level should generate changes at the organizational level. For example, if the coachee was to improve the profitability of his or her unit and increase the number of team-level goals being fulfilled as a result of learning and development achieved through coaching, then it is likely that these improvements at the individual and team levels will filter through into improvements of results at the organizational level.

While outcomes at the results level are arguably most important from an organizational perspective, these are one of the least frequently explored in the coaching literature (Bozer & Jones, 2018). As Kirkpatrick (1996) notes, assessing results-level outcomes is highly complex, which is likely reflected in the shortage of research evidence at this level. Studies that exist on results-level outcomes include goal attainment (Sonesh et al., 2015); retention (Gardiner, Kearns, & Tiggemann, 2013); productivity (Olivero et al., 1997); productivity quality (Parker-Wilkins, 2006); sales performance (Libri & Kemp, 2006); safety performance (Kines et al., 2010); promotion (Feggetter, 2007); selection success (Jones & Andrews, unpublished manuscript); and sickness records (Duijts, Kant, van den Brandt & Swaen, 2008).

Tools and techniques

Following the Jones et al. (2016) framework, each of the four levels (cognitive, skill, affective, results) are further expanded into methods by which to measure each with specific examples.

Measuring cognitive outcomes from coaching

In Kraiger et al.'s (1993) framework, a range of measurement techniques for cognitive outcomes is specified, the first of which is recognition and recall tests. In practice, when evaluating learning from training of the range of cognitive outcome evaluation methods Kraiger et al. discuss, recognition and recall tests are the technique that is most easily applied and therefore the most popular in practice. In the context of cognitive coaching outcomes, as outlined above, recognition and recall tests are the least suitable method, as new verbal knowledge is the least likely cognitive outcome from coaching. However, Kraiger et al.'s other suggested cognitive outcome evaluation methods, such as free sorts to assess mental models (where trainees make judgments of the similarity or closeness among core elements of the course material) and probed protocol analysis (where trainees provide a step-by-step analysis of the necessary stages in successfully completing a task) to assess cognitive strategies, could still be utilized when evaluating coaching. In practice, the highly individualized nature of each coaching intervention means that these evaluation methods would need to be created on a case-by-case basis. It is unlikely that one template technique could be applied across different coachees, making evaluation of coaching at this level practically challenging. This potentially explains the lack of reported cognitive outcomes in the coaching literature.

However, examples of more easily applied techniques to assess cognitive outcomes can be drawn from the coaching literature. For example, Grant (2014) utilizes the Solution-Focused Inventory (SFI; Grant, 2011) to measure solution-focused thinking following coaching. This 12-item scale includes three sub-scales – problem disengagement, goal orientation, and resource activation – that collectively measure an individual's engagement in solution-focused thinking. Also, coachee self-awareness can be measured utilizing the eight-item self-insight scale (Grant, Franklin, & Langford, 2002), which assesses the individual's awareness over the reasons behind their behavior, thoughts and emotions.

Measuring skill-based outcomes from coaching

Skill-based outcomes are demonstrated by the individual's behavior in the workplace and, as such, Kraiger et al. (1993) specify that skill-based outcomes can be measured by behavioral observation. An example of this approach to evaluating coaching is illustrated in the work by Kines et al. (2010), who utilized direct behavioral observations to assess safety behavior on construction sites in order to evaluate the effectiveness of coaching aimed at improving site safety. Kraiger et al. also suggest that skill-based outcomes can be measured using hands-on testing. This form of skill-based evaluation is less frequently seen in the coaching literature; however, Taie (2011) utilized a competency skill test to assess nurses' ability to perform basic life support skills after receiving coaching specifically focused on improving these skills.

A more frequently utilized method of gathering information on an individual's behavior that is described in the coaching literature is the use of 360-degree or multi-source feedback. For example, Luthans and Peterson (2003) utilized the Management Feedback Profile as a 360-degree feedback tool to measure three factors of manager's self-regulatory behavior: behavioral competence (i.e., determines appropriate solutions/resolutions for identified problems); inter-personal competence (i.e., provides timely information and feedback); and personal responsibility (i.e., takes initiative in trying new ideas). Also, Smither et al. (2003) assessed management skills developed as a result of coaching via multi-source feedback. Another variety of multi-source feedback is the 'mini survey' (Goldsmith & Morgan, 2004; Underhill, Koriath, & McAnally, 2007). A mini-360 measures perception of leader improvement over time, focusing on only the specific areas for development chosen by the coachee. By using an improvement scale (i.e., "Did this person improve in their overall leadership effectiveness over the past 6 months?"), surveying the exact same rater group each time is not necessary. The survey is much less time demanding on raters, and results can be aggregated among many leaders for a good view of overall improvement.

A further example of assessing skill-based outcomes can be via self-reported assessment of skill development. This example is frequently seen in the coaching literature (see Bozer & Jones, 2018, for a summary). A specific example of a self-report skills assessment tool is Jones et al's (in press (b)) five-item personal effectiveness scale. This scale is designed to measure the impact of coaching on effectiveness at work, including areas such as prioritization, planning, and flexibility.

Measuring affective outcomes from coaching

According to Kraiger et al.'s (1993) recommendations, affective outcomes should be evaluated by using self-report measures. The field of industrial-organizational psychology benefits from a range of established affective outcome measures, many of which have already been utilized in the coaching literature. For example, Luthans and Peterson (2003) measured organizational commitment as an outcome of coaching using the Organizational Commitment Questionnaire (OCQ; Mowday, Steers, & Porter, 1979); Grant et al. (2009) measured resilience and workplace well-being as coaching outcomes using the Cognitive Hardiness Scale (Nowack, 1990); and Bozer and Sarros (2012) measured coachee career satisfaction using Greenhaus, Parasuraman, and Wormley's (1990) Career Satisfaction Scale. The abundance of suitable self-report scales available in the literature and the ease in which they can be administered mean that evaluating coaching at the affective level is easily implemented in practice.

Recent unpublished presentations have established a potential link between greater employee engagement and coaching. Employee engagement is an increasingly common metric at organizations, measured by quantitative surveys (e.g., Gallup Q12). Questions include such items as "Do you know what is expected of you at work?" or "At work, do your opinions seem to count?" Two presenting organizations have found significantly greater engagement survey scores among employees who have been trained in coaching skills versus a similar population of those who had not.

A further example of assessing affective outcomes is Jones et al's (in press (b)) seven-item work well-being scale. This scale is designed to measure the impact of coaching on coachee perceptions of their work well-being and includes areas such as satisfaction, stress, and engagement.

Measuring results outcomes from coaching

While in theory it is logical that coaching could generate changes at the individual, team, and organizational levels of results, in practice, it is very challenging to evaluate outcomes at these levels. In relation to evaluating training,

Kirkpatrick (1996) explains that there is no easy solution to the problem of evaluating training results. The range of internal and external variables that impact on results, in addition to any changes created as a result of training, mean that it is very difficult to isolate the impact of the training intervention on the results outcome being assessed. These challenges apply equally to evaluating coaching outcomes at the results level. To further confound the issue, the impact of managers and leaders (who are frequently those receiving coaching) on results outcomes is generally not obvious or linear. This may explain why few coaching researchers have attempted to measure results-level outcomes.

The gold standard of results outcomes is the use of objective measures to understand the impact of coaching. These objective measures are those that are not susceptible to subjective interpretation (such as perceptions of performance). Examples of objective results measures include assessing whether coaching has a positive impact on the selection success of undergraduate business students applying for an internship (Jones & Andrews, unpublished manuscript) or the impact of coaching on retention in a sample of Australian doctors (Gardiner et al., 2013) or leaders in the corporate environment (Parker-Wilkins, 2006). A recent unpublished presentation of an objective results measure can be seen with the favorable comparison of average salaries of those leaders receiving coaching versus a similar population of leaders who had not received coaching. The advent of "big data" applied to the human resources profession may make further measurement of coaching results increasingly possible.

A more easily applied tool to assess results outcomes is goal attainment scaling. This technique has been applied in the coaching literature (i.e., Grant, 2014) and requires coachees to specify goals that are personally meaningful and valued at the start of their coaching program. On completion of the coaching, coachees are asked to respond to the question "Up to today, how successful have you been in achieving this goal?" and rate their goal attainment on a scale from 0% (no attainment) to 100% (complete attainment). While this approach to evaluating at the results level is reliant on subjective rather than objective data, it is easily applied and can be utilized to support big data methods where they are available.

When to evaluate?

In this chapter, we have addressed the issue of what outcomes we should evaluate from coaching, theoretically why it is important to evaluate these outcomes, and how we should evaluate outcomes at each level. Our final word relates to when it is appropriate to evaluate. Almost without exception, evaluation in the coaching literature is conducted at the end of the coaching program. This timing of the evaluation is intrinsically linked to the goal of research, which is to evaluate the impact of an intervention over a fixed period. In practice, evaluation need not be confined to these timing restrictions. However, for some outcomes, it makes sense to wait until the final completion of the program to evaluate. For example, due to the distal nature of outcomes, such as the development of new cognitive strategies and skill sets and the impact on results, it is likely that any impact of coaching at these levels will take time to develop. Therefore, evaluation at these levels should be conducted after a sufficient number of coaching sessions have been conducted and time has passed to allow the coachee to implement the new learning from the coaching and changes in behavior and performance to be observed. There is no simple answer to how many sessions are 'sufficient' or how much time is adequate, and this is an area that would significantly benefit from additional research to guide recommendations on the duration of effective coaching programs. On the other hand, affective outcomes are more proximal to the coaching process and more transient in nature, therefore it may be that an impact on affective outcomes can be observed after as little as one coaching session; therefore, practitioners may consider evaluating outcomes at this level more frequently.

Case study

Microsoft has made a large investment in coaching, which has included both affective and skills-based evaluation components (Wallis, Underhill, & Hedly, 2012). Beginning in 2004, it initiated the "Leaders Building Leaders" high-potential development experience, which has been offered to thousands of leaders since its launch.

The program included five developmental components: a leadership orientation, an in-business/profession event, coaching and mentoring, career development, and networking/learning circles. The coaching component included mostly telephone-based sessions for eight months (approximately 7–10 sessions). Coaching began with feedback from the Microsoft 360-degree assessment and any other data points the participant chose to share with their coach. A coaching action plan was then developed, which helped participants to clearly define their coaching goals. The coach, coachee, and manager also conducted a three-way session. Coaching then continued for the next eight months.

Affective outcomes were assessed in the form of a coach satisfaction survey, which was launched at the midpoint of each engagement. Five questions were asked:

How satisfied are you with your coach in the following areas:

- Q1: Identifies clear priorities for my growth and development
- Q2: Genuinely listens to me
- Q3: Provides specific, actionable suggestions/advice
- Q4: Communicates in a direct and concise manner
- Q5: Overall satisfaction with your coaching experience

Overall satisfaction on these questions averaged 97.9%. A "net promoter score" (rating participants' willingness to recommend coaching to others) was also calculated of 175.4, out of a possible 200.

At the end of coaching, a 360-degree 'mini-survey' was also launched to assess skills-based outcomes, asking key stakeholders around the participant leaders whether they noticed improvement over the past eight months. This survey uses a seven-point response scale from "less effective" (−3) to "more effective" (+3). Questions center on the overall leadership effectiveness of the participant, as well as unique, customized questions pertaining to each individual's personal goals. After the first year of the program, 22% of raters indicated that the participants had improved in their personal goals at a +3 level; 59% noted improvement at a +2 or +3 level, and an impressive 89% of raters observed improvement of some form (+1, +2, +3 levels). This aggregated statistic (and others like it) can be shared throughout the organization to indicate positive improvement in leadership effectiveness as a result of the large investment the company had made in the program.

Conclusion

The evaluation of coaching is sometimes an afterthought to the main event of the coaching program itself; however, we have argued here that effectively evaluating coaching is an essential step in understanding whether our coaching practice is effective in achieving the required results. As such, evaluating coaching is important for the individual coach, organizations utilizing coaching as a learning and development tool, coaching researchers, and the profession of coaching as a whole. We have provided a detailed overview of the Jones et al. (2016) framework of coaching outcomes, including the underlying theory which explains why coaching is likely to impact on outcomes at each of these levels. We have explored a variety of tools and techniques to illustrate how coaching can be evaluated at each of these levels, and finally we have provided an indication as to when coaching should be evaluated. Our final recommendation regarding evaluating coaching is perhaps the most important, regardless of at which level you decided to evaluate your coaching program (and we would always encourage you to evaluate at all levels); it is essential that the measures selected are aligned with the goals of the coaching program itself. Close alignment between coaching goals and coaching evaluation will ensure that your evaluation efforts accurately capture the real impact of your coaching practice.

Developing yourself

Suggested readings

Phillips, P. P., Phillips, J. J., & Edwards, L. A. (2012). *Measuring the success of coaching: A step-by-step guide for measuring impact and calculating ROI.* USA: American Society of Training and Development.

Passmore, J., & Velez, M. J. (2015) Training evaluation. In K. Kraiger, J. Passmore, N. R. dos Santos, & S. Malvezzi (Eds.), *Wiley Blackwell handbook of the psychology of training, development and personal improvement.* Chichester: Wiley.

Suggested web links

Sample coach satisfaction survey, to be administered to the leader client. www.coachsource. com/downloads

Sample "mini survey", a short multi rater survey measuring improvement in the eyes of those working with the leader client. www.coachsource.com/downloads

"Coaching with ROI" free webinar with Lisa Ann Edwards. http://coachingwithroi.com.

"Measuring the impact and results of coaching" powerpoint slide show by Brian O. Underhill presented at WBECS 2015. www.coachsource.com/downloads.

Sample cognitive outcome measure: Grant, A. M. (2011). The solution-focused inventory: A tripartite taxonomy for teaching, measuring and conceptualising solution-focused approaches to coaching. *The Coaching Psychologist*, 7(2), 98–106. Available from:

http://citeseerx.ist.psu.edu/viewdoc/download?doi=10.1.1.453.6410&rep=rep1&type=pdf#page=16

References

Alliger, G. M., Tannenbaum, S. I., Bennett, W., Traver, H., & Shotland, A. (1997). A meta-analysis of the relations among training criteria. *Personnel Psychology*, *50*, 341–358. doi:10.1111/j.1744-6570.1997.tb00911.x

Ammentorp, J., Jensen, H. I., & Uhrenfeldt, L. (2013). Danish health professionals' experiences of being coached: A pilot study. *Journal of Continuing Education in the Health Professions*, *33*, 41–47. doi:10.1002/chp.21157

Arthur, W., Bennett. W., Edens, P. S., & Bell, S. T. (2003). Effectiveness of training in organizations: A meta-analysis of design & evaluation features. *Journal of Applied Psychology*, 88, 234–235. doi: 10.1037/0021-9010.88.2.234

Baron, L., & Morin, L. (2010). The impact of executive coaching on self-efficacy related to management soft-skills. *Leadership & Organization Development Journal*, *31*(1), 18–38. doi:10.1108/01437731011010362

Bozer, G., & Jones, R. J. (2018). Understanding the factors that determine workplace coaching effectiveness: A systematic literature review. *European Journal of Work and Organizational Psychology*, *27*(3), 342–361. doi:10.1080/1359432X.2018.1446946

Bozer, G., Joo, B. K., & Santora, J. C. (2015). Executive coaching: Does coach-coachee matching based on similarity really matter? *Consulting Psychology: Practice & Research*, *67*(3), 218–233. doi:10.1037/cpb0000044

Bozer, G., & Sarros, J. C. (2012). Examining the effectiveness of executive coaching on coachees' performance in the Israeli context. *International Journal of Evidence Based Coaching and Mentoring*, 14–32.

Bozer, G., Sarros, J. C., & Santora, J. C. (2013). The role of coachee characteristics in executive coaching for effective sustainability. *Journal of Management Development*, *32*(3), 277–294. doi:10.1108/02621711311318319

Bright, D., & Crockett, A. (2012). Training combined with coaching can make a significant difference in job performance and satisfaction. *Coaching: An International Journal of Theory, Research and Practice*, *5*(1), 4–21. doi:10.1080/17521882.2011.648332

Campbell, J. P. (1988). Training design for productivity improvement. In J. P. Campbell & R. J. Campbell (Eds.), *Productivity in organizations* (pp. 177–215). San Francisco, CA: Jossey-Bass.

Duijts, S. F. A., Kant, I., van den Brandt, P. A., & Swaen, G. M. H. (2008). Effectiveness of a preventive coaching intervention for employees at risk for sickness absence due to psychosocial health complaints: Results of a randomized controlled trial. *Occupational and Environmental Medicine, 50*(7), 765–776. doi:10.1097/JOM.0b013e3181651584

Feggetter, A. J. W. (2007). A preliminary evaluation of executive coaching: Does executive coaching work for candidates on a high potential development scheme? *International Coaching Psychology Review, 2*(2), 129–142.

Gagne, R. M. (1984). Learning outcomes and their effects: Useful categories of human performance. *American Psychologist,* 377–385.

Gardiner, M., Kearns, H., & Tiggemann, M. (2013). Effectiveness of cognitive behavioural coaching in improving the well-being and retention of rural general practitioners. *Australian Journal of Rural Health, 21*(3), 183–189. doi:10.1111/ajr.12033

Goldsmith, M., & Morgan, H. (2004, August). Leadership is a contact sport: The "follow-up factor" in management development. *Strategy + Business,* 36, from https://www.strategy-business.com/article/04307?gko=a260c

Grant, A. M. (2011). The solution-focused inventory: A tripartite taxonomy for teaching, measuring and conceptualising solution-focused approaches to coaching. *The Coaching Psychologist, 7*(2), 98–106.

Grant, A. M. (2014). The efficacy of executive coaching in times of organisational change. *Journal of Change Management, 14*(2), 258–280. doi:10.1080/14697017.2013.805159

Grant, A. M., Curtayne, L., & Burton, G. (2009). Executive coaching enhances goal attainment, resilience and workplace well-being: A randomised controlled study. *The Journal of Positive Psychology, 4*(5), 396–407. doi:10.1080/17439760902992456

Grant, A. M., Franklin, J., & Langford, P. (2002). The self-reflection and insight scale: A new measure of private self-consciousness. *Social Behavior & Personality: An International Journal, 30*(8), 821–836.

Grant, A. M., Green, L. S., & Rynsaardt, J. (2010). Developmental coaching for high school teachers: Executive coaching goes to school. *Consulting Psychology Journal: Practice and Research, 62*(3), 151–168. doi:10.1037/a0019212

Grant, A. M., Passmore, J., Cavanagh, M. J., & Parker, H. (2010). The state of play in coaching today: A comprehensive review of the field. In G. P. Hodgkinson & K. J. Ford (Eds.), *International review of industrial and organizational psychology* (Vol. 25, pp. 125–168). West Sussex, UK: Wiley-Blackwell.

Grant, A. M., Studholme, I., Verma, R., Kirkwood, L., Paton, B., & O'Connor, S. (2017). The impact of leadership coaching in an Australian healthcare setting. *Journal of Health Organization and Management, 31*(2), 237–252. doi:10.1108/JHOM-09–2016–0187

Greenhaus, J. H., Parasuraman, S., & Wormley, W. M. (1990). Effects of race on organizational experiences, job performance, evaluations and career outcomes. *Academy of Management Journal, 33*(1), 64–86.

Gyllensten, K., & Palmer, S. (2005). Can coaching reduce workplace stress? A quasi-experimental study. *International Journal of Evidence Based Coaching and Mentoring, 3,* 75–85.

Gyllensten, K., & Palmer, S. (2006). Experiences of coaching and stress in the workplace: An interpretative phenomenological analysis. *International Coaching Psychology Review, 1*(1), 86–98.

Jones, R. J., & Andrews, H. (unpublished manuscript). Can one-to-one coaching improve selection success and who benefits most? The role of candidate generalized self-efficacy and grit.

Jones, R. J., Woods, S. A., & Guillaume, Y. R. F. (2016). The effectiveness of workplace coaching: A meta-analysis of learning and performance outcomes from coaching. *Journal of Occupational and Organizational Psychology, 89,* 249–277. doi:10.1111/joop.12119

Jones, R. J., Woods, S. A., & Hutchinson, E. (2014). The influence of the Five Factor Model of personality on the perceived effectiveness of executive coaching. *International Journal of Evidence Based Coaching and Mentoring, 12*(2), 109–118. doi:10.1111/j.1744-6570.2003.tb00152.x

Jones, R. J., Woods, S. A., & Zhou, Y. (unpublished manuscript, a). The effects of coachee personality and goal orientation on performance improvement following coaching: A longitudinal field experiment.

Jones, R. J., Woods, S. A., & Zhou, Z. (in press, b). Boundary conditions of workplace coaching outcomes. *Journal of Managerial Psychology*.

Kines, P., Andersen, L. P. S., Spangenberg, S., Mikkelsen, K. L., Dyreborg, J., & Zohar, D. (2010). Improving construction site safety through leader-based verbal safety communication. *Journal of Safety Research, 41*(5), 399–406. doi:10.1016/j.jsr.2010.06.005

Kirkpatrick, D. L. (1967). Evaluation of training. In R. L. Craig & L. R. Bittel (Eds.), *Training and development handbook* (pp. 87–112). New York, NY: McGraw-Hill.

Kirkpatrick, D. L. (1996, January). Great ideas revisited. *Training & Development, 50*, 54–59.

Kolb, A. Y., & Kolb, D. A. (2008). *Experiential learning theory: A dynamic, holistic approach to management learning, education and development*. Department of Organizational Behavior, Case Western Reserve University. Working Paper.

Kraiger, K., Ford, J. K., & Salas, E. D. (1993). Application of cognitive, skill-based, and affective theories of learning outcomes to new methods of training evaluation. *Journal of Applied Psychology, 78*, 311–328. doi:10.1037/0021–9010.78.2.311

Ladegard, G., & Gjerde, S. (2014). Leadership coaching, leader role-efficacy, and trust in subordinates: A mixed methods study assessing leadership coaching as a leadership development tool. *The Leadership Quarterly, 25*(4), 631–646. doi:10.1016/j.leaqua.2014.02.002

Latham, G. P., Locke, E. A., & Fassina, N. E. (2002). High performance cycle: Standing the test of time. In S. Soonentag (Eds.), *Psychological management of individual performance* (pp. 201–228). West Sussex: John Wiley & Sons.

Libri, V., & Kemp, T. (2006). Assessing the efficacy of a cognitive behavioural executive coaching programme. *International Coaching Psychology Review, 1*(2), 9–18.

Locke, E. A., & Latham, G. P. (1990a). *A theory of goal setting and task performance*. Englewood Cliffs, NJ: Prentice Hall.

Locke, E. A., & Latham, G. P. (1990b). Work motivation and satisfaction: Light at the end of the tunnel. *Psychological Science*, 240–246.

Luthans, F., & Peterson, S. J. (2003). 360-degree feedback with systematic coaching: Empirical analysis suggests a winning combination. *Human Resource Management, 42*(3), 243–256. doi:10.1002/hrm.10083

MacKie, D. (2007). Evaluating the effectiveness of executive coaching: Where are we now and where do we need to be? *Australian Psychologist, 42*, 310–318. doi:10.1080/0005 0060701648217

McAdam, S. (2005). *Executive coaching*. London: Thorogood.

Mowday, R. T., Steers, R. M., & Porter, L. W. (1979). The measurement of organizational commitment. *Journal of Vocational Behavior, 14*, 224–247

Neenan, M., & Dryden, W. (2010). *Life coaching: A cognitive-behavioural approach*. London: Routledge.

Nowack, K. (1990). Initial development of an inventory to assess stress and health. *American Journal of Health Promotion, 4*, 173–180.

Olivero, G., Bane, K. D., & Kopelman, R. E. (1997). Executive coaching as a transfer of training tool: Effects on productivity in a public agency. *Public Personnel Management, 26*, 461–469. doi:10.1177/009102609702600403

Parker-Wilkins, V. (2006). Business impact of executive coaching: Demonstrating monetary value. *Industrial and Commercial Training, 38*(3), 122–127. doi:10.1108/00197850610659373

Powell, K. S., & Yalcin, S. (2010). Managerial training effectiveness: A meta-analysis 1952–2002. *Personnel Review, 39,* 227–241. doi:10.1108/00483481011017435

Smither, J. W. (2011). Can psychotherapy research serve as a guide for research about executive coaching? An agenda for the next decade. *Journal of Business and Psychology, 26*(2), 135–145. doi:10.1007/s10869-011-9216-7

Smither, J. W., London, M., Flautt, R., Vargas, Y., & Kucine, I. (2003). Can working with an executive coach improve multisource feedback ratings over time? A quasi-experimental field study. *Personnel Psychology,* 23–42. doi:10.1111/j.1744–6570.2003.tb00142.x

Sonesh, S. C., Coultas, C. W., Marlow, S. L., Lacerenza, C. N., Reyes, D., & Salas, E. (2015). Coaching in the wild: Identifying factors that lead to success. *Consulting Psychology Journal: Practice and Research, 67*(3), 189–217. doi:10.1037/cpb0000042

Sonnentag, S., & Frese, M. (2002). Performance concepts and performance theory. In S. Soonentag (Eds.), *Psychological management of individual performance* (pp. 4–19). West Sussex: John Wiley & Sons.

Spurk, D., Kauffeld, S., Barthauer, L., & Heinemann, N. S. R. (2015). Fostering networking behavior, career planning and optimism, and subjective career success: An intervention study. *Journal of Vocational Behaviour, 87,* 134–144. doi:10.1016/j.jvb.2014.12.007

Swart, J., & Harcup, J. (2013). 'If I learn do we learn?': The link between executive coaching and organizational learning. *Management Learning, 44,* 337–354. doi:10.1177/135050 7612447916

Taie, E. S. (2011). Coaching as an approach to enhance performance. *Journal for Quality and Participation, 34*(1), 34–38.

Tharenou, P., Saks, A. M., & Moore, C. (2007). A review and critique of research on training and organizational-level outcomes. *Human Resource Management Review, 17,* 251–273. doi:10.1016/j.hrmr.2007.07.004

Trathen, S. A. (2007). *Executive coaching, changes in leadership competencies and learning agility amongst Microsoft senior executives.* (PhD Dissertation), School of Education, Colorado State University, Fort Collins, CO.

Underhill, B., Anderson, D., & Silva, R. (2005). Agilent Technologies, Inc. In L. Carter, D. Ulrich, & M. Goldsmith (Eds.), *Best practices in leadership development and organization change* (pp. 1–20). San Francisco, CA: Pfeiffer.

Underhill, B. O., Koriath, J. J., & McAnally, K. (2007). *Executive coaching for results: The definitive guide to developing organizational leaders.* San Francisco, CA: Berrett-Koehler.

Wallis, S., Underhill, B., & Hedly, C. (2012). Leaders building leaders: High potential development and executive coaching at Microsoft. In M. Goldsmith, L. Lyons, & S. McArthur (Eds.), *Coaching for leadership* (3rd ed.). San Francisco, CA: Pfeiffer.

Williams, J. S. (2016). *An investigation of goal-focused and process-oriented approaches to executive coaching using random assignment and switching replications designs.* (PhD Dissertation), Alliant International University, CA.

Wood, R. E., Whelan, J., Sojo, V., & Wong, M. (2013). Goals, goal orientations, strategies and performance. In E. A. Locke & G. P. Latham (Eds.), *New developments in goal setting and task performance* (pp. 90–114). New York, NY: Routledge.

Part 2

Delivering value to clients

Chapter 5

Delivering behavioral change with senior executives

Rebecca Turner, Howard Morgan, and Charles I. Story

Introduction

It is often said that companies reserve their executive coaching resources for high-potential performers and top talent. Therefore coaching to avoid leader derailment is more a thing of the past (e.g., Susing, 2016). While that is true to some extent, many highly successful executives have blind spots that challenge their success in senior roles. This chapter introduces executive coaching approaches and techniques for working with senior leaders who exhibit 'unhelpful' and 'negative' behaviors that can lead to dissatisfaction or unhealthy relationships in the organization. Coaching senior leaders with these behaviors requires careful work on the part of the coach to set the stage for a successful engagement. In this chapter, we outline approaches for success.

Theory and evidence

Negative leadership behaviors

Although 'toxic leadership' is part of the popular lexicon (and is discussed in Chapter 13), we believe it is necessary to describe the broader concept of 'unhelpful' leadership behaviors, which entails the wide spectrum of bullying, conflictual, or negative behaviors (Erickson, Shaw, Murray, & Branch, 2015). In a recent large-scale study, over two thousand employees described negative leader behaviors they had experienced or witnessed at work. Some of the most common were making significant decisions without information, micromanaging and over-control, playing favorites, and being ineffective at coordinating and managing. Less frequently, negative leaders acted in an insular, brutal, or bullying manner, were unable to make appropriate decisions, or were unwilling to change their minds.

Thoroughgood, Padilla, Hunter, and Tate (2012) describe leadership along a *destructive-constructive continuum*. On the destructive side, leadership often entails control, coercion, or manipulation rather than more positive, influential communication. This type of leader most often is selfish in nature and stresses the leader's own goals and objectives over the needs of the organization and its constituents.

'Destructive leadership' results from a failure in perspective taking on the part of leaders. Galinsky and colleagues (Galinsky, Magee, Inesi, & Gruenfeld, 2006; Galinsky, Rucker, & Magee, 2016) found that people who have higher levels of power are more self-centered and self-assured; however, they are also prone to dismiss or misunderstand the viewpoints of those who lack authority. Fortunately, this is not always the case. Powerful people can engage in appropriate perspective taking under certain conditions; for example, when someone can effectively activate in them a sense of responsibility for others (Chen, Lee-Chai, & Bargh, 2001; Overbeck & Park, 2001, 2006) or when an empathic leadership style is emphasized (Schmid Mast, Jonas, & Hall, 2009). In short, while some powerful people have habits that are destructive, the science shows that their behavior can change, especially through an ability to improve their perspective-taking or empathy skills.

Over the years, there have been quite a few descriptions of executives with flawed traits and behaviors, theories about what drives them, and ways that coaches can work with them to alter their behaviors (Crawshaw, 2007; Goldsmith, 2007; Kaplan, 1990; Levinson, 1978; Turner & Goodrich, 2010). Improving leader capabilities in focused areas helps companies reduce leadership issues including derailment, which is enormously costly in terms of employee morale, turnover, engagement, and potentially debilitating lawsuits stemming from dysfunctional relationships (DeVries & Kaiser, 2003; Schyns & Schilling, 2013).

In the 1980s, the Center for Creative Leadership (CCL) launched an impressive program of research on leader derailment (McCall & Lombardo, 1983). After a number of studies were completed, including quantitative ratings of bosses and factor analyses, McCauley and Lombardo (1990) developed a new management feedback instrument to assess managers' strengths and weaknesses. The derailment instrument had the following sub-scales: (1) problems with interpersonal relationships, (2) difficulty building a team, (3) difficulty in making strategic transitions, (4) lack of follow-through, (5) over-dependence, and (6) strategic differences with management.

Balancing the deficiency and positive psychology perspectives

Spurred by the influence of positive psychology theorists such as Martin Seligman and others (see Seligman & Csiksentmihalyi, 2000 for a review; Seligman, Steen, Park, & Peterson, 2005), numerous studies and approaches emerged to analyze character strengths and human virtues such as creativity, hopefulness, fairness, teamwork, authenticity, and open-mindedness (e.g., Kaplan & Kaiser, 2010; Gatling, 2014; Proctor, Maltby, & Linley, 2011; Tse & Mitchell, 2010). Consultants were quick to pick up on these opportunities to encourage their clients to examine themselves by narrowing in on assessing their strengths and how they could use their strengths more effectively in management and in developing themselves as leaders. Throughout the positive psychology movement, many coaches have disputed the idea that an exclusive focus on strengths would be very likely to yield changes in leadership behavior.

And, in recent years, we now have convincing research that focusing too much on strengths will get you in trouble (Kaiser & Overfield, 2011; Kaiser & Hogan, 2011; Kaplan & Kaiser, 2009). This statement may not be completely intuitive. However, consider the fact that much of the research on the relationship between leadership traits and performance is based on correlational techniques, which assume linear relationships between the variables. For example, the trait of conscientiousness is commonly found to be associated with leadership success in a wide variety of settings. However, the relationship between conscientiousness and performance is not linear.

Le and associates (2010) found that increases in conscientiousness were associated with increases in supervisor ratings, but only up to roughly one standard deviation above the mean on conscientiousness. Imagine the person who is extremely high on conscientiousness. These individuals are described as perfectionistic, overly detail-oriented, fearful of making mistakes, and often lacking in creativity. In short, having a very high level of conscientiousness and using it to solve most any or all problems might start to resemble what Levinson (1978) called the "abrasive personality." If leaders cannot rely upon others, accept reasonable mistakes, and delegate important tasks, they will eventually demotivate others and lose credibility. We are firm believers that 360-degree feedback and the focus of coaching always include the leader's strengths as well as needs for development. An exclusive development focus on strengths can leave a person vulnerable to surprises arising from "blind spots" (cf. Seligman et al., 2005).

Aims and processes

Contextual issues surrounding executive coaching for behavior change

Whether the coach is internal or external to the organization, it is important that she learn about the organizational context in which the present destructive behaviors have emerged and been identified. There is always a history behind potential derailment. If the issues that allowed these destructive behaviors to emerge are not understood, then the coaching will have a lower chance of succeeding. We sometimes find that destructive behaviors are allowed to go on for lengthy periods of time before they reach the threshold of someone's intolerance. Despite flaws in their behaviors, these same leaders may be highly charismatic, may be delivering extremely good financial performance, or may be very good at blaming someone or something else.

Experienced coaches not only use active listening, they also go to deeper levels of inquiry, into the nuances to understand root causes of destructiveness in organizations. They question assumptions, their own and others' assumptions, and are not afraid to push back and keep asking hard questions or seeing how people react to their interpretations and suggestions, making adjustments accordingly. Great coaches have agility. Because they are comfortable after years of experience and success as coaches, they may try experiments and go beyond the processes that have been studied and validated in peer-reviewed journal articles. Nevertheless, there is reason for caution here. This work is not about the coach; it is about the leader. Coaches need to keep their egos in check. They must keep the goal in mind and have tried-and-trusted models that guide their work, even though the cases in which they are using them may not fit exactly the context in which they have been studied. If you have deep knowledge and experience and a track record as a coach, you take calculated risks to help the leader 'move the needle.' The challenge is similar to that of a physician with an unusual case who has to rely on educated judgment to help a patient because there is not an evidenced-based protocol.

For example, one of us was asked to coach a scientist/CEO with many awards and patents and great professional distinctions. Almost not noticing the coach was there, for two hours the CEO filled the room with talk about the past, everything that had been achieved and what had surpassed every expectation. The organization was going south. The coach said, "If you are trying to show me how smart you are, I concede." After reflecting a moment, the CEO said, "Well, I like you. You figured me out. How are you going to help?" The coach did not adopt this approach glibly.

It may appear that the rules of empathy were broken in this example. To the contrary, having come across similar situations, the coach experienced real empathy for the client and quickly determined how to intervene in a useful way. The CEO apparently perceived that the coach was there to help him.

The higher up in the organization that leaders go, the more that success is tied to how they manage relationships all around them. Every day, leaders are managing interpersonal micro-moments that are meaningful. Generally speaking, our job as coaches is to help them develop and access managerial courage (Drucker, 2006). Leaders cannot easily hide behind a mask or shy away from conflict or making tough decisions. Yet, sometimes they do.

Let us be clear that destructive leadership does not happen in a vacuum. These leaders have followers who consent or do not resist their leadership tactics. For many reasons, board members or other executives may not be willing to confront undesirable leadership behaviors. Great coaches know when it is time to seek interventions with both the leader and the senior team, or even with board members, rather than focusing only on individual work with the executive. Any such change in the intervention plan has to be managed responsibly and ethically through discussion of confidentiality and a clear understanding of who the client is (Frisch, Lee, Metzger, Robinson, & Rosemarin, 2012).

The theories and models that guide executive coaching for behavior change are generally the same for leaders with a destructive style as they are for most executive coaching cases. However, whether the impetus for coaching comes from the leader or other stakeholders (e.g., the CEO, board members), there is an implied worry or threat that the leader could fail or is blameworthy. A referral to an executive coach for intervening in behavior that has been volatile, emotion-ridden, or inadequate is a high-stakes situation.

The development pipeline for coaching leaders with a destructive style

A small, interview-based study with HR directors from different industries indicated that coaching with senior leaders is less about learning particular skills and more about perspective taking and "changing one's beliefs and assumptions to enable more optimal decision making and behavior" (Susing, 2016, p. 17). The author noted that coaching is perceived to be more impactful at the senior level when the coach goes beyond the purist approach of facilitating self-directed learning and goal attainment. As discussed earlier, at times it is necessary for the coach to be more directive regarding the link between the individual's behavior and the impact on business outcomes.

The "development pipeline" (Hicks & Peterson, 1999; Peterson, 2011), which incorporates the five questions presented below, is a very useful coaching framework describing the core conditions needed for successful leader development. These core conditions also have empirical support (Grant, 2006; 2014). Points relevant to destructive leadership styles are discussed below using the development pipeline framework.

(1) Insight: *Does the leader know what to develop?*

When leaders are destructive, insight about what behaviors to work on and how to work on them is likely to be missing. Wasylyshyn, Shorey, and Shaffin (2012) describe an insight-oriented coaching model for improving success with executives whose behavior patterns are inconsistent and erratic, or toxic. This model integrates an understanding of emotional intelligence (i.e., Goleman, 1998). It is possible to combine key approaches such as cognitive behavioral and insight approaches for behavior change (Kauffman & Hodgetts, 2016; Turner & Goodrich, 2010). Once collaborative and agreed-upon coaching goals are made, it is important to write them down to ensure there is agreement and clarity of intent.

(2) Motivation: *Is the leader willing to invest the time and energy it takes to develop?*

Some leaders believe the pain points will blow over as they have in the past. They may seek alternatives to behavior change in order to try to fix problems. For example, they may blame others, fire them, or remain 'tone deaf.' A first order of business is to ascertain the leader's motivation and curiosity, their willingness to explore some new ways of behaving. In fact, right away, the coach's job is to listen thoroughly and through active listening, engage the leader in a deeper conversation about her own goals and find out what she thinks will happen if she does not make a change. The more the coach understands the leader's values, needs, and motivations, the more the coach will know how to tailor efforts for maximum impact.

(3) Capabilities: *Does the leader have the skills and knowledge they need?*

When senior leaders get into trouble, it is likely that habits that have served them well in the past no longer work because of conditions inside the business, the people involved, the organizational culture, or other external factors have changed. This point reinforces the need for feedback to focus not only on strengths but also specifically on weaknesses, or behaviors that need to change in order to achieve success in the present environment. The coach's role is to support leaders to find opportunities to learn new, alternative ways of handling challenging situations (Cox, 2006; Peterson, 2011).

Many 'old habits'" no longer work in the current zeitgeist. Recently, there has been a sudden escalation in the public's negative attitudes and intolerance toward sexual mistreatment of women in the workplace. Typically, both public opinion and the organizational culture influence the level of tolerance exhibited for this type of leader aggression. It is possible in the future that the "me too" movement will embolden employees to band together and make complaints about other aspects of the workplace environment that they find unacceptable.

(4) Real-world practice: *Does the leader practice the new skills at work?*

Epictetus, an ancient Greek philosopher, maintained that the foundation of all philosophy is self-knowledge. He is quoted as saying, "Man is not disturbed by events, but by the view he takes of them." Thus, changing behaviors often requires changing thought patterns. Cognitive-behavioral approaches to coaching are goal-directed (Palmer & Williams, 2013). They focus on conscious thinking and ways that specific thoughts, or interpretations of events, can lead people to behave in dysfunctional ways. This has to do with how we process information. Cognitive behavioral techniques have strong empirical support, as do positive psychology approaches, active listening, providing support, goal setting, and specific methods of learning/training (deHaan, Grant, Burger, Eriksson, 2016; Grant, 2009; Grant, Curtayne, & Burton, 2009; Locke & Latham, 2013; Peltier, 2010; Peterson, 2008 Rogers, 1961; Taylor, 2008;).

In cognitive-behavioral approaches, executives are asked to apply new skills and understanding in situations that require a conscious effort to implement their new intentions. Coaching sessions focus on preparing action plans that will assist the executive in taking new risks and modulating their responses as appropriate. Follow-up sessions offer space to reflect on how these efforts have transpired and the results achieved, or the various challenges that may have emerged. As described by Peltier (2010), coaching is like conducting an experiment. You collect and analyze data, develop a plan for change, and implement it. Results are then evaluated and fed back into the process. Repetition of new efforts is usually necessary so that they become new habits.

(5) Accountability: *Does the leader internalize the new capabilities to improve her performance and results?*

In order for coaching to succeed, the leader must internalize ('own') the need for change as well as efforts to sustain progress. Not only do leaders need to monitor their own level of self-awareness and behavior but also ensure that they monitor the environment, i.e., the impact they are having on others. This requires learning to read other people's reactions and responses, which is a key step in improving emotional intelligence. Also, seeking regular feedback from stakeholders, especially those who are willing to be candid, will be helpful in maintaining what they have achieved.

Tools and techniques

360 feedback, assessment, and the development plan

While there are a number of good survey-response 360 assessment tools, we use narrative, interview-based 360s when we work with senior leaders. Doing so allows us a window into the context and the organizational dynamics. Interviews also allow follow-up questions so that we really understand the strengths and weaknesses of the executive and examples of how the behavior comes across (Turner & Goodrich, 2010). We learn how people have responded in the past and what impact the executive has had on the organization. Our questions typically include, What is your role and your relationship to the leader? In your opinion, what is working well with the leader? What is not working well? What can she do to improve? What would success look like if everything worked out well in the next 6 or so months? How would you know things are better? What else do I as the coach need to know to be helpful to the leader and the organization?

To launch the 360-degree process, we ask the leader to consider who would be best for us to interview, given that the goal is to obtain useful information for moving ahead. The leader should choose feedback providers because they need to consider their sources credible. Often the leader looks to the coach for suggestions. Typically, you want to interview the person to whom they report, their direct reports, and any peers or others who can comment on their leadership qualities. The problem and the situation give you a good idea as to who would be a good feedback provider. The leader then contacts the feedback providers and asks them to meet with the coach because she will be working with a coach to help her improve her leadership style or abilities.

As stated by Schein (1999, p. 243), "everything you do is an intervention." A 360 assessment is an intervention with consequences. The coach's role demonstrates to the boss, peers, and direct reports that the leader is taking charge of the situation and is open to hearing feedback. The coach should let the interviewees know that the interview information will be integrated across individuals, key themes will be provided to the leader, and specific comments will be anonymous (cf. Turner & Hawkins, 2016). A 360 assessment often raises hopes and expectations in an organization that things may change.

It is recommended that the leader receive a written feedback report, which contains key, specific areas where she is viewed as having strengths and key, specific areas where she has opportunities to develop. After having some initial interviews with the leader ourselves, we may also use a validated assessment tool for personality and/or emotional intelligence. Different coaches have different preferred tools. Before using any tool, be sure that you have the appropriate training, experience, and supervision to use it ethically and, importantly, beneficially for the leader. Utilizing a leadership assessment tool in addition to the narrative feedback can be powerful, because you can examine similarities and differences between the two sources of information (see Hogan, Hogan, & Kaiser, 2011). The benchmarked assessment tool gives you information about general strengths and liabilities, while the interview narrative gives you information about how the person is seen by others in her organization, i.e., how different traits may show up at work. Importantly, the feedback report is provided to the leader only, not to anyone else.

The assessment information provides most of the data needed to work collaboratively with the leader to develop a leadership plan. As is common in the field, only a couple of key objectives are set for development, given that it is hard to focus on more than about two because behavioral patterns are deeply rooted and often take time and real effort to change. Next, we flesh out the objectives. These may include coaching techniques, different sources for learning (e.g., readings, online courses), resources inside the organization, and other efforts. The development plan should be constructed jointly because it is important that the leader buy into the agenda for the next 6 months or so. Our coaching engagements typically are planned for 6 to 9 months and they may be extended. Also, they may be altered over time as new learning occurs and situations shift.

While the assessment report is confidential to the leader, we recommend to leaders that they share their coaching goals with their stakeholders and let them know that they would like ongoing feedback as to how things are going vis-à-vis progress. Sharing this information goes a long way in reassuring others that there is a commitment to change. It also may signal to others that they give the leader a break while she is struggling with the process of changing old behavioral habits that are difficult to change.

Coaching techniques

Coaching is a customized intervention, tailored to meet the needs of the leader. Coaches use their judgment to discern the unique aspects of each engagement and leader predilections. In short, the agenda comes from the leader. Coaches should only use techniques that they are appropriately trained to deliver and should be experienced in the techniques they use. Some of the common techniques are cognitive-behavioral and insight methods (mentioned previously), active listening, homework, role-play, reflective journaling, experiments, and shadowing.

Very often, learning to be a better listener is a goal for leaders with a destructive style (Hoppe, 2006). Given that they tend to be focused on their own goals, it can be difficult for them to offer undivided attention to someone else who wants to communicate complex or nuanced opinions and needs. Role-play exercises can occur between the coach and the leader, or the leader may be given homework to practice how she is going to engage in a challenging situation that she will soon confront, such as having a difficult conversation with a direct report or board member. Reflective journaling is sometimes used so that leaders can keep track of situations and their reactions to them over time. This process may help destructive leaders identify emotional triggers (Cox, 2006; Goldsmith, 2015; Turner & Goodrich, 2010; Ekman, 2003) that drive irrational behaviors or create blind spots for them. Experiments are used to test hypotheses, make decisions, or try out new behaviors in response to old challenges (Herd & Russell, 2011). Leaders often move forward by taking risks and finding out how the outcomes are changed as a result. Coaching meetings involve following up on how things are going in real time and supporting the leader to adjust her thinking, decisions, and behaviors so she will avoid the usual traps and elicit better outcomes.

Coaches sometimes 'shadow' the leader in the work setting. The coach may observe meetings with the leader in order to learn more about how the leader manages challenges in the team, for example. After the meeting, the coach and leader can debrief on how it went and discuss whether alternative communication or other behaviors might yield different team dynamics and outcomes.

Once leaders begin to have success, they may feel rejuvenated and become more engaged than they were earlier. These moments can be a catalyst for further changes and deepened commitment. On the other hand, there will at times be setbacks. The coach's role is to the support the leader in understanding what may have gone awry and deciding how to rectify problems as they arise.

What should not be forgotten is the follow up and assessment of results after a period of coaching. A useful technique is for the coach to go back to each of the stakeholders to ask how the leader is progressing toward her goals. This feedback helps the leader, the stakeholders, and the coach gauge the success of the coaching and consider what additional work may remain. Some coaches do a survey at the midpoint and at the end of coaching. Clarifying whether the coaching goals have been met is an essential step before terminating the engagement.

Case study

The CEO told Jason, a CFO in a large telecommunications company, that he had heard one too many complaints about Jason's arrogance and disrespectful behaviors. These reports had come not only from Jason's peers but also from two board members on the Finance committee. In fact, his peers complained that he was "toxic" to some of their direct reports. These behaviors had been going on for most of Jason's 3 years at the company; however, everyone knew that Jason had a significant role in turning things around after the recent acquisition; he was "untouchable."

The coach listened to Jason's frustrations about his job. He felt no one respected his time and too many people relied on him to weigh in on too many decisions that should be made at lower levels in the organization. He felt extra pressure, especially because he was being criticized for his temper. The coach interviewed seven stakeholders in addition to the CEO. First, stakeholders were in awe of Jason due to his deep experience in finance and his ability to see a way forward during transitions that no one else could see. Also, they believed that Jason was a perfectionist, hard on himself, and that he was obsessive with details. They described their meetings with him. In summary, when people questioned Jason he lost patience with them.

Attempting to deal with Jason by putting a label of "toxic" on his behavior would have only resulted in excuses and frustration. Instead, the coach focused on the reactions of others and their interpretation of how he felt about them. Jason very quickly said that he did not intend to make them feel that way. This allowed the coaching conversation to then focus on the behaviors he chose to use and how he would prefer to be seen in the company. The coach adopted a cognitive-behavioral approach. During sessions, Jason and the coach role-played some of the scenarios with a board member that caused him much angst and anger. He came up with some alternative ways to communicate that would help the board member understand where things stood in Finance. He also learned to detect his triggers for anger, which emanated in part from his interpretation of the situation. In fact, he learned that some of these reactions were the same things he experienced in his personal life.

Over time, Jason got more control over his own interpretations and, after many hours of practice and rehearsal, got much better at communicating differently. There was relief all around him. Did the coaching experience change Jason's personality? No, of course not. His perfectionism was intact, but he was much calmer and began to have a sense of humor about his "OCD." Most of the time he managed very well and when he did not, he was much faster at picking up on it and even apologized for his tone. In fact, his coaching experiences carried over to asserting himself around his peers' direct reports who were passing the buck and not making decisions on their own. Each of these situations improved because the new, alternative behaviors were more effective in getting results through others.

Conclusion

Organizations struggle with senior leaders who are highly effective in some ways and yet destructive to stakeholders and the overall culture. These organizations may hire a seasoned executive coach to work with the leader when replacing the leader is not a desirable or feasible option. In such high-stakes circumstances, coaches have an opportunity to engage the leader and other stakeholders in a change process and to have an impact on the company in a meaningful way. This chapter outlines the necessary conditions and the coaching tools and techniques that will help the coach succeed in engagements with leaders who have a destructive style.

A broad-based understanding and familiarity with cognitive-behavioral approaches, insight-oriented approaches, positive psychology, systems thinking, assessment and feedback methods, as well as specific tools and techniques for coaching sessions are needed. Coaches should be excellent listeners, candid, self-confident, self-aware, experienced and credible, willing to take risks, appropriately humble, and have an ability to think quickly and improvise. They should hold a professional code of ethics related to their practice. High-stakes cases should not be undertaken lightly.

Before exiting, external coaches must leave in place strategies that will reinforce the new behaviors and culture over time.

Resources for developing yourself

Frisch, M. H., Lee, R. J., Metzger, K. L., Robinson, J., & Rosemarin, J. (2012). *Becoming an exceptional executive coach*. NY: AMACOM.

Goldsmith, M. (2008). *What got you here won't get you there*. NY: Hyperion.

Johari Window:
http://changingminds.org/disciplines/communication/models/johari_window.htm

Active Listening:
www.mindtools.com/CommSkll/ActiveListening.htm

SMART Goals:
www.hr.virginia.edu/uploads/documents/media/Writing_SMART_Goals.pdf

Role Playing:
www.mindtools.com/CommSkll/RolePlaying.htm

Narrative 360-Degree Feedback:
www.richardkoonce.com/Executive_Coaching.pdf

Executive Coaching for Behavior Change:
www.youtube.com/watch?v=3szs2X6qUlg&list=PLTcJa38Q-YM9warmBr-iLWlpiuQcpy
DhW&index=1

References

Chen, S., Lee-Chai, A. Y., & Bargh, J. A. (2001). Relationship orientation as a moderator of the effects of social power. *Journal of Personality and Social Psychology, 80*, 173–187.

Cox, E. (2006). An adult learning approach to coaching. In D. Stover & A. M. Grant (Eds.), *Evidence based coaching handbook* (pp. 193–217). Hoboken, NJ: John Wiley & Sons.

Crawshaw, L. (2007). *Taming the abrasive manager: How to end unnecessary roughness in the workplace*. San Francisco, CA: Jossey-Bass.

De Haan, E., Grant, A. M., Burger, Y., & Eriksson, P. O. (2016). A large-scale study of executive and workplace coaching: The relative contributions of relationship, personality match, and self-efficacy. *Consulting Psychology Journal: Practice and Research, 68*, 189–207.

DeVries, D. L., & Kaiser, R. B. (2003, November). *Going sour in the suite: What you can do about executive derailment*. Workshop presented at Maximizing Executive Effectiveness meeting of the Human Resources Planning Society, Miami, FL.

Drucker, P. (2006, February). What executives should remember. *Harvard Business Review, 84*(2).

Ekman, P. (2003). *Emotions revealed: Recognizing faces and feelings to improve communication and emotional life*. New York, NY: Times Books.

Erickson, A., Shaw, B., Murray, J., & Branch, S. (2015). Destructive leadership: Causes, consequences and countermeasures. *Organizational Dynamics, 44*, 266–272.

Frisch, M. H., Lee, R. J., Metzger, K. L., Robinson, J., & Rosemarin, J. (2012). *Becoming an exceptional executive coach*. New York, NY: AMACOM.

Galinsky, A. D., Magee, J. C., Inesi, M. E., & Gruenfeld, D. H. (2006). Power and perspectives not taken. *Psychological Science, 17*, 1068–1074.

Galinsky, A. D., Rucker, D., & Magee, J. (2016). Power and perspective-taking: A critical examination. *Journal of Experimental Social Psychology, 67*, 91–92.

Gatling, A. (2014). The authentic leadership qualities of business coaches and its impact on coaching performance. *International Journal of Evidence Based Coaching and Mentoring, 12*, 27–46.

Goldsmith, M. (2007). *What got you here won't get you there*. New York, NY: Hyperion.

Goldmith, M. (2015). *Triggers*. New York, NY: Crown Business.

Goleman, D. (1998). *Working with emotional intelligence*. New York, NY: Random House.

Grant, A. M. (2006). An integrative goal-focused approach to executive coaching. In D. Stob; er & A. M. Grant (Eds.), *Evidence Based Coaching Handbook* (pp. 153–192). New York: Wiley.

Grant, A. M. (2014). The efficacy of executive coaching in times of organizational change. *Journal of Change Management, 14*, 258–280.

Grant, A. M., Curtayne, L., & Burton, G. (2009). Executive coaching enhances goal attainment, resilience and workplace well being: A randomized controlled study. *The Journal of Positive Psychology, 4*, 396–407.

Herd, A. M. & Russell, J. E. A. (2011). Tools and techniques: what's in your toolbox? In G. Hernez-Broome & L. A. Boyce (Eds.) *Advancing Executive Coaching: Setting the Course for Successful Leadership Consulting*. San Francisco: Jossey.

Hicks, M. D., & Peterson, D. B. (1999). The development pipeline: How people really learn. *Knowledge Management Review, 9*, 30–33.

Hogan, J., Hogan, R., & Kaiser, R. B. (2011). Management derailment: Personality assessment and mitigation. In S. Zedeck (Ed.), *Handbook of industrial and organizational psychology*. Washington, DC: American Psychological Association.

Hoppe, M. H. (2006). *Active listening: Improve your ability to listen and lead*. Greensboro, NC: Center for Creative Leadership.

Kaplan, R. E. (1990). The expansive executive: How the drive to mastery helps and hinders organizations. *Human Resource Management, 29,* 307–326.

Kaplan, R. E., & Kaiser, R. B. (2009). Stop overdoing your strengths. *Harvard Business Review, 87,* 100–103.

Kaplan, R. E., & Kaiser, R. B. (2010). Towards a positive psychology for leaders. In A. P. Linley, S. Harrington, & N. Garcia (Eds.), *Oxford handbook of positive psychology and work* (pp. 107–117). New York and Oxford: Oxford University Press.

Kaiser, R. B., & Hogan, J. (2011). Personality, leader behavior, and overdoing it. *Consulting Psychology Journal: Practice and Research, 63,* 219–242.

Kaiser, R. B., & Overfield, D.V. (2011). Strengths, strengths overused, and lopsided leadership. *Consulting Psychology Journal: Practice and Research, 63, 89–109.*

Kauffman, C., & Hodgetts, W. H. (2016). Model agility: Coaching effectiveness and four perspectives on a case study. *Consulting Psychology Journal: Practice and Research, 68,* 157–176.

Le, H., OH, I. S., Robbins, S. B., Ilies, R., Holland, E., & Westrick, P. (2010). Too much of a good thing? The curvilinear relationships between personality traits and job performance. *Journal of Applied Psychology, 95,* 1–21.

Levinson, H. (1978, May). The abrasive personality. *Harvard Business Review,* 86-94.

Locke, E. A., & Latham, G. P. (2013). *New developments in goal setting and task performance.* New York, NY: Routledge.

McCall, M.W., Jr., & Lombardo, M. M. (1983). *Off the track: Why and how successful executives get derailed.* Greensboro, NC: Center for Creative Leadership.

McCauley, C., & Lombardo, M. (1990). Benchmarks: An instrument for diagnosing managerial strengths and weaknesses. In K. E. Clark & M. B. Clark (Eds.), *Measures of leadership.* West Orange, NJ: Leadership Library of America, Inc.

Overbeck, J. R., & Park, B. (2001). When power does not corrupt: Superior individuation processes among powerful perceivers. *Journal of Personality and Social Psychology, 81,* 549.

Overbeck, J. R., & Park, B. (2006). Powerful perceivers, powerless objects: Flexibility of powerholders' social attention. *Organizational Behavior and Human Decision Processes, 99,* 227–243.

Palmer, S., & Williams, H. (2013). Cognitive behavioral approaches. In J. Passmore et al. (Eds.), *The psychology of coaching and mentoring.* West Sussex, UK: Wiley-Blackwell.

Peltier, B. (2010). *The psychology of executive coaching: Theory and application* (2nd ed.). New York, NY: Routledge.

Peterson, D. B. (2011). Executive coaching: A critical review and recommendations for advancing the practice. In S. Zedeck (Ed.), *APA handbook of industrial and organizational psychology, Vol. 2: Selecting and developing members for the organization.* Washington, DC: American Psychological Association.

Peterson, D. B. (2008, April). *Executive coaching: The psychology behind the best practices for facilitating development.* Master lecture at the annual convention of the California Psychological Association, Anaheim, CA.

Proctor, C., Maltby, J., & Linley, P. A. (2011). Strengths use as a predictor of well being and health-related quality of life. *Journal of Happiness Studies, 12,* 153–169.

Rogers, C. R. (1961). *On becoming a person: A therapist's view of psychotherapy.* New York, NY: Houghton Mifflin.

Schein, E. (2009). *Process consultation revisited: Building the helping relationship.* Reading, MA: Addison Wesley.

Schmid Mast, M., Jonas, K., & Hall, J. A. (2009). Give a person power and he or she will show interpersonal sensitivity: The phenomenon and its why and when. *Journal of Personality and Social Psychology, 97,* 835.

Schyns, B., & Schilling, J. (2013). How bad are the effects of bad leaders? A meta-analysis of destructive leadership and its outcomes. *The Leadership Quarterly*, *24*, 138–158.

Seligman, M. E. P., & Csiksentmihalyi, M. (2000). Positive psychology. *American Psychologist*, *55*, 5–14.

Seligman, M. E. P., Steen, T. A., Park, N., & Peterson, C. (2005). Positive psychology in progress: Empirical validation of interventions. *American Psychologist*, *60*, 410–421.

Susing, I. (2016). Coaching at the top: Optimizing the impact of senior leaders. *OD Practitioner*, *48*, 13–19.

Taylor, S. E. (2008). Fostering a supportive environment at work. *The Psychologist-Manager Journal*, *11*, 265–283.

Tse, H. H. M., & Mitchell, R. J. (2010). A theoretical model of transformational leadership and knowledge creation: The role of open-mindedness norms and leader-member exchange. *Journal of Management & Organization*, *16*, 83–99.

Thoroughgood, C.N., Padilla, A., Hunter, S.T., & Tate, B.W. (2012). *The Leadership Quarterly,* 23, 897-917

Turner, E., & Hawkins, P. (2016). Multi-stakeholder contracting in executive/business coaching: An analysis of practice and recommendations for gaining maximum value. *International Journal of Evidence Based Coaching and Mentoring*, *14*, 48–65.

Turner, R. A., & Goodrich, J. (2010). The case for eclecticism in executive coaching: Application to challenging assignments. *Consulting Psychology Journal: Practice and Research*, *62*, 39–55.

Wasylyshyn, K., Shorey, H. S., & Chaffin, J. S. (2012). Patterns of leadership behavior: Implications for successful executive coaching outcomes. *The Coaching Psychologist*, *8*, 74–85.

Chapter 6

Delivering organizational change

Mary Wayne Bush and John L. Bennett

Introduction

The speed, complexity, and volume of change are increasing, and the demands of change are impacting – and are impacted by – individuals, teams, organizations, and social structures. What used to take decades to evolve may only take weeks. Ways of working together are changing as more work is outsourced and organizations rely more on contract labor and technology (Boudreau, Creelman, & Jesuthasan, 2015; Kotter, 2012; Pfeffer & Sutton, 2006). Changes in organizational structures, operating systems, merger and acquisition integration, and new technologies are just a few examples of change impacting organizations at all levels. A 2016 KPMG survey of CEOs found that

> CEOs believe it's now or never. Globally, 72 percent of CEOs believe that the next 3 years will be more critical for their industry than the last 50 years. Change will be led by technology, connected consumers, and sector convergence. These three forces will upend business models, blur lines between industries and companies, and demand a new way of thinking about business. Much of what will happen is unknowable. What is impossible today will become mainstream tomorrow. (p. 8)

External forces such as emerging technologies, competition, regulation, and customer demands drive organizational change, and effective individual and team leadership is required to meet the demands. However, as important and ubiquitous as change is today, an estimated 60%–70% of organizational change efforts fail to reach their goals (Gibbons, 2015; Jørgensen, Owens, & Neus, 2008; Jørgensen, Bruehl, & Franke, 2014; Kotter, 2012).

This chapter focuses on how coaching supports those who lead change to define and develop their roles in delivering successful organization change. We explore the specific ways that individuals at all levels in the organization can lead and respond to change most effectively. Specifically, we focus on the critical role of the change leader and present an approach to deliver successful change through key processes and goals. We outline how the coach (internal or external to the organization) can most effectively work with the leader to deliver successful change, and we include key approaches and tools. We offer suggestions for coach development, and we include a case study to illustrate leading practices.

Theory and evidence

Change can be defined as making or becoming something different. In today's world, change is a constant state for individuals, groups, and organizations and is occurring at unprecedented rates. This fact is not a surprise, given the impact of dynamic environments, social and global systems, new technology, competition, and scientific discoveries. Entirely new industries are being created and expanded around the globe, while old industries are fading away. For example, who in 1969 would have anticipated the profound impact that the newly invented Internet would have on the world within just a few decades? Or the near-extinction of film cameras, superseded by digital cameras and mobile phones? As an IBM study on global change declared, "Change is the new normal" (Jørgensen, Owens, & Neus, 2008, p. 6).

Change is occurring within all levels of organizations, including the for-profit, not-for-profit, and public sectors. In addition, changes within organizations often occur simultaneously – such as a change in technology systems at the same time two organizations undertake a merger concurrently with a new-product release. Harvard Business School's Kotter (2012) predicted that "The rate of change in the business world is not going to slow down anytime soon. If anything, competition in most industries will probably speed up over the next few decades" (p. 161). Table 6.1 identifies examples of change at the individual, group, and organization levels.

Table 6.1 Examples of change

Level	Change
Individual	• New role or responsibility
	• New process or performance expectation
	• New location or culture
Group	• New or changing membership or team charter
	• Improvement of existing product or policy
	• New process or product
Organization	• New product development
	• New or adjacent market entry
	• New leader/strategy/direction
	• Organization redesign/restructuring
	• Merger/acquisition

By most every measure, Kotter's prediction has turned out to be true. As IBM's study on global change confirms, "Today's dynamic work environment is causing organizations to reframe the traditional view of what 'normal' is" (Jørgensen et al., 2008, p. 6). In effect, there is no "going back to the way things were."

> With the force of constant change impacting leaders, organizations, and team members, change is indeed the "new normal" in organizational life. The challenge is to lead it, manage it, learn from it, and leverage it as an opportunity for continuous improvement. (Bennett & Bush, 2013, p. 282)

Overall, the best strategy for organizations – and people – is to proactively identify and address both internal and external factors that may introduce change.

What causes organizational change?

Change arises from two major sources in organizations. The first source is external (sometimes catastrophic or unexpected), such as when a hurricane destroys an offshore oil drilling platform, or when a change in tax laws causes an organization to modify its cash-management strategies, or when customer expectations shift. The second source of change is internal, such as the planned, strategic response to environmental changes or a transition in leadership.

There are three main reasons that organizations or groups choose to change: performance, development, and transformation.

- *Performance:* accelerating or improving effectiveness and/or efficiency to meet or anticipate external environmental factors or to gain a competitive advantage. Organizational performance can center on operations or financials, meeting the challenge of a new technology introduced to the market, new government regulations, an environmental or global imperative, or a perceived threat from a competitor. For example, the rapid proliferation of the Internet and its use by businesses beginning in the 1980s.
- *Development:* adding, improving, or strengthening an internal resource or capability, such as promoting a leader, implementing a new Material Requirement Planning (MRP) system, or instigating a cost-savings strategy through lean manufacturing. For example, the adoption of lean manufacturing techniques by Duramax Marine, leading to efficiencies and cost savings as jobs are released to the floor and purchase orders are issued more quickly.
- *Transformation:* growth or expansion through new corporate identity and branding, or introduction of a new product or competency, and in organizations, a new territory, merger and acquisition, or market expansion. For example, Amazon's starting out as an online bookstore in 1994 and

becoming one of the world's largest online retail destinations (offering far more than just books), due to founder Jeff Bezos's vision of the potential of the Internet for sales.

Types of change

While it is important to understand the stages of change an individual or group will experience, it is also crucial for a coach to identify the type of change that is planned or is occurring. There are many ways to categorize change, including frequency, strategy, scope or impact, and source. Looking at change through the lens of its intended focus – performance, development, or transformation – can help a coach identify strategies that will facilitate the client's goals.

Jamieson and Sullivan (2011) categorize change into six types:

- Revolutionary. A 'jolt' to the larger system that is rapid and potentially deep, followed by a period of disruption
- Evolutionary. More incremental, often improvement oriented and characterized by being continuous and cumulative
- Transitional. Moving from a current state to a future state without changing some fundamental paradigms of the organization (for example, vision, mission, or culture)
- Transformational. A significant, broad, and deep change that alters an organization's fundamental paradigms
- Strategic. Change that realigns the organization's mission, environment, market, or strategy
- Operational. Altering how the organization does work: processes, systems, workflow, design (pp. 14–18)

Another way scholars look at organizational change processes is the difference between *planned* (episodic) and *performative* (continuous) change models (Tsoukas & Chia, 2000). Planned change is often a replacement strategy whereby a new structure, strategy, or program replaces an old one. In this type of planned change, interventions are orchestrated interruptions intended to correct and/or remove a previous condition to restore balance (i.e., get things back to normal) (Ford & Ford, 1994). Planned change is goal oriented, rational, and intentional. Performative change, on the other hand, consists of smaller, incremental changes that often emerge from experimentation and learning. This type of continuous change is processional, performative, and emergent (Ford, 2008).

The KPMG (2016) survey of CEOs reported that a majority of respondents indicated that, "the force and speed with which technological innovation is moving through the economy is creating an inflection point for the business sector"(p. 5). The impact is so great that 41% expect to be running significantly transformed companies in three years' time. This response rate shows an increase of 12% over CEOs who felt that way in the previous year's survey.

In addition, 82% of those surveyed expressed concern about whether their company's current products or services will be relevant to customers in three years. "Disruption has become every organization's constant companion. Rapidly evolving technology, an ever-growing mountain of data and the increasing need for global integration make it difficult for even the most forward-thinking companies to keep up with increasing change" (Jørgensen et al., 2014, p. 1).

With such a stark reality facing them, organizations are leveraging executive coaching to support effective change. "Coaching – *all* coaching – is about change. Effective coaching facilitates an individual or groups' ability to understand, strategize, and accomplish a specific change. Coaching is designed to elicit the motivation, learning, vision, action and integration to effect successful, sustainable change" (Bush & Bennett, 2018, p. 240). "Coaching is a context that supports change across very large gaps between where a person is and where he or she wants to be" (Rock & Page, 2013, p. xiv). In fact, Bennett and Bush (2014) claim that "Building change capacity must become an ongoing, multi-faceted development focus" for both individuals and organizations, and argue that "developing this capacity can mean a competitive advantage and differentiation in the market for an organization" (p. 133).

Aims and processes: coaching the change leader

Looking across the spectrum of participation in organizational change, distinct change roles become apparent. Each role has a specific function in driving change to successful completion, and each requires a different coaching focus. As described by Conner (2006), there are four roles: Sponsor, Agent, Target, and Advocate. Table 6.2 offers an explanation of these four roles, including key responsibilities, contributions, and items to be taken into consideration for each. Coaches can often support their clients by helping them to identify opportunities to adopt one or more of these change roles.

The key role of the executive coach is to ensure that a client in any of the roles develops and effectively implements a strategy in three arenas of change

Table 6.2 Responsibilities and considerations for roles of change

Role	Responsibility and Contributions
Sponsor	• Decides which changes will happen • Communicates new vision and priorities to the organization • Provides resources to enable the change
Agent	• Executes the change – an individual or group • Develops the plan to deal and deploys the change
Target	• Makes the change – the individual or group that is the focus of the change effort
Advocate	• Individual or group who wants to achieve a change, but without power or position to sanction it

competency: Success of the Change, Stakeholder Engagement, and Self-management. Figure 6.1 illustrates the distinction between the coach's domain and the change leader's domain in successful change.

Table 6.3 clarifies the change leader's responsibilities in each domain.

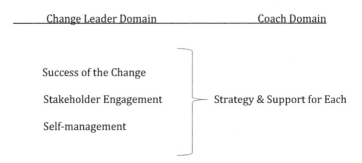

Figure 6.1 Domain distinctions

Table 6.3 Change leader responsibilities

Domain	Change Leader Responsibilities
Success of the Change	• Enabling the compelling vision and charter for the change • Developing and/or observing funding, key milestones, timeline, action and communication plans, metrics, and change sustainment plan
Stakeholder Engagement	• Regular and visible engagement with key stakeholders • Accurate identification of key stakeholders and analysis of their current and desired states of support for the change • Ensuring two-way communication that addresses all stakeholders and groups affected by the change, including regular data gathering and feedback, other engagement strategies (social media, focus groups, town-hall meetings, surveys, website, etc.) • Addressing appropriate reward and recognition to support change momentum and recognize supporters
Self-management	• Management of personal health, fitness, diet, exercise for energy and focus • Continued focus on success in current role or job (if in addition to change project) • Development of skills such as delegation, time management, networking, strategic thinking, leadership presence, mindfulness, facilitation and conflict management • Attention to work-life balance and (if needed) maintaining dual focus on being a change Target as well as fulfilling another role in the change

While each of the roles plays an essential part in the success of change, the role of the Sponsor or change leader most correlates with success in change, and is the focus for this book. Analysis of data from the 2018 ProSci research report shows a direct correlation between the effectiveness of sponsorship and the likelihood of meeting project objectives. And "10 out of 10 times, effective sponsorship was identified as the top contributor to success. And, it wasn't even close – sponsorship beat out the second top contributor by a 3:1 margin" (ProSci, 2018, p. 9).

Experts emphasize the importance of change leadership for the unique – and critical – tasks of setting the vision and other parameters for the change (Conner, 2006; Kotter, 2012; ProSci, 2018). Because of the importance of this role, executive coaching is often requested to support leaders of change projects, not only with the change itself, but to help clarify and sustain their part in successful implementation and to effectively manage his or her time and attention with other duties. Ideally, the coach helps the coachee develop change leadership capability, which, in turn, supports the organization's capacity for change.

The leader provides the vision, parameters, and direction for the change implementation. He or she acts as a "GPS" for the change project: *Guiding*, *Protecting*, and *Sustaining* the project until completion. This involves acting as navigator and compass (providing vision and direction) and clearly outlining expectations (and incentives) for successful completion. In addition, the change leader ensures that the change project is on target and does not get derailed by competing projects, demands for resources, or lack of action. Executive coaching can help change leaders define and communicate their vision for the change, identify and engage key stakeholders, and set up the change infrastructure – including defining metrics for evaluating success and identifying personnel in other key roles. The leader contracts an Agent to manage the project, stipulates the budget and timeframe required, and charters a Change Guiding Team of key stakeholders if needed.

There are many ways in which the change leader must be engaged and knowledgeable about the change in addition to chartering it, analyzing the project's potential strategic implications (both positive and negative), identifying the stakeholder base, defining and communicating the project vision, and outlining what success and sustainment look like for the identified change project. In addition to chartering the change, the leader usually provides the funding for the change project. Any or all of these can become coaching topics. The coach must pay attention to how the change project is going – per identified vision and metrics – as well as how the change project is impacting the leader (positively and/or negatively), and how well the leader is carrying out the role. There is also opportunity to note and discuss how well the leader is building change capability in the organization (and him- or herself) as part of the project.

Specifically, the coach focuses on supporting the executive's awareness, action, and accountability in the three arenas of change competency, ensuring that the executive has a well-designed, personalized, and effective approach to address

Table 6.4 The Change Agenda

Element	Questions to Be Addressed
What?	• What specifically needs to change? • What is its potential impact and outcome/benefit?
Who?	• Who are the key stakeholders in the change? • How will they be affected? • What are their roles? • What information will each of them need?
Where?	• Where will the change be deployed or needed? • In what geographical area or part(s) of the system?
When?	• When must the change be implemented? • How soon? • Is there urgency? • Are there other changes or situations that will be impacted by this change?
Why?	• Why the change? • What are the compelling reasons that this change must be made, and made now?
How?	• How will the change be successful? • What are the milestones, action plan, communications, reward and recognition, and implementation and sustainment plans?

each. For instance, to support success of the change, the coach should first help underscore the scope and importance of the change leader role, as well as help identify areas the leader may excel in or find challenging. For instance, some change leaders are not well versed in defining and communicating a vision for the change. Some are less comfortable in communicating, promoting, or engaging other stakeholders in the change project.

This initial step encompasses the vision, strategic planning, and market exploration that indicate the need for change, and what the change should involve. In this step, a "Change Agenda" (see Table 6.4) is developed, with answers to the basic questions that will be on the minds of all involved: What? Who? Where? When? Why? How? The answers to these questions provide compelling evidence of the need for change, and a timeline and vision for what the change can accomplish. They will also provide foundational content for the change leader's initial communications and messaging across the enterprise.

Tools and techniques

Many tools and techniques can be used by coaching to help clients understand how change works; recognize and support the roles of change; focus on awareness, action, and accountability; and coach the client in the client's role in the change. Here are a few examples to illustrate the approaches that can be employed.

Understand how change works

Coaches should familiarize themselves with change models and theories to better understand and support the change process itself. If the organization has adopted a specific change process or model, the coach should have a thorough knowledge of it. If the organization does not have a process or model for change, the coach can support the exploration of one or more from which to choose. In addition, a coach can help with the implementation of feedback surveys and assessments that will help the client and the organization understand how the change process is going and where challenges might occur.

Tools and resources for understanding how change works include:

- *Leading Change* (Kotter, 2012)
- *The Challenges of Change Whitepaper* (Maurer, 2016)
- *Coaching for Change* (Bennett & Bush, 2014)
- *Our Iceberg Is Melting* (Kotter & Rathgeber, 2016)
- *Immunity to Change* (Kegan & Lahey, 2009)

Recognize and support the change leader role

Coaches should recognize that each change role provides a unique opportunity for support. In addition, coaches should note the size and scope of the change and help the client ensure that there is a clear and agreed-upon change strategy. Having a common change process or model helps align all stakeholders and guide a plan for the change effort. Coaches can assist their clients to identify key stakeholders and guiding team (also called change project team or steering committee) if one exists, and validate that there is a coordinating mechanism for communication and collaboration across the change infrastructure (whether groups or individuals).

Tools for supporting the change leader role include:

- The Energy Bar – a tool to help assess stakeholder engagement in the change process, by Rick Maurer, available at www.energybartools.com/resources
- Diagnostics and change leadership templates from Cohen (2005), including Engaging the Stakeholders: The Enrollment Process, Key Skills and Attributes of Guiding Team Members, Communication Plan Template, Communication Diagnostic, Audience Assessment Template, and Audience Prioritization Matrix

Maintaining the focus on awareness, action, and accountability

Coaching someone in a change role requires a dual focus of accountability on how the coachee is contributing to the success of the change overall and how he or she is fulfilling a specific change role. In some cases, the coachee will have more than one change role (i.e., Agent and Target, or Advocate and Target), and each of these must be addressed. The key elements of role accountability are the accomplishment of the role's function, effective communication with other roles/stakeholders, visible and proactive support of the change, and demonstrated action to make the change successful.

It is important for the coach to separate the role function from the change process in order to help the coachee address effectiveness in both arenas: the success of the change and the effectiveness of the role. Just because the change project is going well, meeting all milestones and moving forward successfully, does not mean that person is optimizing the change role and supporting the change. Also, the coachee can be implementing his or her role impeccably, while the overall change project is not on track. A coach can help the coachee appreciate how their change role offers opportunities for skill development and organizational visibility that would not be available otherwise.

As a coach, ensure that the (coaching) role is clear and distinct from other roles in the change project. Having a clearly worded contract outlining your participation, compensation, and client involvement is key. In addition, avoid dual roles – for example, acting as the coach to the Sponsor as well as being the project Agent, or Communications Specialist.

Tools for maintain the focus on awareness, action, and accountability:

- *The Magic List: Secrets of Successful Organizational Change* (Maurer, www.rickmaurer.com/wp-content/uploads/2013/04/The-Magic-List-V2.pdf)
- Energy Bar Tools (Maurer, www.energybartools.com/images/The-Challenges-of-Change-White-Paper.pdf) – specifically, "Checklist for Sponsors of Change Teams," "Resistance and Support Assessment," "Ability to Make a Case for Change"
- *Coaching with the Brain in Mind* (Rock & Page, 2013)

Coach the person as well as the role

Each of the clients you are coaching is a person who is enacting a role while going through a change process. Often, they need and request coaching about their own experience of the change as well as how to be most effective in their role. It is important to be able to discern what will be the most helpful approach as an executive coach – it may be that a personal issue or misunderstanding is getting in the way of the client fully implementing the role.

Tools for coaching the person as well as the role includes:

- Hougaard, Carter, and Coutts's (2015) *One Second Ahead* is a helpful overview of mindfulness and its applications to corporate life, with easy-to-understand practices and suggestions for daily routines.
- Hacobian (2016) offers helpful advice on "Harnessing the Use of Self" for change agents (i.e., coaches), including "Acknowledging What Is Changing

and Where People Are" (p. 178) and "Understanding What Is Holding the Client's Attention" (p. 179).

- McKnight and Jamieson (2016) advise on use-of-self-as-instrument-of-change, including "Developing Self Awareness" (p. 121) and "Honing Intuition" (p. 123).

Case study

The following is an example of coaching engagement based on an actual case, which illustrates the material contained in this chapter. The names of individuals were changed to protect their identities.

José is the Executive Vice President of Operations for a publicly traded global manufacturing company. The firm recently went public following many years as a privately held business, and much of the company's growth had occurred through acquisitions. At the time that one of the authors began working with José, his company had experienced significant quality and production output challenges, which were lower than planned and disappointing to financial markets. José's primary focus was on installing a quality improvement process with the goal of instilling a common quality culture across the parent company and three new acquisitions. And although José had experience leading large manufacturing operations, this was the first time he faced the challenges of sustained poor quality, disappointing financial performance, continued challenges with merger integration, and the lack of an established quality system. José had the support of the CEO, who chartered him to sponsor this transformational change.

In an initial meeting with his coach, José reflected on his reasons for accepting this project. In addition to benefiting the company and his organization, it would offer an opportunity to manage a large project across divisions, build his network, and showcase his leadership and readiness for a more responsible role in the company. It also became clear that the project scope was broad and the change project was a priority. He would have to delegate some of his current responsibilities in order to make time for the project, as well as keeping his commitment to his family about not working on weekends.

In subsequent meetings with his coach, José clarified his vision and the timeline for the change project, as well as the budget and a specific change methodology. He developed a compelling case for change and an 'elevator pitch' that would be used to communicate the new vision as well as the necessity and urgency of the change. He appointed a change project manager for each of the divisions and the parent company that were adopting the new quality process. These formed a guiding team to oversee change management and progress. The team also included the training and communications specialist, a consulting member from the quality organization, and a data analyst.

In addition, the coach asked what José could do to free up time to focus on the change project and maintain more work-life balance. José chose to delegate several specific tasks to one of his high potential direct reports, Saima. He felt confident that she was equal to the challenge, and he planned to meet with her weekly to go over the projects she was assigned and offer mentoring to her to help her develop her own leadership and management skills. Even including this additional weekly meeting, José estimated that he would gain at least 15 hours of time each week to devote to the change project.

In weekly meetings with his coach, José was able to reflect on the progress with the change project as well as how he was accomplishing his personal goals for leadership visibility and self-management. His change project team was regularly reporting on completion, training metrics, and feedback results. He was ensuring that each key stakeholder was connected with the project, understood its goals and benefits, and was engaging their organization fully. José was also reporting on the project to the CEO and board – garnering praise for his approach and contribution he was making to the company's continued competitiveness.

As the implementation proceeded, José met with his coach to monitor his own goals and reflect on all that he was learning in the process. He used the coaching sessions to think ahead and anticipate what would be most helpful. As a result, he planned a large completion celebration for the change team and key stakeholders. He developed a sustainment plan that would be used to ensure that the quality system continued to meet its targets after implementation. He also devised an ongoing feedback system for any comments, suggestions, or changes that might be needed in future. The feedback system would help ensure that the quality system became part of the company culture.

After seven months, the new system was fully integrated and returning benefits, including cost savings and improved quality. Members of each division, as well as the initial change team, formed a sustainment team, which met quarterly to ensure the system's effectiveness and to address any performance or training issues. José was praised for his leadership and his contribution to making the company more cohesive and competitive.

In the final coaching session, they reviewed what José had learned about himself and the business from his involvement in this project, what new possibilities had become open for him, how he now saw himself as a leader, and how he could best acknowledge those who had helped him. José was pleased that he had achieved his goal of successfully leading the project while also spending every weekend with his family, and he made plans to promote his direct report, Saima. He gave large bonus checks to each of his change team members, and set a date for the change team celebration, including the key stakeholders, to acknowledge their collective accomplishment. José also received a company award for his efforts.

As they parted, José thanked his coach and acknowledged the value that he had received from coaching during this challenging time in his career. "You helped me be my best self and focus on what was important, not just all of the chaos going on around me!"

Coaching helped José stay positive and focused, aware of his strengths and driving the success of the change, stakeholder engagement, and self-management. The coach's role was instrumental in helping ensure that José had a strategy for each and an implementation plan to achieve each goal consistently and thoroughly.

Conclusion

All coaching is about change, whether it is focused on helping individual clients change or helping them lead change. The best strategy is to optimize support for every level of change. In this chapter, we showed how coaching supports key players to define and distinguish their roles in the process. We explored ways that individuals at all levels can lead and respond to change most effectively. Specifically, we showed how coaching can support the critical roles of the change leader to deliver successful change. We outlined how the coach (internal or external to the organization) can most effectively work with the leader to deliver change, and we outlined key approaches and tools. In addition, we offered suggestions for coach development and provided a case study illustrating leading practices.

The ultimate goal of coaching for any change is to assist the coachee in learning to coach themselves and to build their own capacity for dealing with change – while in any role. Since leading and managing change is a skill and a process that can be mastered, coaching can provide tools and resources to help individuals – and organizations – master these skills and continuously build their capacity to deliver successful change.

Developing yourself

There are many articles, books, blogs, and websites that can serve as a resource to those wishing to develop themselves as coaches who work with change leaders. The following list provides some examples of books:

- *Coaching for Change* (Bennett & Bush, 2014)
- *The Change Handbook* (Holman, Devane, & Cady, 2007)
- *Organization Development: A Jossey-Bass Reader* (Gallos, 2006)
- *True Change* (Klein, 2004)
- *Reflective Practice: Writing and Professional Development* (Bolton, 2014)
- *Becoming a Reflective Practitioner* (Johns, 2009)

References

Bennett, J. L., & Bush, M. W. (2013). Executive coaching: An emerging role for management consultants. In A. F. Buono (Ed.), *Exploring the professional identity of management consultants* (pp. 281–299). Charlotte, NC: Information Age Publishing.

Bennett, J. L., & Bush, M. W. (2014). *Coaching for change*. New York, NY: Routledge.

Bush, M. W., & Bennett, J. L. (2018). Organization development in action: Values-based coaching. In D. W. Jamieson, A. H. Church, & J. D. Vogelsang (Eds.), *Enacting values-based change: Organization development in action* (pp. 239–263). London: Palgrave Macmillan.

Bolton, G. E. J. (2014). *Reflective practice: Writing and professional development* (4th ed.). Thousand Oaks, CA: Sage Publications Ltd.

Boudreau, J., Creelman, D., & Jesuthasan, R. (2015). *Lead the work: Navigating a world beyond employment*. San Francisco, CA: Jossey-Bass.

Cohen, A. R. (2005). *The heart of change field guide: Tools and tactics for leading change in your organization*. Boston, MA: Harvard Business School.

Conner, D. (2006). *Managing at the speed of change: How resilient managers succeed and prosper where others fail*. New York, NY: Random House.

Ford, R. (2008, September–December). Complex adaptive systems and improvisation theory: Toward framing a model to enable continuous change. *Journal of Change Management, 8*(3–4), 173–198.

Ford, J. D., & Ford, L. W. (1994). Logics of identity, contradiction, and attraction in change. *Academy of Management Review, 19*, 756–785.

Gallos, J. V. (Ed.). (2006). *Organization development: A Jossey-Bass reader*. San Francisco, CA: Jossey-Bass.

Gibbons, P. (2015). *The science of successful organizational change: How leaders set strategy, change behavior and create and agile culture*. Upper Saddle River, NJ: Pearson Education.

Hacobian, A. (2016). A change agent compass for system transformation. In D. Jamieson, R. Barnett, & A. Buono (Eds.), *Consultation for organizational change revisited* (pp. 171–184). Charlotte, NC: Information Age Publishing.

Holman, P., Devane, T., & Cady, S. (Eds.). (2007). *The change handbook: The definitive resource on today's best methods for engaging whole systems change* (2nd ed.). San Francisco, CA: Berrett-Kohler.

Hougaard, R., Carter, J., & Coutts, G. (2015). *One second ahead: Enhance your performance at work with mindfulness*. New York, NY: Palgrave-Macmillan.

Jamieson, D., & Sullivan, R. (2011, May). *Driving change to get new results*. Chicago, IL: Linkage Organization Development Summit.

Johns, C. (2009). *Becoming a reflective practitioner* (3rd ed.). West Sussex: Wiley-Blackwell.

Jørgensen, H., Owens, L., & Neus, A. (2008). *Making change work*. Somers, NY: IBM.

Jørgensen, H., Bruehl, O., & Franke, N. (2014). *Making change work . . . while the work keeps change: How change architects lead and manage organizational change*. IBM Global Business Services. Retrieved from http://ftp://ftn.software.irb.com/software/nz/downloads/Making_Change_Work_While_the-Work_Keeps_Changing

Kegan, R., & Lahey, L. (2009). *Immunity to change: How to overcome it and unlock the potential in yourself and your organization*. Boston, MA: Harvard Business School Press.

Klein, J. A. (2004). *True change: The outsiders on the inside get things done in organizations*. San Francisco, CA: Jossey-Bass.

Kotter, J. (2012). *Leading change*. Cambridge, MA: Harvard Business Review Press.

Kotter, J., & Rathgeber, H. (2016). *Our iceberg is melting: Changing and succeeding under any conditions* (2nd ed.). New York, NY: Penguin Random House.

KPMG. (2016). *Now or never: 2016 global CEO outlook*. KPMG. Retrieved from https://home.kpmg.com/content/dam/kpmg/pdf/2016/06/2016-global-ceo-outlook.pdf

Maurer, R. (2016). *The challenges of change whitepaper*. Retrieved from www.energybartools.com/images/The-Challenges-of-Change-White-Paper.pdf

McKnight, L., & Jamieson, D. (2016). The critical role of use of self in organization development consulting practice. In D. Jamieson, R. Barnett, & A. Buono (Eds.), *Consultation for organizational change revisited* (pp. 115–128). Charlotte, NC: Information Age Publishing.

Pfeffer, J., & Sutton, R. (2006). *Hard facts, dangerous half-truths and total nonsense: Profiting from evidence-based management*. Brighton, MA: Harvard Business Review Press.

ProSci. (2018). *Best practice report 2018*. Fort Collins, CO. Retrieved from https://cdn2.hub spot.net/hubfs?367443/2018-Best-Practices-Report/2018-Best-Practices-Executive-Summary.pdf?t_1518736678755

Rock, D., & Page, L. (2013). *Coaching with the brain in mind*. Hoboken, NJ: John Wiley & Sons.

Tsoukas, H., & Chia, R. (2000). On organizational becoming: Rethinking organizational change, *Organization Science, 13*(5), 567–582.

Chapter 7

Delivering value in coaching through exploring meaning, purpose, values, and strengths

Ole Michael Spaten and Suzy Green

Introduction

The changes society has been through over the past few decades has had a profound impact on the individual's professional and personal life; it seems that encountered problems grow in complexity, and hence there's a growing demand for the helping professions (Hill, 2014), such as psychotherapy and coaching. An increasing number of people seek help through therapy or coaching when their own resources are inadequate or do not appear appropriate for solving the problem (Schreyögg & Schmidt-Lellek, 2017). Engaging in a dialogue with an understanding friend no longer seems to be sufficient, and therefore professionals are called into consultation; the growth of these offerings have been well-known for many years (Renton, 2009; ICF, 2012; Schreyögg & Schmidt-Lellek, 2017).

Executive coaching is an example of such offerings. Executive coaching has since its inception been utilized not only to enhance an executive's performance to support broader organizational goals but for the explicit aim of increasing self-awareness and self-management as a leader. Executive coaching at the senior leadership level has often been referred to as 'developmental' or 'transformational' coaching. Increasingly, this type of coaching includes a focus on executive well-being, by placing emphasis on values, meaning, and happiness.

Similarly at the broader organizational level, with increased pressure on the individual in the globalized and VUCA (volatile, uncertain, complex, and ambiguous) world, organizations have increasingly been looking to support well-being as a lever for improved performance, based on the rationale that a happy worker is a productive worker (Steger, 2017). As organizations compete on salary and benefit terms, more and more organizations are looking to other incentives to attract and retain top talent. Additionally, an increasing number of leaders appear to be seeking meaningful work and may expect their organizations to provide it (Sverko & Vizek-Vidovic, 1995). One study stated that finding meaning in one's work is as important as level of pay and job security (O'Brien, 1992). How can organizations meet these challenges, namely leaders seeking meaningfulness in their work?

With constant change becoming the norm for individuals, teams, and organizations, a focus on values and meaning in executive coaching can be an opportunity for greater levels of self-awareness for the coachee, as well as an opportunity to better align coachee goals and actions to their inner core values and ethical compass (Stelter, 2016; Bush, Ozkan, & Passmore, 2013) to increase overall well-being and optimal functioning. Similarly, organizations who support meaning-based approaches for senior leaders may also benefit (Steger, Littman-Ovadia, Miller, Menger, & Rothmann, 2013). In this chapter, we will argue that by providing senior leaders the opportunities to engage in executive coaching, not only can they increase their own levels of meaning, but they may also, through their influential roles, assist their organizations in creating greater levels of meaning for those who work there.

Theory and evidence

Meaningful work

Steger (2017), a leading scholar in the study of meaning and meaning at work, argues that meaning-based approaches hold the promise of being the next huge groundbreaking area for organizations seeking to improve organizational effectiveness (p. 60). Steger further suggests that organizations provide fertile conditions for the growth of meaningful work and hence enhanced well-being and performance by executives and their teams.

While there may be many approaches to fostering meaningful work in organizations, we would argue that evidence-based executive coaching, particularly at the c-suite or senior level, is a powerful means of doing so, at the individual as well as at team levels.

Meaning-based executive coaching

The uptake of executive coaching has increased during the last 30 years (Buschi, 2016). Similarly, the field of coaching psychology has experienced significant growth in both research and practice literature. Three meta-analysis studies (Theeboom, Beersma, & van Vianen, 2014; Jones, Woods, & Guillaume, 2015; Sonesh et al., 2015) and one systematic review (Lai & McDowall, 2014) have provided evidence that coaching is effective. Collectively these studies show that coaching has significant positive effects on areas such as performance and skills, well-being, coping, work attitudes, and goal-directed self-regulation.

People are seeking executive coaching for various reasons, and as many senior leaders move towards their "afternoon of life" (Jung, 1970), a common developmental area is that of the search for meaning and purpose. Many senior leaders also are looking to leave a legacy as they prepare for their inevitable departure from the corporate world.

Overview of meaning at work research

The scientific research base for meaning and purpose, in general, has increased in recent years. The literature relating to the application of meaning-centered approaches in evidence-based coaching practice has also grown (Buschi, 2016; Podolny, Khurana, & Hill-Popper, 2005).

Long before research into meaning at work occurred, psychological research existed on meaning in life, which has been identified as a primary personal resource. It has consistently been found to be associated with mental health and psychological well-being throughout the human lifespan (Steger, Oishi, & Kashdan, 2009).

Meaning has been defined as the intrinsic value and joy a person feels when they are able to apply their strengths and values with a sense of purpose, efficacy, and self-worth by contributing to society (Baumeister & Vohs, 2002). However, it is important to note there are different definitions of meaning, and the terms meaning and purpose are often used interchangeably. There has also been debate and differences among academics concerning definitions about the concept of meaning at work (Steger, 2017). In summarizing, Steger suggests that the common thread across all definitions is "the idea that for work to be meaningful, an individual worker must be able to identify some personally meaningful contribution made by his or her effort" (Steger, 2017, p. 60). To the c-suite leader, this element of meaning may be especially relevant because of the significant periods of time spent working, but also as a way to orientate in a rapidly changing world (Stelter, 2009). This means that the work and effort the c-suite leader puts into a company may be harder for the leader to keep track of in a dynamic workplace. The role of the c-suite leader may also change in accordance with changes in the company, or the leader may be new to the company and may have been specifically hired to create and implement change. Often the change of role will also have an influence on values, and therefore the work on meaning and values must be seen as a continued process by both the leader and the coach (Spero, 2006).

C-suite leaders' ability to lead a team may also be positively affected by pursuing meaning as a part of coaching. The leader's ability to understand, respond, and communicate appropriately in emotional situations depends on the leader's own knowledge about his or her own reactions (West-Leuer, 2017). Furthermore, the c-suite leader's ability to create an environment that supports employee well-being and ability to find their work meaningful may create better performance (Podolny et al., 2005). This ability then also provides further rationale as to why a c-suite leader could benefit from coaching on meaning, values, and emotions.

In recent years, there has been an increasing research base surrounding meaning and purpose and its associated application in the workplace. Research suggests that there are a number of key outcomes of meaningful work. These include productivity, increased strengths utilization, increased career commitment, increased experiences of 'flow' at work, high intrinsic work motivation, high job satisfaction, high-quality performance, and low levels of absenteeism and turnover (Steger, 2017). Therefore, it can be in the interest of both the company and the leaders to work with meaning as an element of coaching. In addition, with an aging population and workplace participation extending beyond the traditional retirement years, we would argue that meaningful work might become more important. The later years of life can be seen as a traditional adult developmental period where individuals are looking to make a positive difference, leave behind a legacy and are reflecting on their lives to determine if they have lived their life to the fullest (Erikson, 1950). The CEO may therefore question life decisions and everyday decisions both in his or her personal and professional life. In this natural process of growing older, the meaning and values in life may be questioned and have an influence on career choices (Yates, Oginni, Olway, & Petzold, 2017). There's also accruing research that suggests that finding a purpose for your life may add years to it. A study by Hill and Turiano (2014) found that purposeful individuals lived longer than their counterparts did during the 14 years after baseline assessment.

Meaning in coaching research

Concerning specific research on the study of meaning in coaching, there have been limited studies. A PsycINFO search revealed only seven studies using the keywords "meaning" and "coaching" and "executive." Recommendations and key findings from available current evidence-based coaching research (Buschi, 2016; Bush et al., 2013; Shams, 2011; Oliver, 2010; Gelona, 2008; Pooley, 2006; Sztucinski, 2002) will be pinpointed below: "Issues of meaning and identity are foundational" arise in all coaching for both individuals and groups (Bush et al., 2013). In executive coaching, core skills include self-reflection and the ability to help the coachee to "develop productive patterns" in the system of communication, e.g., people in the coachee "network of business concern, conversation and relationship" (Oliver, 2010). When the coach gains insight into the "life cycle of a coaching relationship," then the coach determines how this relationship "can release leadership potential and resources." Further areas of high awareness and essential elements in executive coaching are goals and achievement, self, confrontation, emotions, and bonds (Sztucinski, 2002).

Other topics related to the study of meaning, such as values, emotions, and happiness, have also only recently become a focus of research and application in executive coaching and coaching in general with the emergence of the complementary field of positive psychology (Green & Palmer, 2018). Previously, there was a traditional tendency to understand emotions as an unimportant element in work, and therefore emotions and values have not been seen as elements to increase production (Bachkirova & Cox, 2007).

Although some researchers have identified values as an important element in empowering individuals and groups in coaching in the postmodern society

(Stelter, 2016; Spero, 2006), Stelter argues the need for recognizing the importance of values in our work life if it is not to become a superficial chain of actions (Stelter, 2016). Other researchers identify the motivational component of meaning in life pointing to a sense of goal directedness or purposefulness (Emmons, 2003).

Others point to feelings of happiness, meaning, and motivation as central elements in successful coaching (Dik, Byrne, & Steger, 2013; Gelona, 2008; Akrivou & Bradbury-Huang, 2011). All these different aspects point towards a focus not only on productivity, but also towards work as part of a key identity marker in the Western world (Bush et al., 2013) and a key pathway to experiencing greater levels of positivity at work and in life (Green, McQuaid, Purtell, & Dulagil, 2016).

In the last 50 years, the emphasis on productive teams and employees in companies decreased the interest in creating meaningful working environments (Podolny, Khurana, & Hill-Popper, 2005). It is argued, however, that it might be time to return to those aspects of meaning and make them become important once more (ibid.). Not only for the purpose of productivity, but also for a broader noble purpose, where the workplace is seen as an institution that has an important societal role to play in supporting the health and well-being of its people and the community it exists in. This noble purpose for a c-suite or senior leader can become a realistic objective or specific goal within an executive coaching context. In fact, coaching may be essential in terms of providing the space within a c-suite leader's hectic schedule to create a specific goal and action plan from what may have initially been a broader dream or desire. We would also argue that there are real and growing opportunities for c-suite leaders, who yield positive energy and influence, to make a difference not only in their own organizations or communities but in the world at large.

Development of meaning in evidence-based executive coaching

We suggest that there are three primary approaches to exploring meaning in evidence-based coaching with senior leaders:

1   Values-Based Approaches (e.g., Values Clarification, Self-Concordant Goal Setting)
2   Vision-Based Approaches (e.g., Developing longer term goals or an overarching purpose/mission)
3   Strengths-Based Approaches (e.g., Strengths Assessments, Job Crafting)

We suggest that meaning-based executive coaching can be both goal and non-goal related. In the early stages of the development of the coaching relationship and coaching alliance (O'Broin & Palmer, 2006), the exploration of values and "working identity" (Ibarra, 2003) are primarily for the purposes of enhanced self-awareness; hence, it may be argued that this phase of coaching is non-goal related or non-goal-focused. Early sessions and homework may be more reflective in nature with the aim of enhanced self-awareness and personal growth preceding goal-setting (particularly to support self-concordance) and goal-striving behavior. However, the creation of personally meaningful goals and the implementation of action plans and actionable behaviors aligned to values and overall purpose in life is goal-related.

Values-based approaches

Values crystallization and prioritization

As noted earlier, the interest in and use of values in coaching is not new. However, with the emergence of therapeutic techniques such as ACT (acceptance and commitment therapy), there has been a revival of sorts regarding the interest and application of values in coaching (Anstiss & Blonna, 2014). Collis and Winters (2018) argues, that similar to many other positive psychology approaches to coaching, the focus of ACT is helping clients select and pursue autonomous and valued goals and develop richer and more meaningful lives. In ACT, 'values' are defined as "intentional qualities that join together a string of moments into a meaningful path" (Hayes, 2005, p. 155). Collis and Winters (2018) argues, that if a choice is made to behave in ways that are consistent with a person's values over time, the result is a meaningful life. Anstiss and Blonna (2014) suggest that values clarification may be one of the first activities an ACT coach does with a coachee, with values then referred to throughout the coaching process to ensure values-congruent action and the creation of a meaningful life.

Generally, though, we would argue that values crystallization and prioritization has always been a common activity in coaching. The use of values clarification exercises in the early stages of coaching or as a homework task can be a conversation starter and a powerful tool to commence executive coaching conversations relating to meaning and will also aid the creation of self-concordant goals (Sheldon, 2004). This does require an investment of time in coaching and outside of coaching (such as set homework) where the coachee is asked to consciously reflect on and select their core values (life and/or work). Values lists or card sorts are commonly utilized. Alternatively, a tool such as a "letter from the future"(Grant & Greene, 2005), a milestone birthday description, or a "writing your eulogy" exercise would work: in these exercises, the coachee is asked to describe their reflection on the years preceding, how they would want others to perceive them, and the impact their actions have had on others and the world. This can be a useful tool to clarifying what matters most in life, i.e., core life values.

In the case of the c-suite leader, values may have been an activity they have utilized previously as part of a leadership development program or previous executive coaching experiences. Regardless of prior experience, we would strongly recommend that a rationale be provided by the coach as to why revisiting values is crucial when it comes to the topic of meaning and purpose. Upon further exploration of values, it is our experience that a senior leader may in fact gain insight as to the importance or lack of what appeared to be important values or valued goals in the past. It is not uncommon that through the process of coaching, a coachee may in fact determine new values and/or let go of old ones that no longer are relevant or reflective of their new emerging authentic self.

Self-concordant goal setting

Locke and Latham's (1984) foundational work in goal setting is a useful tool for building meaning in executive coaching. In particular, through self-concordant goal setting (Sheldon, 2002), i.e., goals aligned to core life values, coachees are able to tap into intrinsic motivation and remain energized while working toward the achievement of their desired goals.

Sheldon (2014) argues that the topics of deeper purpose and more accurate self-knowledge have received relatively little attention in the research literature on personal goals and idiographic goal strivings. Sheldon, a leader in the field, outlined the "self-concordance model" (Sheldon, 2004), which emerged from a significant body of research on self-determination theory (Deci & Ryan, 1998)

The self-concordance model (SCM; Sheldon, 2004; Sheldon & Gunz, 2009; Sheldon & Elliot, 1999) of goal setting and goal striving is of utmost importance when it comes to the consideration of meaning in executive coaching. SCM research has found, that some goals are better for people's mental health, well-being, and maturation than are other goals (Ryan, Sheldon, Kasser, & Deci, 1996), because they better express the person's underlying interests, values, talents, needs, and motives. Sheldon argues that "a central struggle for most people, at least at some point within their lives, involves overcoming ignorance to discover what they really want and what is truly most important to them" (Sheldon, 2014, p. 2).

As such, we would again suggest that when coaching c-suite leaders on the topic of meaning, the important linkages between values and self-concordant goals should be made, highlighting again the need for the c-suite leader not to rush the values clarification/prioritization process, as it is essential in creating self-concordant and meaningful goals.

Vision-based approaches

As noted earlier, links have been made between the motivational components of goals with the suggestion that meaning or purposefulness reflects the extent to which people perceive themselves as living in alignment with their overarching goals through their daily lives (Emmons, 2003).

In addition, the development of longer-term goals or the creation of an "inspirational fuzzy vision" (Grant & Greene, 2005) can also help create a sense of purpose or direction for coachees. Little (1989) uses the terms "magnificent obsessions" to differentiate from "trivial pursuits." The distinction separates pursuits of a typical Tuesday (e.g., "checking e-mails") to the magnificent obsessions of a lifetime (e.g., "liberate my people"). Executive coaching can especially be used to explore these, thereby providing opportunities for a deeper exploration into what really matters and hence the topics of meaning and purpose. The means for doing so, for instance, can be asking the coachee to complete writing tasks for homework. This can also assist in meaning making, exploring one's self-knowledge, and identifying one's "magnificent obsessions." Research has shown that when people are asked to imagine and write about their future selves as working hard and accomplishing their goals, they show a significant increase in positive mood (Lyubomirsky, 2008). The very act of writing prompts people to organize their thoughts in a systematic manner that requires analysis, and by doing so builds meaning (Lyubomirsky, 2008). In coaching a c–suite leader on the topic of meaning, the articulation of an inspirational vision that incorporates an overarching purpose aligned to values is essential in the meaning-making process. So too is identifying specific actions that are aligned both to core life values and an inspirational and meaningful vision. In fact, we would argue that meaning arises from the daily recognition that one is living a values-congruent life and making progress towards a meaningful goal and future.

Strengths-based approaches

Character strengths

While it may be argued that executive coaching has always been strengths-focused, it is the explicit use of strengths tools in coaching that has become increasingly popular (Biswas-Diener, 2010). Many different strengths assessments and tools are utilized in coaching contexts. However, with the emergence of positive psychology, there has been a focus on the concept of character strengths in particular. As the c–suite leader explores the topic of meaning, identity becomes a key topic of discussion. We would suggest that character strengths might be a useful approach to exploring identity and in addition be a useful tool for the coach to assist the coachee in identifying natural character strengths that could be utilized and/or lesser strengths that may need development to create greater levels of meaning.

A multitude of peer-reviewed studies have explored the identification, measurement, and development of character strengths and pointed to character strengths as a foundational pathway to human flourishing (Park, Peterson, & Seligman, 2004; Seligman, Steen, Park, & Peterson, 2005; Gander, Proyer, Ruch, & Wyss, 2012; Wood, Froh, & Geraghty, 2010; Gander, Proyer, Ruch, & Wyss, 2013). For example, research has found that people who use four or more of their top character strengths at work are more likely to experience job satisfaction, pleasure, engagement, and meaning in their work (Littman-Ovadia & Steger, 2010; Wrzesniewski et al., 1997; Harzer & Ruch, 2012).

The creation of a meaningful life for a c-suite leader can be on both a personal and a professional level. The c-suite leader (as a central person) can also support the creation of meaning for employees. Meaning might be seen as an important element in a more general sense of well-being for employees, and this process of creating meaning will also be helpful in closing in on well-being as a connection between the professional and personal life.

Using strengths assessments early on in the executive coaching process can also assist in goal selection (i.e., setting goals that can either leverage signature strengths or alternatively develop 'lesser strengths') and in the goal-striving process (leveraging strengths to take action).

Job crafting

'Job crafting' has emerged as a theoretical approach that expands perspectives on job design to include proactive changes that employees make to their own jobs (Wrzesniewski & Dutton, 2001). Job crafting is defined as "the physical and cognitive changes individuals make in the task or relational boundaries of their work" (Wrzesniewski & Dutton, 2001, p. 179). By altering task and relational boundaries, employees can change the social and task components of their jobs and experience different kinds of meaning of the work and themselves, from the most routine to the most complex jobs, and from the lowest to the highest tiers of an organization (Berg, Wrzesniewski, & Dutton, 2010).

Research points to job crafting having positive effects on employees' degree of psychological well-being (Berg, Grant, & Johnson, 2010), work engagement, and performance (Tims, Bakker, & Derks, 2012). This suggests that job crafting matters for a number of key individual and organizational outcomes.

While job crafting may seem more applicable to general staff and not necessarily senior leaders who may have more autonomy over their roles, we would suggest that a knowledge of this research and practice is crucial for a senior leader to impart to his organization if the broader desire and perhaps goal of coaching is to create greater levels of meaningful work within the organization.

Wrzesniewski, LoBuglio, Dutton, and Berg. (2013), a leader in the field, suggests that job crafters shape the boundaries that define their jobs in three main ways:

1   *Task Crafting* – Job crafters may change the physical or temporal boundaries around the bundle of tasks that they consider to be their job. Task crafting consists of adding or dropping tasks, adjusting the time or effort spent on various tasks, and redesigning aspects of tasks (e.g., a teacher who spends time learning new classroom technology to fulfill his passion for IT).

2 *Relational Crafting* – Job crafters may redefine the relational boundaries that define the interpersonal interactions involved in performing their jobs. Relational crafting consists of creating and/or sustaining relationships with others at work, spending more time with preferred individuals, and reducing or completely avoiding contact with others (e.g., a marketing analyst forming a relationship with someone in sales to better understand the impact of his work on salespeople).

3 *Cognitive Crafting* – Job crafters may reframe the cognitive boundaries that ascribe meaning or purpose to the tasks and relationships that comprise their jobs. Cognitive crafting consists of employees' efforts to perceive and interpret their tasks, relationships, or job as a whole in ways that change the significance of their work (e.g., a custodian who thinks of his job as enabling education by providing clean, distraction-free classrooms for students).

As above, while the concept may not appear relevant to the c-suite leader, it is our experience that even at the very senior levels of organizations, leaders may have a disconnect between their job descriptions and their raison d'être. Introducing the research and honing in on the 'cognitive crafting' component may be extremely relevant for the senior leader who may wish to 'reframe' the perception of what they're aiming to do in their current role and/or organization in terms of creating a meaningful work life.

Aims and processes in purpose-based and meaning-based executive coaching

Issues of meaning and identity are important to increase self-awareness and are therefore foundational to all coaching. We suggest that these topics are of utmost importance in times of change: "Issues of meaning and identity take centre stage during organizational change" (Bush et al., 2013, p. 64). As such, an important task for the coach is to assist the executive's effectiveness in creating a meaningful work environment. To do so, the coach should allow time and support for the executive to focus and reflect upon what is meaningful in their position (Gelona, 2008). To some leaders, these topics as part of coaching may be new, having never worked with their own meaning making. To some leaders, it may be areas that have been part of coaching or leadership development seminars earlier on and therefore part of continued development. Regardless of the coachee developmental stage, it is important for the coach to get to know and adapt to the coachee.

If the coachee is already experienced in working with values and meaning, it can be worth revisiting the c-suite leader's values and the elements that may have changed over time, since the coachee is part of the coaching process. There may have been changes in the coachee's professional or personal life that requires a new perspective on earlier values or on meaning. It could also be a new job where skills or values that have been hard to incorporate in an earlier job can now be revisited and taken in as a part of a new strategy. It may also help the coachee to look at what well-being means under new circumstances. Here the models on well-being in the models section can be a way to investigate different elements that can have an impact on the creation of meaning.

On a practical note, when coaching individuals on issues concerning meaning and identity, it has been argued that the coach typically waits for such issues to arise naturally in the coaching process (Bush et al., 2013). We would argue that increasingly coachees may seek coaching for the specific purposes of creating meaningful work and a meaningful life and hence an explicit discussion and preparedness by the coach to address this topic will become increasingly important. We would suggest to coaches, however, that the topic of meaning can be a sensitive one and should not be rushed or covered superficially. A strong working alliance built in the early stages of the coaching relationship will allow for deeper and perhaps more expressive and challenging conversations relating to meaning and purpose.

In the process of change, the coach needs to be continually aware of the emotional transfer and the power balance in the coaching relationship. In order for the coach to be aware of this, the coach should get regular supervision in order to work on his or her own feelings and emotional transfer (Cox & Bachkirova, 2007). In coaching coachees, the relationship to the coach is a core element in a positive coaching experience (Machin, 2010). The coachee appreciates connecting with an empathetic, trustworthy, and non-judgmental coach (Machin, 2010). Especially in sensitive areas, e.g., the work with values and meaning, such coach qualities are very important. This makes the coachee's continued work on his or her own development key.

While the raising of self-awareness has been and will continue to be a core component of the aims and processes relating to coaching, this is particularly so when it comes to the topic of meaning, as it is this topic that engages the coachee in deep reflection and exploration of their core values, their authentic self, and their "way of being" (Rogers, 1980). Some leaders will have had extensive training in different types of leadership and ways to improve companies' economic performance. But this training may not have had any influence on or worked with the leaders' core values. This means that even experienced c-suites leaders may have very different starting points in working with meaning as a part of coaching.

We would argue then that discovering and creating meaning in work and life become a core part of becoming an authentic leader and "authentic leadership" (Luthans & Avolio, 2003). Fusco, Palmer, and O'Riordan (2011) point to the authentic leader as a leader who is self-aware and thereby able to act in accordance with their own values. Such an awareness can also be a help for executives who want to improve their communication (West-Leuer, 2017). Furthermore, West-Leuer points out that executives often fail to improve their communication with their employees if they are not aware of or do not reflect upon their own values and emotional reactions (West-Leuer, 2017).

Both for groups and individuals who work in the globalized VUCA world, the concept of meaning can be central when constant change is part of everyday life. The individual leader often works within a team, and the ability of a team to have a common understanding of the members, group identity, and group values can have a significant impact on both the well-being of the team members and on their ability to reach their common goal (Bush et al., 2013). When changes are implemented in companies, the employees and executives often find that change opens a row of questions about the meaning and identity of individuals and the team. On these occasions, the coach can help the executive to be clear about the communication of the new strategies in the company (Bush et al., 2013). If the executive wants to retain company employees, this process of meaning making can be of uttermost importance. At the same time, research points to meaning as one of the factors that makes individuals change career (Yates et al., 2017). These notions will be elaborated in the following paragraph.

In order to promote development on meaning and identity, Bush et al. (2013) point out four existential "inflection points" where the coach can support and direct the executive's focus through coaching during times of organizational change.

First, the coach can help the executive assess and evaluate changes and understand how these changes affect the identity of the organization. At this stage, the executive might need support in disconnecting from the previous organizational vision and identity to be able to formulate a new meaning and identity coherent with the change.

Second, the coach can help the executive to process the new or refined structure coherent with the new organizational vision and then communicate this identity to significant people in the organization. This communication can likewise support the executive to help employees in the organization find their new coherent work identity.

Third, the coach might make the executive more aware about their own behavior and thereby supporting the executive in adopting subsequent more helpful or appropriate behaviors consistent with the new vision and identity of the organization.

Fourth, the coach can initiate reflections on how the executive can advocate and represent the change in work patterns, both inside and outside the company. In this way, it will help the executive, and employees, in creating meaning and identity, and at the same time in fostering a sense of belonging and the experience of being a valuable member of the team.

Working with these four areas, the new organizational identity is sustained through "communication, celebration of successes, and reinforcement of the soundness of the new identity and meaning and the reasons for the change" (Bush et al., 2013, p. 65).

Besides, the coach's aim should be at helping the executive regard him- or herself as self-determined and self-determining. How the executives deal with emotions are of great importance for their own thriving, the employees' well-being, and the work outcome of both groups (Löwer-Hirsch & West-Leuer,

2016). The coach should therefore aim to help their client perceive and deal with emotions during work on meaning, goals and identity, making self-awareness of the coach an important aspect (Bachkirova & Cox, 2007).

Tools and techniques in coaching for meaning, purpose, and strengths

In addition to the above-mentioned self-awareness of the coachee, we would argue that prior to conducting meaning-based executive coaching, the coach invests in his or her own personal growth regarding topics as values, strengths, vision, and the broader concept of meaning, particularly when coaching at the c-suite level, where the executive may expect coach maturity and completion of associated developmental work.

Models

Numerous models can be explicitly utilized in an executive coaching engage-ment focused on the development of meaning. The ones we have chosen to highlight below directly focus on either meaning and purpose or the key role that meaning and purpose play in the broader sense of well-being or living a flourishing life, which may be the ultimate aim of meaning-centered coaching. When coaching a senior executive on the topic of meaning, it will be impor-tant to establish quickly the rationale for the introduction of the models to coaching and that some aspects of the model/s may not be as relevant to the coaching process.

PERMA (Seligman, 2012)

Seligman's multidimensional approach to well-being forms the acronym PERMA. Seligman argues that well-being can be strengthened when people plan positive actions within each of the five domains: (1) positive emotions, (2) engagement, (3) relationships, (4) meaning, and (5) accomplishment. In the utilization of PERMA as a model in coaching, the coach should highlight the importance of meaning in creating high levels of overall well-being. The coachee may also believe that 'accomplishment' is irrelevant if they've reached the pinnacle of their career. However, it may lead to a discussion with the coachee around making accomplishment more meaningful or where accom-plishment becomes a legacy for others rather than just oneself.

Ryff's model of psychological well-being (1995)

Ryff and Keyes (1995) developed a multidimensional approach to psychological well-being that defined six different aspects of human actualization: autonomy, personal growth, self-acceptance, life purpose, mastery, and positive relatedness.

Life purpose refers to the idea that the person has goals in life and a sense of directedness. While this model can be introduced to explore the importance of life purpose, it can also be used to explore the topic of well-being more broadly for a coachee. The other five aspects identified in Ryff's model can also be explored in terms of their impact on the creation of a meaningful life. For example, how well a coachee is doing in terms of 'positive relatedness' and what the role of positive relatedness is when it comes to meaning making for the senior executive who has an ever-present battle with juggling work/life issues.

SPIRE and CARMA (Steger, 2017)

The tools outlined in the figure below provide the evidence-based executive coach with a framework to assist their coachees in finding pathways to more meaningful work and assist the organizations the executives work in with strategies (based on research) to foster meaningful work for employees. Given that

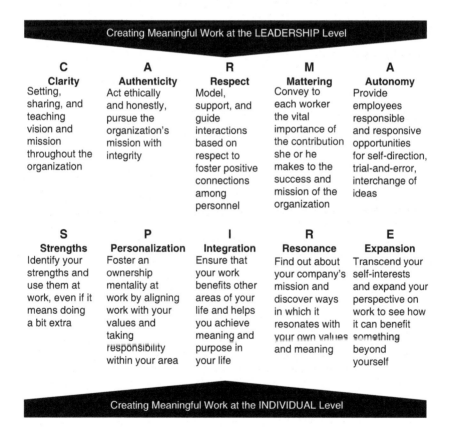

Figure 7.1 Creating meaningful work at the leadership level

executive coaching is not solely focused on professional and personal outcomes for the executive but simultaneously seeks outcomes for the executive's team and broader organization, both models may be useful in a coaching context.

Tools

There are numerous values cards and lists available either freely online or for purchase (e.g., www.thelangleygroup.com.au, www.thepositivityinstitute.com.au). A job-crafting exercise is available from the Center for Positive Organizations (http://positiveorgs.bus.umich.edu/cpo-tools/job-crafting-exercise/).

Assessments:

- Work and Meaning Inventory (WAMI) – Steger, Dik, and Duffy (2012).
- Purpose in Life Test – Crumbaugh and Maholick (1964/1981).
- VIA Character Strengths Assessment – Peterson and Seligman (2004).
- Strengths Profile – www.strengthsprofile.com.
- Strengths Finder – Rath (2007).

Conclusion

In this chapter, we have sought to provide a broad introduction to the topic of meaning as it relates to executive coaching and an overview of the current research base. We provided an overview of three key approaches a coach may explore the topic via 1) values-based approaches; 2) vision based approaches; and 3) strengths-based approaches. We have also provided relevant models and tools that might be helpful when executive coaching senior leaders in this area.

As the research base on meaning in life and meaning at work grows and so too does the interest in the workplace, both from employees and employers, coaches will increasingly be required to have conversations relating to values, strengths, emotions, meaning, and purpose. We have argued for the need for coaches to commit to ongoing professional development in this area, together with a commitment to one's own personal growth and exploration of meaning.

It is our hope that we might stimulate further interest on the topic of meaning-based executive coaching and that through further research specifically within an evidence-based coaching context (which is notably lacking at this stage) that the field itself flourishes and supports the creation of greater meaning at work for individuals and supports the creation of meaningful and flourishing workplaces. We hope we have also highlighted the important role a c-suite or senior leader may play in terms of increasing overall meaningfulness in the workplace.

Developing yourself

The following are recommended books and websites on this topic.

Books

- Purpose and Meaning in the Workplace (Dik et al., 2013)
- Man's Search for Meaning by (Frankl, 1946)

Websites

- www.drpaulwong.com
- www.positiveorgs.bus.umich.edu

Videos

- What Makes Life Meaningful – a TEDX talk by Michael Steger.
- The Meaning of Life: What Makes Life Meaningful – a TEDX talk by Frank Martela – www.youtube.com/watch?v=rdKBZbTCVFY

References

Akrivou, K., & Bradbury-Huang, H. (2011). Executive catalysts: Predicting sustainable organizational performance amid complex demands. *The Leadership Quarterly, 22*(5), 995–1009. Netherlands: Elsevier.

Anstiss, T., & Blonna, R. (2014). Acceptance and commitment coaching. In J. Passmore (Ed.), *Mastery in coaching: A complete psychological toolkit for advanced coaching* (pp. 253–276). London: Kogan Page Publishing.

Bachkirova, T., & Cox, E. (2007). Coaching with emotion in organisations: Investigation of personal theories. *Leadership & Organization Development Journal, 28*(7), 600–612.

Baumeister, R. F., & Vohs, K. D. (2002). The pursuit of meaningfulness in life. In C. R. Snyder & S. J. Lopez (Eds.), *Handbook of positive psychology* (pp. 608–628). New York, NY: Oxford University Press.

Berg, J. M., Grant, A. M., & Johnson, V. (2010). When callings are calling: Crafting work and leisure in pursuit of unanswered occupational callings. *Organization Science, 21*, 973–994.

Berg, J. M., Wrzesniewski, A., & Dutton, J. E. (2010). Perceiving and responding to challenges in job crafting at different ranks: When proactivity requires adaptivity. *Journal of Organizational Behavior, 31*, 158–186.

Biswas-Diener, R. (2010). *Practicing positive psychology coaching: Assessment, diagnosis and intervention*. New York, NY: John Wiley & Sons.

Buschi, A. E. (2016). *How executive coaches' meaning making informs their choices in coaching sessions*, (76), ProQuest Information & Learning, US.

Bush, M. W., Ozkan, E., & Passmore, J. (2013). The development of meaning and identity within coaching. In J. Passmore, D. D. Peterson, & T. Freire (Eds.), *The Wiley-Blackwell handbook of the psychology of coaching and mentoring* (pp. 58–67). Chichester, West Sussex, UK: John Wiley & Sons.

Collis & Winters (2018). Applications of acceptance and commitment training in positive psychology. In S. Green & S. Palmer (Eds.), *Positive psychology coaching in practice*. London, UK: Routledge.

Cox, E. & Bachkirova, T. (2007). Coaching with emotion: How coaches deal with difficult emotional situations. *International Coaching Psychology Review, 2*(2), 178–189.

Crumbaugh, J. C., & Maholick, L. T. (1964). An experimental study in existentialism: The psychometric approach to Frankl's concept of noogenic neurosis. *Journal of Clinical Psychology, 20*, 200–207.

Deci, E. L. & Ryan, R. M. (1998). Self determination theory and the facilitation of intrinsinc motivation, social development, and well-being. *American Psychologist*, 55(1), 68–78.

Dik, B. J., Byrne, Z. S., & Steger, M. F. (Eds.). (2013). *Purpose and meaning in the workplace.* Washington, DC: American Psychological Association.

Emmons, R. A. (2003). Personal goals, life meaning, and virtue: Wellsprings of a positive life. In C. Keyes & J. Haidt (Eds.), *Flourishing: Positive psychology and the well-lived life* (pp. 105–128). Washington, DC: American Psychological Association.

Erikson, E. H. (1950). Growth and crises of the "healthy personality." In M. J. E. Senn (Ed.), *Symposium on the healthy personality* (pp. 91–146). Oxford: Josiah Macy, Jr. Foundation.

Fusco, T., Palmer, S., & O'Riordan, S. (2011). Can coaching psychology help develop authentic leaders? Part two. *The Coaching Psychologist*, 7(2), 127–131.

Gander, F., Proyer, R. T., Ruch, W., & Wyss, T. (2012). The good character at work: An initial study on the contribution of character strengths in identifying healthy and unhealthy work-related behavior and experience patterns. *International Archives of Occupational and Environmental Health, 85*(8), 895–904.

Gander, F., Proyer, R. T., Ruch, W., & Wyss, T. (2013). Strength-based positive interventions: Further evidence for their potential in enhancing well-being and alleviating depression. *Journal of Happiness Studies, 14*(4).

Gelona, J. (2008). What motivates coaching clients? A practitioner's view. *The Coaching Psychologist*, 4(2), 72–77.

Grant, A., & Greene, J. (2005). *Coach yourself @ work*. Sydney, NSW: ABC Books.

Green, S., McQuaid, M., Purtell, A., & Dulagil, A. (2016). The psychology of positivity at work. In L. G. Oades, & J. Passmore (Eds.), *Handbook of positivity & strength-based approaches at work*. Hoboken, NJ: Wiley-Blackwell.

Green, S., & Palmer, S. (2018). *Positive psychology coaching in practice*. London: Routledge.

Harzer, C., & Ruch, W. (2012). When the job is a calling: The role of applying one's signature strengths at work. *The Journal of Positive Psychology*, 7(5), 362–371, UK: Taylor & Francis.

Hayes, S. C. (2005). *Get out of your mind and into your life*. In S. C. Hayes & S. Smith (Eds.). Get Out of Your Mind and Into Your Life. The New Acceptance and Commitment Therapy (p. 155). Oakland, CA: New Harbinger Publications, Inc.

Hill, P. L., & Turiano, N. A. (2014). Purpose in life as a predictor of mortality across adulthood. *Sage Journal, 25*(7), 1482–1486, New York, NY: Sage Publications Ltd.

Hill, Clara E. (2014). *Helping skills. Facilitating exploration, insight and action.* (4th ed.). Washington: American Psychological Association.

Ibarra, H. (2003). *Working identity: Unconventional strategies for reinventing your career*. Boston, MA: Harvard Business School Press.

International Coach Federation. (2012). *2012 ICF Global coaching study*. Executive summary. Retrieved January 20, 2018 from https://coachfederation.org/app/uploads/2017/12/2012ICFGlobalCoachingStudy-ExecutiveSummary.pdf

Jones, R. J., Woods, S. A., & Guillaume, Y. R. F. (2015, January 10–19). *Measuring the immeasurable: The perceived coaching effectiveness scale*. British Psychological Society Division of Occupational Psychology Annual Conference, Glasgow.

Jung, C. G. (1970). *Four archetypes; Mother, rebirth, spirit, trickster*. Princeton, NJ: Princeton University Press.

Lai, Y. L., & McDowall, A. (2014). A systematic review (SR) of coaching psychology: Focusing on the attributes of effective coaching psychologists. *International Coaching Psychology Review, 9*(2), 120–136, London UK: The British Psychological Society.

Little, B. R. (1989). Personal projects analysis: Trivial pursuits, magnificent obsessions, and the search for coherence. In D. M. Buss & N. Cantor (Eds.), *Personality psychology*. New York, NY: Springer.

Littman-Ovadia, H., & Steger, M. (2010). Character strengths and well-being among volunteers and employees: Toward an integrative model. *The Journal of Positive Psychology, 5*(6), 419–430.

Locke, E. A., & Gary, P. L. (1984). *Goal setting: A motivational technique that works!* New Jersey: Prentice-Hall.

Löwer-Hirsch, M., & West-Leuer, B. (2016). *Psychodynamic coaching for executives: Individual and group coaching in theory and practice*. Berlin: Springer-Verlag.

Luthans, F., & Avolio, B. J. (2003). Authentic leadership development. In K. S. Cameron, J. E. Dutton, & R. E. Quinn (Eds.), *Positive organizational scholarship* (pp. 241–258). San Francisco, CA: Berrett-Koehler.

Lyubomirsky, S. (2008). *The how of happiness: A scientific approach to getting the life you want*. New York, NY: Penguin Random House.

Machin, S. (2010). The nature of the internal coaching relationship. *International Journal of Evidence Based Coaching and Mentoring, 4*, 37–52.

O'Brien, G. E. (1992). Changing meanings of work. In J. F. Hardey & G. M. Stephenson (Eds.), *Employment relations: The psychology of influence and control at work* (pp. 44–66). Oxford: Blackwell.

O'Broin, A., & Palmer, S. (2006). The coach-client relationship and contributions made by the coach in improving coaching outcome. *The Coaching Psychologist, 2*(2), 16–20, UK: Cambridge Publishers Ltd.

Oliver, C. (2010). Reflexive coaching: Linking meaning and action in the leadership system. In *The coaching relationship: Putting people first* (pp. 101–120). New York, NY: Routledge/Taylor & Francis Group.

Park, N., Peterson, C., & Seligman, M. E. (2004). Strengths of character and well-being. *Journal of Social and Clinical Psychology, 23*(5), 603–619.

Podolny, J. M., Khurana, R., & Hill-Popper, M. (2005). Revisiting the meaning of leadership. *Research in Organizational Behavior, 26*, 1–36. Amsterdam, Netherlands: Elsevier.

Pooley, J. (2006). Layers of meaning: A coaching journey. In *Executive coaching: Systems-psycho dynamic perspective* (pp. 113–130). London: Karnac Books.

Rath, T. (2007). *Strengths finder 2.0*. New York, NY: Gallup Press.

Renton, J. (2009). Coaching and mentoring: What they are and how to make the most of them (Vol. 21). New Jersey: John Wiley & Sons.

Rogers, C. R. (1980). *A way of being*. Boston, MA: Houghton-Mifflin.

Ryan, R. M., Sheldon, K. M., Kasser, T., & Deci, E. L. (1996). All goals are not created equal: An organismic perspective on the nature of goals and their regulation. In P. M. Gollwitzer & J. A. Bargh (Eds.), *The psychology of action: Linking cognition and motivation to behavior* (pp. 7–26). New York, NY: Guilford Press.

Ryff, C. D., & Keyes, C. L. M. (1995). The structure of psychological well-being revisited. *Journal of Personality and Social Psychology, 69*(4), 719–727.

Shams, M. (2011). Key issues in family business coaching. In *Coaching in the family owned business: A path to growth* (pp. 1–11). London: Karnac Books.

Seligman, M. E. (2012). *Flourish: A visionary new understanding of happiness and well-being.* New York, NY: Simon & Schuster.

Seligman, M. E. P., Steen, T. A., Park, N., & Peterson, C. (2005). Positive psychology progress: Empirical validation of interventions. *American Psychologist, 60*(5), 410–421.

Schreyögg, A., & Schmidt-Lellek, C. (Eds.). (2017). *The professionalization of coaching: A reader for the coach.* New York, NY: Springer.

Sheldon, K. M. (2002). The self-concordance model of healthy goal striving: When personal goals correctly represent the person. *Handbook of self-determination research,* 65–86.

Sheldon, K. M. (2004). *Optimal human being: An integrated multi-level perspective.* UK: Psychology Press, Taylor & Francis.

Sheldon, K. M. (2014). Becoming oneself: The central role of self-concordant goal selection. *Personality and Social Psychology Review, 18*(4), 349–365.

Sheldon, K. M., & Elliot, A. J. (1999). Goal striving, need satisfaction, and longitudinal well-being: The self-concordance model. *Journal of Personality and Social Psychology, 76*(3), 482.

Sheldon, K. M., & Gunz, A. (2009). Psychological needs as basic motives, not just experiential requirements. *Journal of personality, 77*(5), 1467–1492.

Sonesh, S. C., Coultas, C. W., Lacerenza, C. N., Marlow, S. L., Benishek, L. E., & Salas, E. (2015). The power of coaching: A meta-analytic investigation. *Coaching: An International Journal of Theory, Research and Practice, 8*(2), 73–95.

Spero, M. (2006). Coaching as a transitional process: A case of a lawyer in transition. Executive Coaching: Systems-Psychodynamic Perspective, 217.

Steger, M. F. (2017). Creating meaning and purpose at work. In *Wiley Blackwell handbook of the psychology of positivity and strengths-based approaches at work* (pp. 60–81). West Sussex, UK: John Wiley & Sons, Ltd.

Steger, M. F., Dik, B. J., & Duffy, R. D. (2012). Measuring meaningful work: The Work and Meaning Inventory (WAMI). *Journal of Career Assessment, 20,* 322–337.

Steger, M. F., Littman-Ovadia, H., Miller, M., Menger, L., & Rothmann, S. (2013). Engaging in work even when it is meaningless. Positive affective disposition and meaningful work interact in relation to work engagement. *Journal of Career Assessment, 21*(2), 348–361.

Steger, M. F., Oishi, S., & Kashdan, T. B. (2009). Meaning in life across the life span: Levels and correlates of meaning in life from emerging adulthood to older adulthood. *Journal of Positive Psychology, 4,* 43–52.

Stelter, R. (2009). Coaching as a reflective space in a society of growing diversity – towards a narrative, postmodern paradigm. *International Coaching Psychology Review, 4*(2), 209–219.

Stelter, R. (2016). The coach as a fellow human companion. In *Coaching Psychology: Metatheoretical perspectives and applications in multicultural contexts* (pp. 47–66). New York, NY: Springer International Publishing.

Šverko, B., & Vidović, V. V. (1995). Studies of the meaning of work: Approaches, models and some of the findings. In *Life roles, values and careers.* San Francisco, CA: Jossey-Bass.

Sztucinski, K. (2002). *The nature of executive coaching: An exploration of the executive's experience.* (62), ProQuest Information & Learning, US.

Theeboom, T., Beersma, B., & van Vianen, A. E. (2014). Does coaching work? A meta-analysis on the effects of coaching on individual level outcomes in an organizational context. *The Journal of Positive Psychology, 9*(1), 1–18.

Tims, M., Bakker, A. B., & Derks, D. (2012). Development and validation of the job crafting scale. *Journal of Vocational Behavior, 80*(1), 173–186.

West-Leuer, B. (2017). Emotions in the context of coaching. In A. Schreyögg & C. Schmidt-Lellek (Eds.), *The professionalization of coaching: A reader for the coach* (pp. 249–263). New York, NY: Springer Science + Business Media.

Wood, A. M., Froh, J. J., & Geraghty, A. W. (2010). Gratitude and well-being: A review and theoretical integration. *Clinical Psychology Review, 30*(7), 890–905.

Wrzesniewski, A., McCauley, C., Rozin, P. & Schwartz, B. (1997). Jobs, careers and callings: People's relations to their Work. *Journal of Research in Personality, 31*, 21–33.

Wrzesniewski, A., & Dutton, J. E. (2001). Crafting a job: Revisioning employees as active crafters of their work. *Academy of Management Review, 26*(2), 179–201.

Wrzesniewski, A., LoBuglio, N., Dutton, J. E., & Berg, J. M. (2013). Job crafting and cultivating positive meaning and identity in work. In *Advances in positive organizational psychology* (pp. 281–302). UK: Emerald Group Publishing Limited.

Yates, J., Oginni, T., Olway, H., & Petzold, T. (2017). Career conversations in coaching: The contribution that career theory can make to coaching practice. *Coaching: An International Journal of Theory, Research and Practice, 10*(1), 82–93.

Chapter 8

Delivering value to the organization

Doug Riddle

Introduction

We see two people in a room, perhaps an office in a massive industrial center or maybe a professional office. They are deeply engaged in conversation in the room. Or perhaps they are in different parts of the world and talk by phone or see each other in the blue light of a videoconference. In the popular mind, it is always two people when we are speaking of executive coaching. If this is executive coaching or leadership coaching, we imagine one coach skillfully exploring, challenging, and supporting the other person, whom we might call the coachee or client.

The coachee's company has made this coaching engagement available to the executive, but how can we identify the value to the organization?

Although coaching in its modern incarnations traces its roots through all kinds of helping professions, including Edgar Schein's process consultation (Schein, 1988) and other group and team processes (Brock, 2012; Berman & Bradt, 2006; Bader, 2009), in the popular mind and among coaches themselves, it has been dominated by this dyadic frame: one coach helping one client. In many, perhaps most contexts, that set of conversations has been funded by the organization employing the person being coached and is believed to have value for the organization. Clearly, the sheer amount of coaching provided by organizations and the costs associated with this premium intervention should indicate that executive coaching has high value for the organizations who sponsor it (Sherman, 2004; Bower, 2012; Grover & Furnham, 2016; Abel, Ray & Nair, 2016). In this chapter, we will explore what coaches can do to make the value to the organization more obvious and direct rather than depend on causal chains that are hard to tease apart and harder to demonstrate with evidence.

Theory and evidence

In this section, I will review the theoretical frame and evidence for the contributions a systems view can make for coaches and coaching. Executive coaching claims to have indirect benefits for the organization, but measuring those results is fraught with difficulty. I suggest that a systems approach that targets the organization itself can make the value proposition more visible and reliable.

We target the organization by thinking of the organization as the client in all our leadership coaching. What difference will that make in the processes associated with coaching, including contracting, initiating the relationship, doing the work, and modifying the kinds of assignments given to coachees?

Organizational effects of individual coaching

The fundamental premise underlying the value of individual executive or leadership coaching is that better leaders make better organizations (Institute of Coaching, 2017; Hilgart, 2014; Cooke & Hilton, 2015). Attempts to quantify that contribution have been beset by methodological and logical problems (Phillips & Phillips, 2005; De Meuse, Dai, & Lee, 2009; Grant, Passmore, Cavanagh, & Parker, 2010; Grant, 2012, 2013; Passmore & Fillery-Travis, 2011; Kombarakaran, et.al., 2008; Leonard-Cross, 2010; Schlosser, Steinbrenner, & Hunt, 2006; Sonesh, et.al., 2015). Most often, this effect is assumed rather than stated directly, but there are some logic models that propose reasonable mechanisms (Crompton, Smyrnios, & Bi, 2012; Grant, 2016; Leedham, 2005; Levenson, 2009). For instance, the assertions of coaching's benefits tend to focus on a dependable set of competencies (Theeboom, Beersma, & van Vianen, 2014; Greif, 2007; Reeves, 2006; Coutu, et.al., 2009; Ely, et.al., 2010), specifically performance/skills, well-being, coping, work attitudes, and goal-directed self-regulation. Unfortunately, these factors are generally measured by global subjective ratings of improvement (Turner, 2006), which are known to be strongly affected by social desirability. Also important is the fact that it is in the coachee's interest to see improvement in skills, competencies, or attitudes that have been identified as opportunities for improvement. When the organization has invested considerable time and funding for the coaching intervention, the pressure is greater to show improvement (Stern & Stout-Rostron, 2013; Reeves, 2006). The Institute of Coaching proposes the following benefits of individual coaching to organizations:

- Empowers individuals and encourages them to take responsibility
- Increases employee and staff engagement
- Improves individual performance
- Helps identify and develop high-potential employees
- Helps identify both organizational and individual strengths and development opportunities
- Helps to motivate and empower individuals to excel
- Demonstrates organizational commitment to human resource development
(https://instituteofcoaching.org/coaching-overview/coaching-benefits)

How firm is the evidence for a causal relationship between these characteristics and increased organizational effectiveness or performance? (Meuse & Dai, 2009; O'Connor & Cavanaugh, 2013, p.561) For instance, shouldn't it be obvious that taking personal responsibility is essential for organizational performance? However, there might be multiple potential causes for poor performance, and the fact that poor performers also report a low sense of personal responsibility is not a significant indicator of a causal relationship. It may be just as likely that poor performers lack essential skills or preparation or have a lousy relationship with their manager, and their lack of success has led to disengagement. Our work is rife with these assumptions about what is cause and what is effect, and they are so deeply embedded in our cultural assumptions that it seldom occurs to anyone to challenge them.

Retention of executives

Often claimed is that executive coaching has a beneficial effect on retention of top staff, although our experience has demonstrated that it is not uncommon to have separation from the organization as an outcome of the increased self-awareness, self-efficacy, and sense of personal responsibility/autonomy that is associated with coaching (Riddle, 2013). One of the ways coaching is marketed is to compare the cost of replacing a top executive with the cost of coaching. This analysis is fraught with complexity, not least that a different executive may provide significantly better results than one who is unhappy or whose personal style is at odds with the prevailing or desired culture. The cost of maintaining the involvement of someone who is not happy with the organization or other leaders may outweigh the benefits of retention (Boushey & Glynn, 2012). So many of coaching's results lack controls for Hawthorne effects that it is nearly impossible to distinguish assertions that are scientifically demonstrable from those that should be seen as marketing hyperbole (McCambridge, Witton, & Elbourne, 2004).

Leader effects on team performance/climate

We have substantial evidence that team leaders have significant impact on the performance and climate within their teams (Miles & Mangold, 2002; Sauer, 2011; Durham, Knight, & Locke, 1997). The team seems a logical bridge between individual change and group performance. But what kinds of leadership have the best effect on team performance? Once again, the answer appears to be "it depends." If leaders are actually better equipped as agile learners because of coaching, there may be measurable effects. The challenge here is that the range of kinds of teams and the huge variety of measures of performance do not lend themselves to clear causal models. The caution of Cooke and Hilton (2015) is that

> The consistent theme from this research is that no single leadership style or behavior can be prescribed for effective leadership and management of science teams, but rather, a combination of approaches is required. This

combination encompasses: shared and hierarchical leadership; contingency and dynamic leadership that recognize the cyclical and temporal needs of a team as it develops and evolves over time; goal alignment; and the management of fault lines within and between teams that manifest as conflict, including conflict that drives innovation.

(Cooke & Hilton, 2015)

In other words, to the extent that executive coaching enables a leader to flexibly adapt to the changing needs of her team's circumstances on an ongoing basis, it may very well be of high value to the organization.

However, the research is still mixed on the connection between leader behavior and team performance. Burke et al. (2006) found small but significant effects in a large meta-analysis of team leadership research on several leader behaviors. Thirty percent of the variance in team learning was accounted for by empowerment behaviors by the team leader. On the other hand, Inez Makaske (2015) found no relationship between positive leader behavior, team climate, and team performance when observational data was included in the analysis (see also Ulla Kinnunen, Feldt, & Mauno, 2016). This returns us to the concern that the introduction of observers who do not have a stake in demonstrating success tends to undermine our sanguine assumptions. Why is this a problem?

Problems with ratings of observers of improvement

The question of who are the right observers of change in organizational interventions (including coaching) is a fundamental problem with much social science research. This has led to problems that have gained much attention in the last decade with the inability to reproduce the positive effects of many studies (Ioannidis, 2005). A group of 270 collaborators provided 100 examples of this phenomenon (Aarts et al., 2015). Reproduction tended to show much weaker effects than the original research.

William Shadish's (2006) summary of the effects of bias in program evaluation is germane. The observers or raters of improvement are also those who have chosen the program of executive coaching. This dynamic affects the estimates of coaching impact that purport to demonstrate a large return on investment. It is not unusual for coaching organizations to trumpet returns on investment from seven to 30 times the original investment (McGovern, et.al., 2001). We should be cautious about these estimates for the reasons mentioned.

Problems with identifying organizational impact with individual model

It may very well be that we are asking the wrong questions about the organizational impact of executive coaching. The organization is seldom the immediate focus of the intervention in executive coaching, so we may be well advised to turn from concern with the organizational impact of the individual coaching and focus our attention on the ways that coaches may have a more clear and direct effect on the organization; one that is visible to and involves the participation of decision-makers. This will require a systems orientation and a change in our usual thinking about who is the client.

Why should we move from an individual focus? An individual focus presents some unique problems in executive coaching because of the question of who is the client (EASC, 2017). If we are concerned with value to the organization, we open the door to the authority and responsibility of the organization to monitor its investment. We have seen dramatic changes in the thinking and expectations of organizations about what information should be made available to them and how it might be used in decisions about career or employability of coachees. For psychologists bound by the ethical code of the American Psychological Association or similar professional bodies, this has posed major challenges. From the viewpoint of the HR leader who may be contracting for coaching, there is no clear reason that they shouldn't have access to all the information generated by the coaching experience. In many part of the world, employees have no expectation of privacy with respect to their working space, their email, their product generation, or their phone calls. In fact, those with company-supplied phones often are subject to company information technology policies that explicitly describe the company as the owner of the data they contain (Sahadi, 2015). Why should coaching be different? From the point of view of the HR leader, more transparency about the concerns, development, and opportunities of the talent they are supposed to be managing must be valuable.

While this whole line of thinking may fill coaches with horror, it illustrates the importance of sharpening our conceptual frameworks so that claims made on behalf of coaching's value do not lead us into broad assertions that open the door to sabotage of the whole human development initiative. In particular, the claims about the organizational benefit of individual coaching are predicated on a wide foundation of untested assumptions.

Ethical and practical problems with an individual view

Let's dig a little deeper into the rationale for a systems view. For instance, I previously mentioned the often-promised benefit to organizations of greater retention as a consequence of executive coaching. It is well known that one of the infrequent outcomes of a substantial coaching engagement is the decision by the coachee to seek other employment. From the individual view, this is no problem so long as the interests of the coachee are pre-eminent. However, few organizations would engage a coach to help a talented leader realize that he or she should work somewhere else. As "getting the right people to leave" is seldom a benefit advertised by coaches (see Passmore, 2007), coaches are forced into an elegant justification dance relying on an untestable hypothesis that we merely surfaced a 'bad fit.'

Just as other helping professions have developed sophisticated philosophical edifices that justify every possible outcome as if it were what was intended after all (usually by blaming the person being "helped" viz., "resistance," "not ready," "not therapeutically minded," etc.), executive coaching could easily yield its soul by creating a class of inerrant priests. More worthwhile is connecting the efforts of the coach to the mission and objectives of the organization and its success on behalf of the whole ecosystem of shareholders, leaders, employees/ workers, and customers. Value has to be calculated in the cauldron of competing interests by acknowledging and addressing all of them while making informed choices about managing the tensions involved.

Aims and processes: increase value of the coach to the organization

To increase the value of the coach to the client organization, a systems view will manifest in five initiatives:

1   Recognition of the multiple forces at work and acknowledgement of one's role in the larger enterprise
2   A deliberate choice of the organization as client
3   Employment of systems-oriented interventions in the individual executive coaching engagement (network effects, power dynamics, etc.)
4   Strategic engagement with the largest possible set of actors in the organizational context
5   Expansion of the role of the coach

Recognition of the complex interplay of forces and interests

It has become standard practice in most executive coaching engagements to have meetings in advance with a human resources or learning and development manager and some kind of alignment meeting with the coachee's manager or boss. However, the expectations associated with each of those meetings are not predetermined. It would be easy to see these meetings as simple discovery on the part of the coach. A coach who is thinking systemically will recognize that these meetings require reciprocal sharing of information. Outcomes must include agreements on the purpose for the coaching, the patterns of information sharing that will be followed, and the impact expected on the behavior or outlook of the coachee as well as the effect on the teams she may lead and relationships with others in the organization. A coach with a systems framework will be identifying all the key stakeholders who are affected by the leadership of the coachee and the organizational factors that are going to affect and be affected by the coaching engagement. The coach will be interested in how the coaching engagement is supposed to contribute to the succession management plans of the organization and what the business benefits anticipated from a successful outcome will be.

Perhaps the coach will even have a visual model of the network of people and forces that he uses to help shape the planning for the coaching intervention in the form of an influence map (Hanneman & Riddle, 2005). At the least, the coach will be keeping in mind the multitude of influences and effects that are in the stream of activity that led to this engagement and will continue throughout the coaching engagement. This also ought to occasion a certain humility about one's role in the ongoing process. An executive coach who understands the dynamics of systems will recognize that she is an important element in the developmental culture of the organization, but not the only one. She will also realize that much of her impact is going to be the result of relationships and conversations with people other than her coachee. She will work with the people surrounding her coachee to prepare them to adapt to changes from the coaching. She will also shape the coaching to bring the larger political and social context into the sessions with her coachee.

Deliberate choice of the organization as the client

For executive coaching, we are wise to think of the organization as the primary client rather than the person being coached. The person being coached is in the engagement because the organization believes it is in the organization's best interest for the person to be coached and is willing to make an investment of time, money, and other resources for this. The assumption for all this is that there is a reasonable business case for the executive coaching and that basis establishes a moral context for the work.

Why is this important? Executive coaching has inherited certain assumptions from its grandparent, psychotherapy (Jordan & Livingstone, 2013). The therapist is generally free to address all of her attention to the patient or client without concern for others who might be involved. Ethically, this means that confidentiality can be assured for all communications between therapist and patient, apart from mandated reporting of abuse. Third-party payers may require a diagnosis and treatment plan, but other matters of content are absolutely restricted. As Brian O. Underhill has pointed out, this may be parallel to the company's need to know the developmental target and coaching plan for a coaching engagement (personal communication).

In executive coaching, there are no legal protections for what is discussed in sessions and the sponsoring organization may be intimately involved in the kinds of goals for coaching, what outcomes are acceptable, and the level of commitment demonstrated by the person being coached. Perhaps more important are the ethical imperatives associated with the insistence that coaching is a justifiable business expense. While it is entirely possible to insist that the coach is completely committed to the well-being or advancement of the coachee, when conflicts arise between the interests of the individual and the organization, psychotherapeutic practices provide little practical guidance for action. As a result, the organizations with mature experience in coaching often have sophisticated rubrics that maintain the healthy balance of limited privacy with ensuring direct value to the business. They 'interfere' with selection of coaches, matching with coachees, defining acceptable outcomes, setting limits on the amount and appropriate targets for coaching, and insisting on significant reporting about goals, progress, engagement, and results. The individual being coached is never the only client.

In coaching senior executives, I make explicit with my coachees that I am morally bound to work with them in their capacity as leaders of the organization (Knights & Poppleton, 2007). While personal matters always surface, the well-being of those for whom the leader is the steward is the priority. One executive thanked me for his coaching and I reminded him that "I'm not doing this for you." His shocked expression led me to remind him that we were both doing it on behalf of the hundreds of people just outside his office whose livelihoods were in his hands. "We do it for them, their families, and your customers." I want my coachees to prosper, but not at the expense of healthy organizations.

Bring the organization into the coaching session: employment of systems-oriented interventions in the individual executive coaching engagement

A systems mindset has practical implications for the conversations and experiments that are proposed for the coaching itself. If we are looking to increase the impact within the organization, the coaching questions and the 'homework' or milestones between sessions provide a valuable set of opportunities. Coaches with a systems viewpoint will frequently incorporate tools such as network analysis (Alireza, 2014) and tools for boundary-spanning leadership (Ernst & Chrobot-Mason, 2010).

How does one get better at working the politics within human organizations? Encouraging the client to strategically build her network is a first step. When an executive has been given a coaching engagement for development, the organization has opened a number of opportunities for connections that might otherwise seem awkward or inappropriate to pursue. For instance, let us say a coachee has been encouraged to develop a more strategic or enterprise mindset. It is clearly beneficial to that effort for him to interview senior leaders who are known for their strategic acumen or for the way they conceptualize their leadership in terms of leading the whole enterprise as well as their particular functional role. A coachee may now have an entrée to conversations and the development of a relationship with a variety of leaders with special skills or positions of importance.

Developing the coachee's professional network to include people who are in different subgroups, representing different gender, age, ethnic, or cultural groups, has been shown to be associated with increased leader impact (Hunt, 2015).

Assigning a series of interviews with more senior leaders within the organization or leaders in different sectors or regions can serve to increase the visibility of the coachee, but also can draw attention of senior leaders to issues of concern to the person being coached.

Similarly, the importance of developing a diverse boundary-spanning network should be obvious if the leadership impact of the coachee deserves expansion. Interventions that focus the attention of the coachee on the value of alliances for creating strategic value represent another avenue of organizational impact. Coaching questions like "Who are you enlisting to help shape your innovative solutions?" keep the collective nature of leadership and the importance of group involvement and action front and center. In all of these, we are encouraging the coachee to think about and extend effort to group contexts beyond one-on-one relationships.

It may be said that the agent and target roles are shifted in this picture. As executive coaches, we want to move away from therapeutic models that focus on the 'identified patient' or the individual target of change and growth. We are moving toward a model that involves the coachee as the agent of change within the organization and the coach as collaborator with that coachee. It is true that the coachee will learn new attitudes, behaviors, and competencies, but they ought to be in service of greater impact within the organization.

I often remind my coachees that the coaching engagement provides a catalyst for their greater involvement in strategic and cross-boundary influence. They can use the fact that they are working with a coach to take actions to gain access to decision-makers and actors outside their normal range of influence. "I have been asked to interview three members of the executive team about the focus on strategic execution," says one coachee. In the same way that students in graduate programs are likely to gain audience with leaders throughout a field, so a coachee may leverage the commitment to development for connections to people throughout the organization for learning opportunities.

Strategic engagement with the widest set of actors

Because the client is the organization, it is reasonable to expect a high degree of involvement by others who interact with the coachee. It has now become common practice to insist on a joint meeting early in the coaching engagement with the coachee's manager and human resources business partner or the client lead for executive coaching. Too often, these meetings focus only on the goals for change for the coachee and miss the opportunity to contract for specific actions by the others, such as the line managers, sponsor, or wider network. As coach, I may inquire about what contribution each of these groups and individuals makes to the coaching process and press for contracted agreements about the practical steps each will take.

The simplest demand should be for regular feedback to the coachee as the coaching engagement proceeds. This provides accountability for the coachee, but it also creates a mechanism by which contextual factors affecting the leadership of the coachee may be addressed. The absence of a succession plan or the neglect of basic career guidance are circumstances that can contribute uncertainty and undermine confidence of the coachee. Additionally, the attention to these organizational practices and internal systems can be a source of stimulation to examine whether more disciplined practices could have a beneficial impact on a larger group of leaders than just the current coachee. By inquiring about how coaching will fit into these systems (whether they exist or not), the coach raises important questions about the organization's commitment to development and its readiness to support the growth of the coachee (as well as other leaders).

Similarly, the coachee's manager is in an ideal position to guide the expansion of the coachee's professional network in consultation with the human resources business partner. She can identify opportunities for exposure to good models of leadership effectiveness. She can make introductions that reduce the chance that the coachee will be seen as over-reaching or stepping out of bounds in organizations for which that is a concern. Meanwhile, the involvement of these two people (and others as needed) sets in motion joint actions toward development. The coach, by involving these individuals, sets an expectation that development will be a core obligation of the organization's leaders and that it is important to collaborate in this way for organizational benefit.

We have often asked for and received meetings with much more senior leaders in the organization as part of the discovery process for the coaching engagement. In recent years, I've also taken the coachee into these discovery meetings as well as the HR business partner. Partly this allows me to model healthy ways of asking difficult questions, but it also gives visibility to our client contacts and adds weight to their work. Very senior leaders are often happy to have the chance to spell out their thinking about the kind of leadership needed in the present and future and be willing to play a role in giving feedback or communicating their view of progress toward culture and climate goals.

Expansion of the role of the coach

The executive coach who is willing to just be the 'hired hand' fixing the broken or developing the promising is neglecting the opportunity to make a significant direct difference in the working of the organizational client. The old distinction between the consultant to who comes to analyze a problem and prescribe a solution and the coach who is a companion in development is of declining usefulness. A coach who uses coaching approaches to consultation is consulting and should be prepared to play advisory and other roles to contribute high value to the organization (Schein, 1997).

What are the additional roles that a coach may offer? The most obvious is an advisory role on the integration of coaching with other developmental processes and programs within the organization (Riddle, 2015; Joo, Sushko, &

McLean, 2012). In the contracting phase, the coach will always ask how the coaching contributes to the existing developmental processes within the organization. Does the coachee have a mentor or mentors? Is he part of a cohort of high-potential leaders tagged for specific developmental opportunities? What leadership development programs has the organization already provided for him? How will the coaching be incorporated into the other talent management processes of the organization? If these questions result in a bewildered stare, it can be useful to propose some conversations with decision-makers to increase the impact of the coaching and ensure that it is integrated into existing talent and leadership initiatives (Wheeler, 2011). Seldom do learning and development professionals or human resources leaders intentionally choose fragmented processes that may be at odds with each other.

As a coaching expert, the executive coach also can contribute to the increased competence and effectiveness of internal coaches (Gurchiek, 2016). Most large organizations (and many small ones, as well) have invested in developing internal coaching pools of professionals who either do some coaching as part of their work or are full-time coaches for the appropriate levels of leader and kinds of development. These programs are beset with challenges, such as who the appropriate subjects are for internal coaching. The ethical and role confusion issues associated with internal coaches can be substantial during times of major change or market disruption, and trust is easily lost when something goes badly. The external executive coach can make important contributions to the ongoing training of internal coaches (Grant & Hartley, 2013), to advising the managers of internal coaching on sticky issues, and to improving the rubrics by which choices of internal or external, mentor or peer support, etc., are determined.

Tools and techniques to increase organizational value

I've mentioned a number of specific techniques as we've proceeded through the case for organizational value, but I will gather a few of the most effective in a brief survey here. As noted earlier, these generally need to be introduced at the contracting phase of the engagement if they are to be accepted within the organization. Otherwise, they may be too disruptive of existing processes.

- Alignment meetings with manager, human resources business partner, coachee, and coach. It is my preference that these meetings are run by the members of the meeting, either the human resources business partner or the coachee herself. I always prepare each of the participants in advance so they are prepared to contribute at the right level and ensure that organizational value is front and center. My role is entirely clarification when it appears necessary and ensuring that some agreement about objectives is concluded.
- Coachee runs discovery process. In line with my concern that any interventions I propose in an engagement initiate a practice that could continue

without my involvement, I try to avoid doing discovery interviews about a coachee without him being there. My preference is that the coachee and I structure interview questions and the clear purpose and outcomes of the interviews and then have the coachee do them on his own. If I have reason to believe that his level of defensiveness or impaired self-awareness is sufficiently extreme that this won't work, then I will accompany him. The point is that having the coachee ask the questions changes the inter-personal dynamics of the relationships in a positive direction and gives the people interviewed a clear stake in the outcomes of the coaching. Once a coachee has been able to ask some difficult questions and listen fully, there is a higher probability that there can be further conversations about tough issues. This also anchors the coaching conversations in the expressed concerns and viewpoints of others in the organization and reduces the possibility of the coaching becoming captive to the self-aggrandizing sub-jectivity of the coachee.

- Focus coaching on specific organizational talent processes. It is likely that coaching that supports a clear organizational need is going to be seen as more valuable to the organization (Walker-Fraser, & Stanhoe, 2011; Walker-Fraser, 2011). Many coaches have developed specific programs of coaching that speak to the challenges that learning and development leaders face throughout their work. Examples include the onboarding of executives, other transitional coaching for leaders, and triage consulting on problem situations. The high numbers of failures or derailments among promoted leaders gives everyone pause. Yet we know many of the factors that con-tribute to increasing success (Riddle, 2016; Grant, 2017; Hoover, 2015)).
- Shape the discovery process for greater access to decision-makers. If we believe that executive coaching and coaching approaches can make valuable contributions to the climate and culture of an organization, it is smart to involve higher-level executives in the coaching engagement. In consulta-tion with the client contact responsible for managing coaching services, I design discovery processes that ensure interviews with leaders at least two levels above that of the coachee. The coachee is then equipped with ques-tions about the larger leadership vision of the organization as well as the opportunity to develop sponsor relationships with more senior leaders. Par-ticularly with women and other marginalized groups, these opportunities are critical to creating more equitable environments within organizations.

Case study

A colleague and I were engaged by a $6B company's governing board to pre-pare the chief operating officer to become the CEO. A not-uncommon situ-ation had led to the engagement: the senior leader was a brilliant strategist, widely respected in the field who had led the day-to-day management of the system through several very challenging market changes. Under his leadership, the company had acquired multiple small regional companies in its field and expanded its reach throughout a significant region to become the second largest company in its market. However, there were doubts about his ability to make the shift in mindset and behavior needed for the CEO role. Complaints that he was too much in the weeds and that his impatience with people left those around him feeling bruised, battered, and inadequate concerned the board. A deep coaching engagement was seen as a way to address the competing views of his leadership.

The coaching was successful in that it resulted in increased confidence on the part of the board and he was selected to become CEO. From the beginning, we recognized and contracted with the expectation that the organization was the client. This was made explicit in conversations with board leadership as well as with the coachee. As a part of this partnership model, we established regular meetings with the human resources and talent leadership of the organization to ensure that the work was consistent with their goals and mission. This also had the purpose of elevating the importance of these leaders and ensuring the visibility of their role in the leadership development process of the organization. The long-term outcome was an expectation that the relationship the new CEO had with these HR leaders would grow and expand so my work as an outside coach could terminate.

By addressing the systems context of the coaching, it quickly became apparent to the coachee that his executive team was going to need help stepping up to the pace and changing market environment the organization was facing. This led to coaching for the senior team and, because of our commitment to elevating the value of internal resources, the head of talent was enlisted to be the co-coach for the team coaching. Over several years, the executive team went through developmental processes to equip them for the volatile and complex changes in their markets.

During this time, the discovery interviews and alignment meetings with the prior CEO and the board chairs led the board chair to call for advice and consultation on board relationships and managing the succession. The board composition was an artifact of an earlier incarnation of the organization when it was a small, regionally contained company. I was able to encourage the board chair to recognize that a different member composition was needed for the company as it now existed and the nominating committee adopted new plans for future board composition.

The question of the value of the executive coaching was addressed in cases like this by forming the right kind of relationship with the organization sponsoring the coaching and by clarifying the differing roles and the obligations associated with the various relationships involved. An executive coach with a systems approach and a clear view of the organization as first client has much to offer of value to the whole organization while improving the leadership capacity of her coachee at the same time.

Conclusion

Executive coaching has the potential to have significant organizational impact, but it will require some important shifts in the thinking and practice of executive coaches. These shifts include a mindset that insists on a greater partnership between the coach and the organization based on the recognition that – if leadership is the focus – the organization must be seen as the client. Consequently, the way contracting, discovery, the coaching itself, and the ongoing patterns of interaction with key organizational players are undertaken will reflect a systems view. It will also require that coaches courageously expand the roles they assume and the services they provide to their clients. It is time for executive coaching to grow up and leave its narrowly individualistic heritage in favor of a high-impact role in organizational success.

References

Aarts, A. A., Anderson, J. E., Anderson, C. J., Attridge, P. R., Attwood, A., Axt, J., . . . Zuni, K. (2015). Estimating the reproducibility of psychological science. *Science, 349*(6251). https://doi.org/10.1126/science.aac4716

Abel, A., Ray, R., & Nair, S. (2016). *Global executive coaching survey 2016: Developing leaders and leadership capabilities at all levels.* New York: The Conference Board.

Alireza, A., Wigand, R. T., & Hossain, L. (2014). Measuring social capital through network analysis and its influence on individual performance. *Library Information Science Research, 36*(1), 66–73.

Bader, M. (2009). The differences between coaching and therapy is greatly overstated. *Psychology Today.* Retrieved from www.psychologytoday.com/blog/what-is-he-thinking/200904/the-difference-between-coaching-and-therapy-is-greatly-overstated

Berman, W. H., & Bradt, G. (2006). Executive coaching and consulting: "Different strokes for different folks". *Professional Psychology: Research and Practice, 37*(3), 244–253. https://doi.org/10.1037/0735-7028.37.3.244

Boushey, H., & Glynn, S. G. (2012). *There are significant business costs to replacing employees.* Retrieved from www.americanprogress.org/issues/economy/reports/2012/11/16/44464/there-are-significant-business-costs-to-replacing-employees/.

Bower, K. M. (2012). Leadership coaching: Does it really provide value? *Journal of Practical Consulting, 41,* 1–5. Retrieved from www.regent.edu/acad/global/publications/jpc/vol4iss1/JPC_Vol4Iss1_Bower.pdf

Brock, V. G. (2012). *Sourcebook of coaching history.* Charleston, SC: Create Space Independent Publishing.

Burke, S. C., Stagl, K., Klein, C., Goodwin, G., Salas, E., & Halpin, S. M. (2006). What type of leader behaviors are functional in teams? A meta analysis *The Leadership Quarterly, 17,* 288–307. https://doi.org/10.1016/j.leaqua.2006.02.007

Cooke, N. J., & Hilton, M. L. (2015). *Team science leadership.* Retrieved from: www.ncbi.nlm.nih.gov/books/NBK310381/

Coutu, D., Kauffman, C., Alexander, G., Alvey, S., Annunzio, S., Applegate, L., & Zucker, R. (2009). *The realities of executive coaching HBR research report | the realities of executive coaching.* Retrieved from www.warriormindcoach.com/Coaching-Benefits.pdf

Crompton, B. M., Smyrnios, K. X., & Bi, R. (2012). Measuring the influence of business coaching on fast-growth firms. *Small Enterprise Research, 19*(1), 16–31. https://doi.org/10.5172/ser.2012.19.1.16

De Meuse, K. P., Dai, G., & Lee, R. J. (2009). Evaluating the effectiveness of executive coaching: Beyond ROI? *Coaching: An International Journal of Theory, Research and Practice, 2*(2), 117–134. https://doi.org/10.1080/17521880902882413

Durham, C. C., Knight, D., & Locke, E. A. (1997). Effects of leader role, team-set goal difficulty, efficacy, and tactics on team effectiveness. *Organizational Behavior & Human Decision Processes, 72*(2), 203–231.

EASC. (2017). *EASC-ethical guidelines short form.* Retrieved from www.easc-online.eu/fileadmin/content/dokumente/verein/de/Kurzfassung_Ethikrichtlinien_EASC_DE_EN_web.pdf

Ely, K., Boyce, L. A., Nelson, J. K., Zaccaro, S. J., Hernez-Broome, G., & Whyman, W. (2010). Evaluating leadership coaching: A review and integrated framework. *The Leadership Quarterly, 21*(4), 585–599. https://doi.org/10.1016/j.leaqua.2010.06.003

Ernst, C., & Chrobot-Mason, D. (2010). *Boundary spanning leadership.* Greensboro, NC: Center for Creative Leadership.

Grant, A. M. (2012). ROI is a poor measure of coaching success: Towards a more holistic approach using a well-being and engagement framework. *Coaching, 5*(2), 74–85. https://doi.org/10.1080/17521882.2012.672438

Grant, A. M. (2013). The efficacy of coaching. In *Wiley-Blackwell handbook of the psychology of coaching and mentoring.* Hoboken, NJ: Wiley-Blackwell.

Grant, A. M. (2016). What can Sydney tell us about coaching? Research with implications for practice from down under. *Consulting Psychology Journal: Practice and Research, 68*(2), 105–117. https://doi.org/10.1037/cpb0000047

Grant, A. M. (2017). The third "generation" of workplace coaching: Creating a culture of quality conversations. *Coaching: An International Journal of Theory, Research and Practice, 10*(1), 37–53. https://doi.org/10.1080/17521882.2016.1266005

Grant, A. M., & Hartley, M. (2013). Developing the leader as coach: Insights, strategies and tips for embedding coaching skills in the workplace. *Coaching: An International Journal of Theory, Research and Practice, 6*(2), 102–115. https://doi.org/10.1080/17521882.2013.824015

Grant, A. M., Passmore, J., Cavanagh, M., & Parker, H. (2010). The state of play in coaching. *International Review of Industrial & Organizational Psychology, 25*, 125–168.

Greif, S. (2007). Advances in research on coaching outcomes. *International Coaching Psychology Review, 2*(3), 222–249. Retrieved from www.researchgate.net/profile/Siegfried_Greif/publication/200735401_Advances_in_research_on_coaching_outcomes/links/09e4150b9d04bd9e9e000000/Advances-in-research-on-coaching-outcomes.pdf#page=6

Grover, S., & Furnham, A. (2016). Coaching as a developmental intervention in organisations: A systematic review of its effectiveness and the mechanisms underlying It. *PLoS One.* https://doi.org/10.1371/journal.pone.0159137

Gurchiek, K. (2016). *Should your organization use internal coaches?* Retrieved October 15, 2017, from www.shrm.org/resourcesandtools/hr-topics/organizational-and-employee-development/pages/does-your-organization-use-internal-coaches.aspx

Hanneman, R. A., & Riddle, M. D. (2005). *Introduction to social network methods.* Riverside, CA: University of California.

Hilgart, E. (2014). *Coaching for organizational culture change: Can it work? – Hilgart*. Retrieved October 15, 2017, from http://hilgart.co/journal/coaching-culture-change-can-work/

Hoover, J. (2015). *The ten commandments of contextual coaching how coaching through an organizational lens aligns what individual leaders do best with what organizations need most*. Retrieved from www.partners-international.com/wp-content/uploads/2015/03/Direct-from-The-Conference-Board-Coaching-Summit-2015-Ten-Commandments-of-Contextual-Coaching.pdf

Hunt, V., Layton, D., & Prince, S. (2015). *Diversity matters*. McKinsey & Co. (white paper). Retrieved from www.mckinsey.com/~/media/mckinsey/business%20functions/organization/our%20insights/why%20diversity%20matters/diversity%20matters.ashx

Ioannidis, J. P. A. (2005). Why most published research findings are false. *J.P.A. PLoS Medicine, 2*(e124). Retrieved from https://journals.plos.org/plosmedicine/article?id=10.1371/journal.pmed.0020124.

Joo, B. K. (Brian), Sushko, J. S., & McLean, G. N. (2012). Multiple faces of coaching : Manager-as-coach, executive coaching, and formal mentoring. *Organization Development Journal, 30*(1), 19–38. https://doi.org/10.1080/13678860802102534

Jordan, M., & Livingstone, J. B. (2013). Coaching and psychotherapy in health and wellness: Overlap, dissimilarities, & the potential for collaboration. *Global Advances in Health and Medicine, 2*(4). Retrieved from www.ncbi.nlm.nih.gov/pmc/articles/PMC3833547/

Kinnunen, U., Feldt, T., & Mauno, S. (2016). Authentic leadership and team climate: Testing cross-lagged relationships. *Journal of Managerial Psychology, 31*(3), 331–345.

Knights, A., & Poppleton, A. (2007). *Coaching in organisations*. London, UK: Chartered Institute of Personnel and Development.

Kombarakaran, F. A., Yang, J. A., Baker, M. N., & Fernandes, P. B. (2008). Executive coaching: It works! *Consulting Psychology Journal: Practice and Research, 60*(1), 78–90. https://doi.org/10.1037/1065-9293.60.1.78

Leedham, M. (2005). The coaching scorecard: A holistic approach to evaluating the benefits of business coaching. *International Journal of Evidence Based Coaching and Mentoring, 3*(2). Retrieved from www.authentic-change.com/wp-content/uploads/2017/03/coaching-scorecard.pdf

Leonard-Cross, E. (2010). Developmental coaching: Business benefit - fact or fad?: An evaluative study to explore the impact of coaching in the workplace. International Coaching Psychology Review. 5(1), 36-47.

Levenson, A. (2009). Measuring and maximizing the business impact of executive coaching. *Consulting Psychology Journal: Practice and Research, 61*(2), 103–121. https://doi.org/10.1037/a0015438

Makaske, I., Hoogeboom, D. A. M. G. M., Wilderom, C., & Wilderom, C. P. M. (2015). *The effect of leadership behavior on work climate and team effectiveness*. Retrieved from http://essay.utwente.nl/67485/1/Makaske_BA_faculty.pdf.pdf

McCambridge, J., Witton, J., Elbourne, D. (2014). Systematic review of the Hawthorne effect: New concepts are needed to study research participation effects. *Journal of Clinical Epidemiology, 67*(3), 267–277.

McGovern, J., Lindemann, M., Vergara, M., Murphy, S., Barker, L., & Warrenfeltz, R. (2001). Maximizing the impact of executive coaching: Behavioral change, organizational outcomes, and return on investment. The Manchester Review., 6(1).

Meuse, K. P. D., & Dai, G. (2009). What we can learn from the research literature. *The Korn-Ferry Institute*, 2–17.

Miles, S. J., & Mangold, G. (2002). The impact of team leader performance on team member satisfaction: The subordinates perspective. *Team Performance Management, 8*(5/6), 113–121.

O'Connor, S. & Cavanaugh, M. (2013). The coaching ripple effect: The effects of developmental coaching on wellbeing across organisational networks. *Psychology of Well-Being: Theory, Research and Practice, 3*(2).

Passmore, J. (2007). Addressing deficit performance through coaching: Using motivational interviewing for performance improvement in coaching. *International Coaching Psychology Review, 2*(3), 265–279.

Passmore, J., & Fillery-Travis, A. (2011). A critical review of executive coaching research: A decade of progress and what's to come. *Coaching: An International Journal of Theory, Research and Practice, 4*(2), 70–88. https://doi.org/10.1080/17521882.2011.596484

Phillips, J. J., & Phillips, P. P. (2005). Measuring ROI in executive coaching. *International Journal of Coaching in Organizations, 3*(1), 53–62. Retrieved from www.roiinstitute.net/wp-content/uploads/2014/12/Measuring-ROI-in-Executive-Coaching.pdf

Reeves, W. B. (2006). The value proposition for executive coaching. *Financial Executive.* Retrieved December 9, 2017, from http://blogs.wayne.edu/ioadventures/files/2013/12/The-Value-Propostion-For-Executive-Coaching.pdf

Riddle, D. D. (2013). Unpublished informal survey of coaching practice leaders from 3 coaching organizations.

Riddle, D. D. (2015). Creating an integrated coaching system. In D. D. Riddle, E. Hoole, & E. Gullette (Eds.), *Center for creative leadership handbook of coaching in organizations.* Hoboken, NJ: John Wiley & Sons Ltd.

Riddle, D. D. (2016). *Executive integration: Equipping transitioning leaders for success.* (white paper) Greensboro, NC: Center for Creative Leadership.

Sahadi, J. (2015). *Can your employer see everything you do on your company phone?* Retrieved March 18, 2018, from http://money.cnn.com/2015/08/27/pf/using-smartphones-from-work/index.html

Sauer, S. J. (2011). Taking the reins: The effects of new leader status and leadership style on team performance. *Journal of Applied Psychology, 96*(3), 574–587.

Schein, E.H. (1997). The concept of client from a process consultation perspective: A guide for change agents. Retrieved from https://dspace.mit.edu/bitstream/handle/1721.1/2647/SWP-3946-36987393.pdf

Schein, E.H. (1988). *Process consultation: Its role in organization development, Vol. 1* (2nd ed.) Boston: FT Publishing.

Schlosser, B., Steinbrenner, D., Kumata, E. & Hunt, J. (2006). The coaching impact study : Measuring the value of executive coaching. *International Journal of Coaching in Organizations, 4*(3), 8–26.

Shadish, W. R. (2006, January). *The common threads in program evaluation.* Retrieved November 5, 2017, from www.ncbi.nlm.nih.gov/pubmed/16356356

Sherman, S. A. (2004). The wild west of executive coaching. *Harvard Business Review, 82*(11), 82–90. Retrieved from www.hbr.org

Sonesh, S. C., Coultas, C. W., Lacerenza, C. N., Marlow, S. L., Benishek, L. E., & Salas, E. (2015). The power of coaching: A meta-analytic investigation. *Coaching: An International Journal of Theory, Research and Practice, 8*(2), 73–95. https://doi.org/10.1080/17521882.2015.1071418

Stern, L., & Stout-Rostron, S. (2013, February). What progress has been made in coaching research in relation to 16 ICRF focus areas from 2008 to 2012? *Coaching: An International Journal of Theory, Research and Practice, 6*, 72–96. https://doi.org/10.1080/17521882.2012.757013

Theeboom, T., Beersma, B., & van Vianen, A. E. M. (2014). Does coaching work? A meta-analysis on the effects of coaching on individual level outcomes in an organizational context. *The Journal of Positive Psychology*, *9*(1), 1–18. https://doi.org/10.1080/17439760.2013.837499

Turner, C. (2006). *Ungagged: Executives on executive coaching*. Retrieved October 15, 2017, from https://iveybusinessjournal.com/publication/ungagged-executives-on-executive-coaching/

Walker-Fraser, A., & Stanhoe, N. (2011). An HR perspective on executive coaching for organisational learning. *International Journal of Evidence Based Coaching and Mentoring*, *9*(2). Retrieved from www.business.brookes.ac.uk/research/areas/coachingandmentoring/

Walker-Fraser, A. (2011). Coaching and the link to organizational performance: An HR perspective on how to demonstrate return on investment. *Development and Learning in Organizations: An International Journal*, *25*(4), 8–10.

Wheeler, L. (2011). How does the adoption of coaching behaviours by line managers contribute to the achievement of organisational goals? *International Journal of Evidence Based Coaching and Mentoring*, *9*(1). Retrieved from www.business.brookes.ac.uk/research/areas/coachingandmentoring/

Chapter 9

Delivering value through cross-cultural team coaching

Philippe Rosinski

Introduction

Weaving a cultural perspective into the coaching of executive teams is crucial, not only because executive teams are increasingly culturally diverse but also because when teams tap into their hidden intercultural potential, they become more creative and more effective.

Yet, executive team coaches able to integrate interculturalism into their craft remain until now the exception rather than the norm.

In this chapter, I will build upon my previous work in this area (2003, 2010), and introduce a process (10-Co steps) for coaching intercultural teams, focusing on executive teams in particular. Most of all, my aim here is to invite advanced practitioners to more systematically leverage cultural differences and to offer them a practical way to do so by using the Cultural Orientations Framework (COF) assessment. The case studies in particular should give you a sense of how coaching across cultures can be deployed in practice and how culture enriches the executive team coaching process.

I will refer to the traditional view of diversity (i.e., external/internal diversity) and will introduce the notion of explicit/implicit diversity. I will argue that all teams are culturally diverse, at least in some latent fashion, and that therefore team coaching needs to become intercultural team coaching. I will also suggest that coaching executive teams with lasting impact implies embracing the holographic/organic/complexity paradigm and addressing complexity faced by senior teams from multiple, interconnected perspectives ranging from the physical to the spiritual (Rosinski, 2010). The cultural perspective works best in combination with other perspectives, which together form a powerful, integrated, global form of team coaching.

Theory and evidence

As an early team coach, my practice has been informed by group dynamics. This was a time when literature on teams, let alone on team coaching, was almost nonexistent. In the last decade, several books have appeared that divulge best practices and research findings (see notably Salas, Rico, & Passmore, 2017, which provides a wide-scale literature review of team and group processes).

Group dynamics

A group is not equivalent to the sum of its individual members. It takes a life of its own: at its best, the group makes the most of individual contributions and achieves synergy; at its worst, it produces conformism or polarization. These notions, which team coaches are now all familiar with, weren't evident before the emergence of "group dynamics," defined as "the influential actions, processes, and changes that occur within and between groups; also, the scientific study of these processes" (Forsyth, 2014 (6th ed.), p. 2). Kurt Lewin coined the term "group dynamics" and is widely considered as having pioneered this field in the 1940s (Anzieu & Martin, 1990 (9th ed.), p. 11; Forsyth, p. 24). Lewin explained behaviors of group members as a function of the interaction between their personal characteristics and environmental factors. Psychologists, sociologists, and social psychologists conducted research that highlighted pitfalls as well as ways for groups to improve: for example, Kenneth Benne and Paul Sheats on functions and roles in a group (Benne & Sheats, 1948; Anzieu & Martin, pp. 370–372), Robert Bales (1950) on examining behaviors that positively or negatively affect the group, Solomon Asch on the pressure to conform (1956), Marvin Dunnette, Campbell, and Jaastad (1963) on group creativity, and Ivan Steiner on comparing the productivity of groups to that of individuals for various tasks (1972), to name but a few.

The concept of 'group' has been defined in numerous ways. Donelson Forsyth shows a sampling and defines a group as "two or more individuals who are connected by and within social relationships" (p. 3). A team can be defined as "any group of people who work together" (*Collins Dictionary*). In practice, a team may be more clearly defined as a group that is small in size, cohesive, and focused on achieving specific goals. However, this distinction is not always made and the terms 'group' and 'team' are sometimes used interchangeably. For example, in dysfunctional teams, cohesion and/or focus may be absent. Furthermore, for Forsyth, cohesion, goals, as well as interaction, interdependence, and structure characterize groups, not just teams (p. 11).

Sometimes 'teams' are opposed to 'groups.' Jon Katzenbach contrasts working groups in which "performance is a function of what the members do as individuals" and team performance, which "calls for both individual and mutual accountability" (Katzenbach & Smith, 1993, p. 4). This view contradicts Forsyth's noted above. However, as a practitioner, it is important not to get bogged down by academic disagreements on definitions, but to focus on the authors' practical solutions. What matters to clients is that the coach helps them to achieve sustainable high performance and to serve their stakeholders with impact.

Team coaching

I started to work with individuals and teams over a period of time (typically one year), helping them articulate their goals, overcome their challenges, and access their own resources to do so. The coaching approach I developed seemed like a natural extension of classical training and group meeting facilitation and a new vehicle to obtain a lasting impact. Clients were not left alone to figure out how to put into practice what they had learned during a training workshop. Being supported throughout the journey, they were less tempted to return to business as usual and enabled instead to overcome obstacles along the way.

One advantage perhaps of not having been trained in a specific team coaching methodology is that I have continuously sought to enrich my practice from various disciplines, to question assumptions, and to integrate multiple perspectives to serve my coachees and their stakeholders.

As important as academic literacy of the subject matter is, it is not a substitute for personal development if you want to coach individuals, let alone teams. Having a healthy and mature ego (confident without arrogance, humble without lacking in self-esteem), an OK-OK attitude (Harris, 1969), is essential to engage with clients in a constructive, benevolent, and fluid fashion. Different avenues exist to develop this quality of being. Undergoing psychotherapy can be formative. Participating in group therapy with a master allows you to grow as well as learn about group dynamics. Being coached or supervised are alternatives: group supervision can serve as a laboratory to prepare for team coaching.

Although I had coached teams for some years already, it wasn't until 1998 that the first European coaching conference was organized.[1] I spoke there with Peter Leyland, business director of the Baxter Renal Healthcare Division, on "Coaching Teams for High Performance." I had the privilege to coach Peter and his team from 1997 until 1999. The story of their success has been featured in the *Sloan Management Review* in 2000 by Sandra Vandermerve, professor at the Management School, Imperial College (London). Peter Leyland received various support on his journey but, in his view, the team coaching proved most important in helping him achieve a spectacular turnaround (1998). At the time of the conference, a 50% increase in growth and significantly higher levels of perceived morale had been obtained.

Several "principles of effective team coaching" that I shared at the 1998 conference have been articulated in subsequent years by various authors: serving multiple stakeholders, adopting a systemic view, and framing team coaching interventions as a high-performance journey rather than isolated events, etc. For example, while Peter Hawkins's "level 3 – systemic coaching"[2] concept is not new (see "I invited team members to put themselves in the shoes of their various stakeholders, drawing graffiti on flip charts representing each group's hopes and frustrations" Rosinski, 2003, p. 18), it nevertheless has the merit of encouraging prospective team coaches to opt for an "outside-in" approach that systematically considers the "dynamic relations between the team and its wider systemic context." What is more, Peter Hawkins proposes a level 4 ("eco-systemic team coaching"),[3] which brings us to a new level of coaching teams of teams.

With rare exceptions – notably (Longin, 1998), which I discovered later – it is only in the past 10 years that books on team coaching have appeared. Krister Lowe (2017b) compiled a list of five recommended readings, highlighting the specific value each book brought for him: *Leadership Team Coaching* (Peter Hawkins, 2011–2014, 2nd ed.), *Coaching the Team at Work* (David Clutterbuck, 2007), *From One to Many* (Jennifer Britton, 2013), *High-Performance Team Coaching* (Jacqueline Peters & Catherine Carr, 2013) and *Group and Team Coaching* (Christine Thornton, 2010–2016, 2nd ed.).

Lowe makes the important point that becoming a successful team coach requires more than reading books and getting trained "in a 3 day or even year-long team coach certification program"; most critically, it requires "getting out there and working with real teams," ideally combined with some supervision, peer learning with another team coach, etc.

Cultural perspective

If team coaching, particularly at the executive level, were not hard enough, two additional factors of complexity increasingly need to be considered: cultural diversity and geographic distance. Strangely enough, there is still little literature, let alone research, on intercultural team coaching.

Coaching across Cultures (Rosinski, 2003) was the first book to systematically link coaching and interculturalism. This built upon the work of anthropologists, communication experts, and cross-cultural consultants, including Florence Kluckhohn and Fred Strodtbeck (1961), Edward Hall (1976), Geert Hofstede (2001), and Fons Trompenaars (1997), among others. *Coaching across Cultures* addresses both individual and team coaching, particularly at the executive level. I defined coaching as the "art of facilitating the unleashing of people's potential to reach meaningful, important objectives" (2003, p. 4). Coaching across cultures enables the unleashing of the additional human potential residing in cultural diversity through an intercultural approach.

"Intercultural coaching" has two goals:

1   As you would expect, to enable more effective work across cultures (though not only in an international sense).
2   More fundamentally, to offer in essence a more creative and complete form of coaching. The approach challenges cultural assumptions in all situations. It propels you, the coach, and your coachees beyond previous limitations. It offers new options in the form of alternative ways of thinking, communicating, managing time, and engaging in your various activities (Rosinski, *Global Coaching*, 2010, pp. 121–122).

The debate has been developed in other texts (Moral & Abbott, 2009; Passmore, 2013).

Cultural diversity

An important difficulty with the concept of cultural diversity is that various things exist under this headline (Meyer, 2017, p. 155; Harrison & Klein, 2007).

Cultural diversity may be external (i.e., visible differences such as ethnicity, gender, or age) and internal (i.e., cultural preferences regarding time management, communication, thinking, organizing, etc.). This dichotomy is related to the known surface-level/deep-level diversity distinction (Meyer, pp. 153, 157)

This distinction is useful in that it allows us to describe and then enlarge our inner territory. By expanding our worldview, we have access to new external choices and become more effective. However, the separation is apparently an illusion and reality is not that simple. It is more interconnected and complex than we think (Rosinski, 2010, p. 178). In line with the holographic/complexity/organic paradigm (Rosinski, 2010, Chapter 9) that transcends the still-prevalent mechanistic worldview without excluding it, I propose a complementary dichotomy: cultural diversity is *explicit* (i.e., manifested) or *implicit* (i.e., hidden but nevertheless potentially available to the team). In other words, a team might come across as relatively homogeneous and would not be considered diverse under the usual definitions (referring to visible characteristics or to internal/cognitive diversity). However, from a holographic standpoint, which accounts for notions such as Carl Jung's collective unconscious as well as coaches' belief in the vast – yet largely untapped – human potential, this apparent homogeneous team would be still considered diverse and heterogeneous, albeit in an implicit, enfolded sense.

Intercultural team coaching applies to all forms of diversity. Since diversity is always present, I argue that, to be most effective, all team coaching should become intercultural team coaching. Systematically weaving a cultural perspective into team coaching represents a formidable opportunity to deploy the human potential in its rich cultural diversity, even when these cultural differences are still latent rather than unfolded.

Cultural diversity for better and for worse

Cultural diversity is a double-edge sword. Randall Peterson (2017) reviewed the research and concluded that a team's level of performance is independent from the level of (explicit) diversity within it. Peterson suggested the relationship was more subtle and depended on how diversity was managed. Poorly handled, it becomes a problem, which drives performance down. Effectively exploited, it becomes a source of progress. In his correspondence with me on 26 June 2017, he mentioned several sources and references to support his claims: Bowers, Pharmer, and Salas (2000), Webber and Donahue (2001), Harrison, Price, Gavin, and Florey (2002), Horwitz and Horwitz (2007), Stahl, Maznevski, Voigt, and Jonsen (2010), Bell, Villado, Lukasik, Belau, and Briggs (2011), and Klein (2017).

Dana Verhoeven, Cooper, Flynn, and Shuffler (2017) reach similar conclusions:

> Empirical studies have linked aspects of cultural diversity in relation to team outcomes, to assess increases or decreases in performance. Both positive and negative aspects of team diversity have been included in team effectiveness research (Staples & Zhao, 2006). Specifically, increased creativity, innovation, and flexibility have been progressive outcomes of team diversity (Jehn, Northcraft, & Neale, 1999; Lau & Murnighan, 1998; McLeod, Lobel, & Cox, 1996). In contrast, increased cultural diversity causes communication difficulties, misunderstandings, decreased cohesion and increased conflict, and ultimately decreases performance (Hambrick, Davison, Snell, & Snow, 1998; Lau & Murnighan, 1998; Williams & O'Reilly, 1998).

Michelle Humes and Anne Reilly (2008) make a similar case:

> Intercultural teams have the potential to become the most effective and productive teams in an organization when their diversity becomes an asset and a productive resource for the team (Kirkman & Shapiro, 2001; Earley & Mosakowski, 2000). Functional intercultural teams bring more perspectives and more alternatives to a task as well as strengthen commitment to the group's task (Adler, 2002). However, because of the potential for misunderstanding, miscommunication, and conflict, poorly managed intercultural teams can also become the least productive teams in an organization (Matveev & Nelson, 2004). The group dynamics in an intercultural team may be complex and time-consuming, also adversely affecting the team's productivity. Communication issues such as information overload and geographic distance between team members are also challenges to team performance (Gillam & Oppenheim, 2006; Jarvenpaa & Leidner, 1998).

Cass Sunstein and Reid Hastie (2015) found that the cognitive biases at the individual level were often amplified in a group or team context. They argued that there were means to reduce these effects:

> One of our central themes is the immense importance of diversity, not necessarily along demographic lines, but in terms of ideas and perspectives. We are speaking above all of cognitive diversity.
> Leaders can do a great deal to increase diversity, both by creating the right culture and by hiring the right kind of people.
> One of the particular advantages of diversity and dissent is that they promote two things that institutions need: creativity and innovation.
> When minority voices are heard, well-functioning groups are likely to be jolted out of their routines, and fresh solutions, even a high degree of innovation can follow.

When dissent and diversity are present and levels of participation are high, groups are likely to do a lot better.

(p. 104)

Whereas these academics have shown the merits of tapping into alternative cultural viewpoints, coaching across cultures offers a practical way to access the richness to promote creativity and synergy.

Polarization and pressures to conform

When we have more (explicit) diversity, we have greater risk of polarization due to misunderstanding, conflict, etc. In addition, a more subtle phenomenon, called confirmation bias, reinforces the polarization: we tend to pay more attention to information that confirms what we believe and to dismiss information that contradicts what we consider to be true (as was shown in a striking experiment at Stanford University by Lord, Ross, & Lepper, 1979). Merely giving team members a chance to express their opinions is not sufficient to help them come together. It can even pull them apart.

What is more, when team members do converge, it may take the form of uniformity rather than unity (Rosinski, 2003, p. 41). Social psychologists have studied for a long time the pressures to conform that manifest themselves in pitfalls such as the "Abilene paradox" (group members not voicing their preferences/reservations, not objecting to a course of action that is ultimately satisfactory for no one – Harvey, 1974) and "groupthink" (tendency toward uniformity and censorship – Janis, 1972).

Coaching across cultures is invaluable to turn team diversity into an asset, considering that all teams are diverse to various degrees. It is also helpful to inject/unfold alternative perspectives into/from relatively homogeneous teams, which risk overlooking fruitful possibilities outside their current explicit and limited worldviews.

Multiple levels and perspectives

Working at multiple levels (individual-team-organization-society) enables coaches to uncover complex interrelations and to have a greater impact. This systemic approach promotes alignment while eliminating stalemates originating from conflicting messages (Hackman, 2003; Rosinski, 2003, 2011; Meyer, 2017, pp. 165–166).

In my experience, what distinguishes the executive level from operational management is the high complexity and multifaceted nature of challenges faced. Challenges may be complicated for operational teams without necessarily being complex (e.g., it is all connected). But, for sure, this is not to say that executive teams are the only ones facing complexity.

I have developed an integrated, multidimensional team coaching approach suited for embracing complexity (Rosinski, 2010). It calls upon six interlinked coaching perspectives (i.e., physical, managerial, psychological, political, cultural, and spiritual) and adopts an organic/holographic view of reality more appropriate for dealing with its "VUCA" experience (i.e., volatile-uncertain-complex/chaotic-ambiguous). Given the increasing pace of change, greater connectivity, diminishing resources, etc., the pressure on executive teams is getting higher and higher.

How can we help them take care of themselves so they can sustain these high demands? The physical perspective, which is often overlooked in team coaching, is about promoting health and fitness. In turn, we also help executive teams promote physical well-being in their organizations as a goal in itself and as a foundation for everything else.

At the other end of the spectrum, the spiritual perspective helps the executive team members conduct their organization and their own lives purposefully, and to discern what is truly important. This allows them to radiate positive energy toward others, to impart a sense a meaning, to inspire and to elicit genuine engagement.

Some senior executives may fall prey to ego challenges (e.g., narcissism, obsession): the very qualities that enabled them to rise to the top (e.g., drive, discipline) risk becoming liabilities. Focusing on the psychological perspective fosters constructive relationships and healthy cooperation. We want to preserve leaders' ego while encouraging them to embrace their shadow part so their self, a more complete form of their ego, can emerge (Jung, 1923/1971). The psychological perspective, from a different angle, stimulates flow, also known as the zone, when executives are completely absorbed in what they do, feel energized, and achieve high performance almost effortlessly (Seligman & Csikszentmihalyi, 2000).

The managerial perspective is usually better known. It focuses teams on achieving results and adding value. It involves setting the right goals, measuring progress, and adapting leadership styles to various situations.

The political perspective, at the team level, helps executive teams to systematically muster the necessary support from various stakeholders so the team can achieve its goals and team members can achieve theirs, while also serving the various stakeholders. One R&D management team I worked with crafted its message to highlight the value it was producing for the organization and its clients, approached select top executives on that basis, and obtained the additional resources it had unsuccessfully asked for before.

In the rest of this chapter, I will focus on the cultural perspective. In practice, the perspectives are combined and called upon as appropriate. Being able to juggle with the various perspectives and to flexibly provide the executive team with what will, in the moment, best help it move forward, is the hallmark of excellent global team coaching.

Global coaching brings team coaching to the next level. It invites team coaches to venture outside their current areas of specialization, to learn from a wide range of fields, and to work with teams in an interdisciplinary manner.

Aims and processes in cross-cultural team coaching

Executive team coaches help teams achieve sustainable high performance: reaching their targets and producing high-quality work to serve multiple stakeholders (themselves, team members, internal and external 'clients,' and hopefully society overall). Intercultural coaches help teams achieve greater results through the synthesis of diverse cultural viewpoints.

Aims are defined more precisely for each team coaching project, but they typically involve helping team members:

- Develop mutual understanding, trust, and pleasure in working together;
- Increase their awareness of current team performance;
- Become conscious of personal strengths, weaknesses, preferences, and the implications for teamwork;
- Sharpen their communication and interpersonal skills;
- Foster creativity and leverage diverse viewpoints to effectively address complex business challenges;
- Articulate their contribution to the organization, taking into account the overall vision and strategy, forces in the external environment, internal culture, competencies, structure, and systems;
- More generally, articulate how their work will serve various stakeholders and how it will make the world a better place for future generations (social, environmental, and economic benefits);
- Develop their commitment around a common purpose and concrete action plans; and
- Enhance their ability to work together (including cross-culturally and remotely).[4]

As I was reflecting on the process I use for coaching executive teams, it appeared that I could describe it in the form of 10 steps and that each step could be labeled with a word starting with the same two letters: 'Co.' These seem particularly appropriate since 'co' (meaning 'with' in Latin) perfectly expresses the notion of 'togetherness' at the heart of teamwork.

'Co' is also found in 'complexity,' which characterizes the type of challenges faced at the executive level but can also be found in other teams (e.g., multidisciplinary team of experts and researchers addressing a complex societal challenge). However, while the 10-Co steps process is described linearly, its deployment needs to occur from a complexity outlook to be effective. It has to be flexibly adjusted along the way to address emerging threats and seize new opportunities, "to sense which way things are moving and how to best fit into them" (Grof's "watercourse way"; Rosinski, 2010, pp. 190–191), to be fully present to what is happening as the team coaching unfolds. Coaching remains an art that transcends technique and it cannot be reduced to a fixed prescription (Rosinski, 2003, p. 4).

The 10-Co steps process applies to executive teams and can be adjusted in other contexts (e.g., when the team is meant to be short-lived). Although team life is always dynamic with new members joining while others leave along the way in an ever-changing context, I expect a certain level of stability that justifies the investment in team coaching, as it is described in this chapter, for immediate as well as lasting results.

10-Co steps for coaching executive teams

1. Contracting

I am often contacted by the team leader himself or herself,[5] or by the person in charge of HR who introduces me to the team leader. Even if they want to call upon me to coach their executive team, I first want to explore the pertinence of a team coaching engagement and the conditions for making the investment worthwhile for them[6] and for their stakeholders. Cultural orientations already play a role here: rather than acting out of cultural habit for better but sometimes for worse, you want to choose the best option even when it means going outside your cultural comfort zone.

Why do you want to build your team in the first place? In *Coaching across Cultures* (pp. 136–138), I shared the example of a president of a vast territory: each team member was an executive in charge of a specific region. Encouraging autonomy, and even some healthy competition between members, made a lot of sense, as there were limited opportunities for synergies. Team members did not cooperate much but they really did not have to. Therefore, it was probably not worth investing in team coaching. On the other hand, the president recognized that collaboration had to be reinforced among his team of direct reports located at the company's headquarters. They had to become more united to drive the whole business forward. Team coaching made much more sense here.

Is your team composition right or at least acceptable? Team leaders often don't get to compose their own team. While we can usually not expect every member to be super-skilled and fully committed to the team's success, it is reasonable to require a sufficient level of task proficiency as well as an open and constructive attitude. If a team member lacks in basic emotional intelligence, displays contempt towards team members from other cultures, or promotes sterile conflicts, the team leader needs to first deal with the situation. For example, he could state clear expectations for behavioral change within a certain timeframe and offer support. If this is not sufficient, termination is the next option. We want to avoid spending time dealing with this individual type of problem during the team coaching meeting, thereby distracting the team from what should be its real priorities.

Here are more useful questions for team leaders to examine before they engage in the team coaching journey:

Do you have sufficient support from key decision-makers in your organization, not just to invest in the team coaching effort but also to foster the conditions for success afterwards? How would this team coaching effort fit into the overall vision and strategy?

What do you hope to gain from the team coaching? How will you know it is successful? Who are your various stakeholders and how should they benefit from this team coaching?

Considering the targets you are aiming for, are you prepared to devote the necessary time for your team coaching? The danger here is to perpetuate the cultural 'time is scarce' outlook, trying to cram too much in too little time and overlooking the potential benefits of slowing down. By considering that 'time is plentiful,' you create an opportunity to build relationships within the team and to clearly discern what your priorities should be, what truly matters. Intercultural coaches strive for effectiveness (step back to do the right things) as well as efficiency (be productive by doing things right). If coaches are not mindful of these cultural variations, they may simply follow the dominant cultural norm without challenging it.

Finally, as a team coach, I want to work on projects that are meaningful to me. The ideal scenario is when I can help a team accomplish something that, beyond its immediate stakeholders, will serve society and the world at large. I am fortunate to have the opportunity to work on projects of this sort. But in our imperfect world, we also make a purposeful contribution whenever we help a team in bringing joy to people or in promoting some progress (notably economic, environmental, and social).

2. Context

Once a contract has been signed, outlining goals, steps, scope, conditions, and timing, the coach will study the context in more depth, asking the team leader and his colleagues to provide background information: vision, strategy, values, products and services, organizational chart, and mapping out of various key stakeholders, etc.

Coaches are not consultants, but they still need to understand the context in order to discern threats and opportunities and to help coachees discover avenues for success or choose their path to sustainable high performance.

3. Connecting

Establishing a close and trustful relationship with the team leader is of utmost importance. The team leader needs to feel comfortable in sharing personal aspirations, wishes, and concerns. Cultural awareness and savviness are necessary to establish this quality of connection with culturally diverse leaders. For example, in 2016, I had the chance to coach medical directors in Haiti for Doctors Without Borders. The time spent there was critical for me to better understand the situation and to start building trusting relationships. In one-to-one exchanges, the Haitian leaders would regularly test the waters with me with an allusion or a non-verbal expression. This generally signaled that they wanted to share delicate information or a dilemma. Being attentive to these cues was of course essential, but I also made sure to communicate my genuine respect and admiration. These people devote their energy to save human lives under difficult circumstances and do a remarkable job. I believe they saw my deep respect and started to confide in me. To ease the process, I would reformulate their implicit communication and kindly tease them: "If I understand between the lines, what you are saying is . . ." followed by a more explicit version of their message. Their subsequent smile would signal that I had gotten it! (Leadership & Coaching Global, 2018, p. 363).

In any event, I make clear to each team leader that I want to serve him/her personally (in addition of course to serving the team overall and its stakeholders).

4. Consultation

I use a combination of assessments and interviews to obtain a clear view of the situation, which allows me to design a tailored program likely to be perceived as relevant, valuable, and focused on the important issues.

One assessment is meant to visualize how the team is doing in various areas that matter for its sustainable success. Krister Lowe has compiled a list of recommended surveys (2017a). I typically use one that is not on his list: the Campbell-Hallam Team Development Survey™ (TDS™) (Hallam & Campbell, 1994; Rosinski, 2010, pp. 15–16).

Another assessment is specifically looking at the team cultural profile. I use the COF assessment,[7] which I have specifically designed for intercultural team coaching. As good as general team assessments are, they don't address the cultural perspective and need to be complemented with a cultural assessment.

TDS and COF results are treated strictly confidentially. Each participant will have access to his own individual results, but individual results will not be shared with anyone else. Only aggregate results will be presented and discussed.

If possible, I like to see the assessment results prior to the interviews. However, assessments and interviews can also be run in parallel.

I meet on a one-on-one basis with each team member to conduct interviews (for about 45 minutes to 1 hour with each member). Alternatively, those conversations can take place over the phone or videoconference.

The interviews are open-ended and confidential. The purpose is to get a feel for the motivators, issues, zones of opportunities, and areas of resistance. The discussions allow me to clarify expectations as well as potential contributions to the program success. The nature of the interviews enables participants to talk openly and candidly about their needs and concerns.

The interviews are an opportunity to build rapport with each team member and to convey the message that the program is meant to be in the service of multiple stakeholders: the team overall and each team member, the organization, and its stakeholders, not to mention society overall.

5. Conception

Based on the agreed goals, information about the context, personal discussions with the team leader (and HR executive when possible and appropriate), the TDS and COF results, and the interviews, the coach designs the intervention: specific objectives plus the outline with the various activities and the flow. Slideshows and worksheets will usually be prepared in the later construction stage, during which materials will be made ready as well.

6. Coaching and co-design

This one-to-one session takes two to three hours in total. First, the team coach presents his findings to the team leader, focusing on key themes emerging from the interviews and assessments. This is a delicate moment, particularly when the TDS reveals sub-par team performance (compared to a benchmark) and when feedback for the team leader specifically is difficult. I try to put team results in perspective: what matters is what you and the team will do about the results. Sometimes low team scores can act as a wake-up call, and I mention that I have personally witnessed remarkable team transformations. Conversely, high team scores don't guarantee long-term success: complacency followed by decline can indeed occur when teams are tempted to rest on their laurels. The same message applies to the team leader individually.

Examining both aggregate COF results and the individual team leader COF during this feedback session sheds light on cultural tendencies that might enable team success or inhibit it.

The team coach presents his tentative design for the team coaching process in general and first team coaching meeting/retreat in particular. The team leader suggests possible changes, and this becomes a co-design effort.

Importantly, they discuss how the team leader will act upon the feedback received and, by changing his behavior, encourage team members to venture outside their comfort zone to grow as well.

They also discuss their respective roles throughout the process. The coach typically acts as a facilitator and manages the process. The team leader frames the coaching intervention in its broader context, sets the parameters (e.g., clarifies what the team can decide and what is beyond its authority), and acts as a contributor (just like other team members).

I may ask the team leader to do some preparation work: for example, articulating a vision for the team that will serve as a starting point for a team discussion.

We agree on a project plan to ensure the proper management of all the logistics.

We also agree on a time schedule. My team coaching usually consists of at least an initial two-day retreat and a one-day follow-up.

7. Construction

This is the preparation time: slideshows, worksheets, ordering and gathering materials for various activities, and a detailed outline.

I also liaise with my client who reserves the venue (if it has not been done yet), takes care of travels (as necessary), and organizes special additional activities (such as go-karting or simply sharing nice evening meals).

8. Coming together

The actual flow of the team retreat is an output of the design and is flexibly adjusted during the team meeting as the process unfolds.

The retreat typically includes three parts: raising the team awareness about its current assets and obstacles to sustainable high performance (as well as tapping into the members' experience and creativity to identify ways to make the most of assets and overcome obstacles), building specific competencies (those that are most needed for progress) through inputs from the coach and experiential activities, and crystallization in the form of a shared vision, an action plan, and concrete engagements from team members.

9. Commitments

It is crucial to ensure that team members leave the retreat with concrete commitments that will benefit the team and its stakeholders. The more these pledges reflect authentic desires in service of a meaningful common purpose, the easier it will be for team members to make good on their promises.

These actions should also take advantage of the diverse and complementary skills available in the team and necessary for its success.

10. Continuing

Sometimes, despite their best intentions, team members get caught up in their daily routines and overlook the actions they had committed to. The team leader needs to instill the necessary discipline, rigor, courage, and perseverance to maintain if not amplify the momentum.

Team members also have a proactive role to play. A sign of high-performance teams is when team members feel mutually accountable for their success (Katzenbach, 1993).

Several follow-ups can be scheduled with the external team coach, as appropriate. They can take the form of a new retreat, when the team has to address a new set of challenges, notably due to changing conditions in the marketplace (Rosinski, 2003, p. 130).

Tools and techniques used in topic area

In working with teams, it is possible to use a wide variety of tools, depending on context, issue, and individuals. These might include experiential activities, action learning team projects, group discussions, videotaped team activities followed by a review with self-disclosing and feedback exchanges, individual reflections, peer coaching, and group facilitation.

For experienced coaches, I will look at three specific techniques. I touched on the first one, "Capturing the voices of various stakeholders with images/graffiti" earlier. Stakeholders are mainly external to the team with the exception of team members themselves, which constitute a category of stakeholders too.

The second technique also involves inductive activities such as drawing, looking at postcards, or creating collages. However, these artistic expressions are focused inward. They constitute powerful ways to reveal individual cultural characteristics as well as common cultural themes, which can unite team members (Rosinski, 2003, pp. 65–68, 114–116).

Let me elaborate on the third technique, which is deductive rather than inductive and focused on using the Cultural Orientations Framework™ assessment (COF™) (Rosinski, 2010) as a means of raising awareness about cultural orientations manifested in everything team members do and of inviting them to consider alternative cultural perspectives when these could be beneficial. Other cultural assessment tools exist, but their primary focus is on establishing country cultural profiles and comparing individual preferences with a range of national cultures (e.g., Hofstede Insights Culture Compass™, GlobeSmart®, Cultural Orientations Indicator®) rather than on helping individuals grow by learning from cultural differences of various kinds.

The COF is available at www.COFassessment.com, and the underlying model (Figure 9.1) is explained in detail in Rosinski (2003). Here I will focus on how the executive coach might use the tool to help teams increase their versatility, creativity, and effectiveness. The underlying dynamic and inclusive view of culture enables us to build unity in diversity by leveraging cultural differences. It contrasts with traditional binary and static intercultural approaches, which sometimes inadvertently reinforce stereotypes.

Catherine Carr and Lily Seto wrote the following:

> We selected Rosinski's COF as a conceptual framework and primary assessment tool for several reasons (cultural categories transcend typical categorization, team profile can be utilized for future initiatives, cost

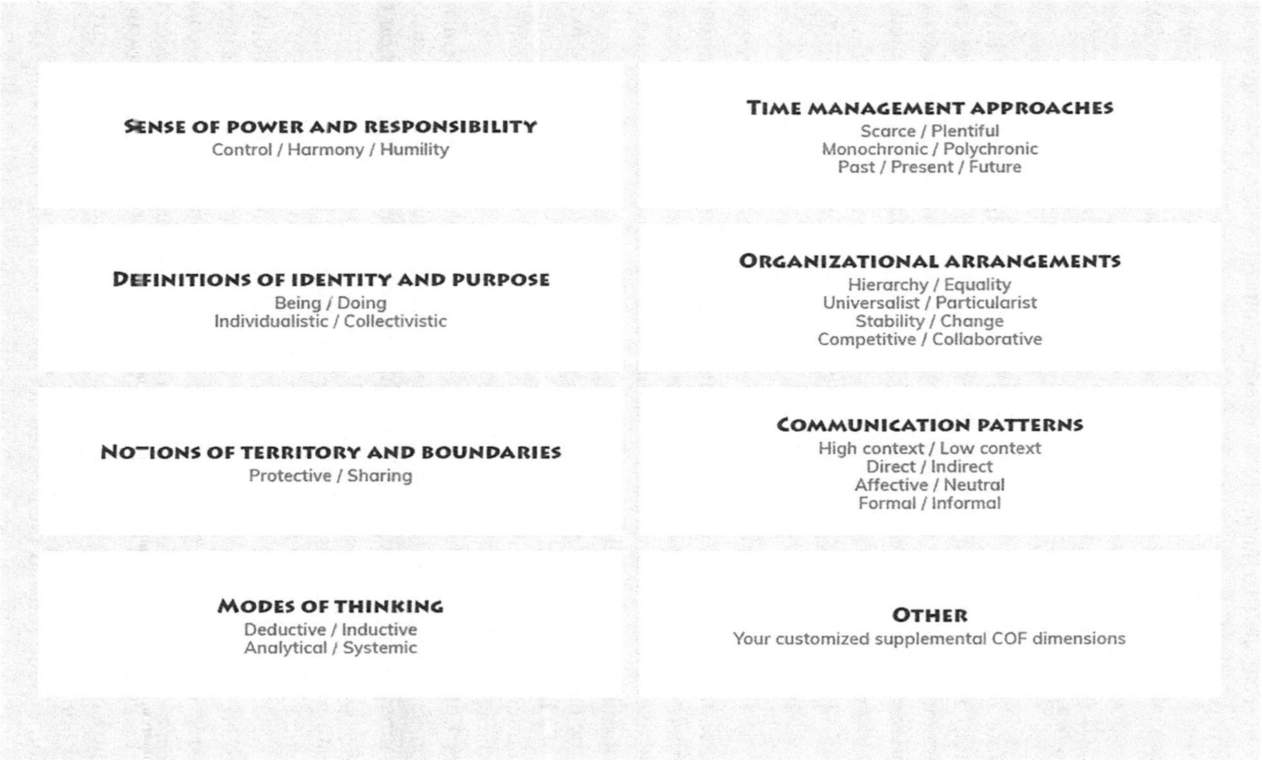

SENSE OF POWER AND RESPONSIBILITY
Control / Harmony / Humility

DEFINITIONS OF IDENTITY AND PURPOSE
Being / Doing
Individualistic / Collectivistic

NOTIONS OF TERRITORY AND BOUNDARIES
Protective / Sharing

MODES OF THINKING
Deductive / Inductive
Analytical / Systemic

TIME MANAGEMENT APPROACHES
Scarce / Plentiful
Monochronic / Polychronic
Past / Present / Future

ORGANIZATIONAL ARRANGEMENTS
Hierarchy / Equality
Universalist / Particularist
Stability / Change
Competitive / Collaborative

COMMUNICATION PATTERNS
High context / Low context
Direct / Indirect
Affective / Neutral
Formal / Informal

OTHER
Your customized supplemental COF dimensions

Figure 9.1 Cultural Orientations Framework (COF)

effectiveness . . .). Other models were considered, however the COF framework seemed particularly designed for coaches to have coaching conversations that facilitate leveraging cultural differences and creating new possibilities.

(An Action Research Study on Coaches' Cultural
Awareness in the Public Sector, 2013)

For each cultural dimension, the COF assessment examines two aspects (see Figure 9.2):

1   Your *orientation* (e.g., clear "Control" on the "Control-Humility" dimension) is neither good nor bad. It just reflects your preference. For each dimension, it can be represented by a position on a horizontal axis. All orientations have merits. However, they can sometimes be overused or underused.

2   For each possible orientation, an *ability* can be represented by a position on a vertical axis. It reflects how you are currently capable of using the specific orientation.

The results come from a self-assessment, which has limitations but constitutes nevertheless a useful basis for a conversation. Results don't matter per se. The fruitful exchange, which raises self-awareness and opens up new options for the participants, is what counts.

At the team level, the COF assessment aggregates the individual results in the form of a histogram. Team members can visualize the team profile for each cultural dimension (e.g., Figure 9.3) and see how their individual scores compare with the rest of the team.

This European executive team was seen as an exemplary high-performance team in its organization. To his credit, the team leader did not take this success for granted. Instead, he engaged in a team coaching process. The results on the Control-Humility dimension revealed a clear preference for control (reflecting team members' beliefs that they were essentially in charge of their destiny) combined with an ability for control (the capacity to make things happen). The team was indeed ambitious and confident in its capacity to reach ambitious targets. However, they saw that humility was less present (the belief that power is outside of us, the recognition of our inevitable limitations, and the ability to accept these limitations and to let go). This clearly signaled the danger for them: everything was still going well but some members had realized that their current hard-working rhythm was not sustainable. Some were already starting to run out of steam.

Another slide showed their preference for polychronic time (doing several things at the same time): they were conducting many projects in parallel. Looking at both slides, the solution became evident for the team: eliminating non-essential projects so they could pace their efforts, working at 80% rather than

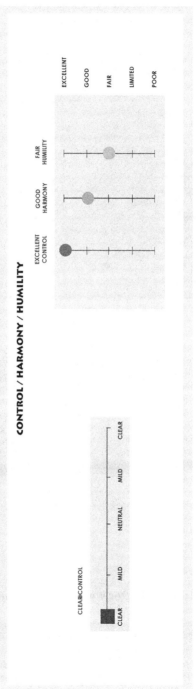

SENSE OF POWER AND RESPONSIBILITY

CONTROL / HARMONY / HUMILITY

Figure 9.2 Orientation and abilities

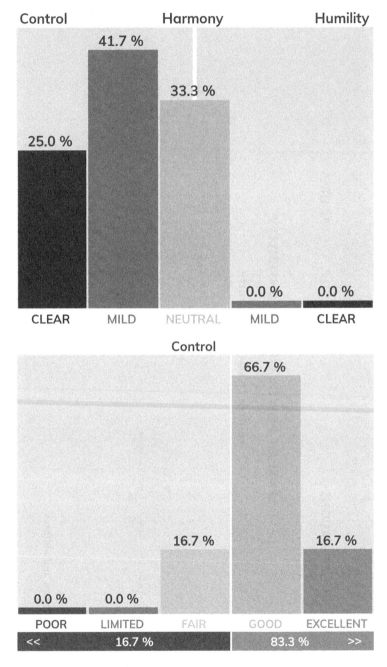

Figure 9.3 COF aggregate results – coaching of a senior international European team (N = 12). Above: Preferred cultural orientations – Below: Abilities for each possible orientation.

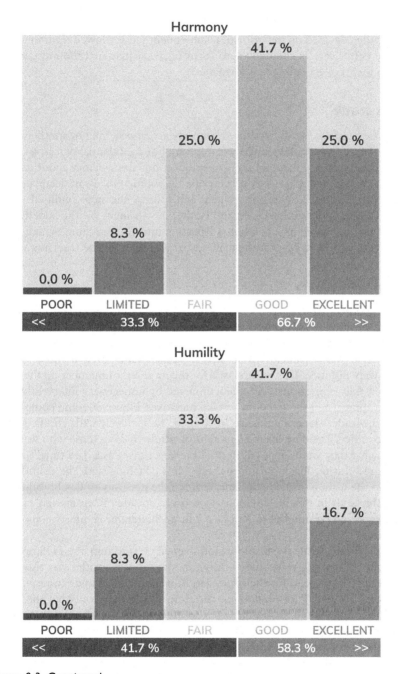

Figure 9.3 Continued.

120% of their personal capacity. During the last day of our team coaching retreat, they decided on the priorities. Subsequently, this allowed team members to take better care of themselves, to focus on what mattered the most, and to sustain their collective high performance.

Case study

The following case study is adapted from my actual coaching of another international executive team (primarily European). For confidentiality reasons, I will neither mention the name of the organization nor the specifics about its context. In this limited space, I won't describe the whole process in detail: it refers to executive team coaching in general and follows the steps outlined earlier in the "Aims and processes" section. Rather, I will focus on the added value obtained from weaving a cultural perspective into the coaching, which often led to breakthroughs first for the team leader and then for the team as a whole.

Hierarchy-equality

Team members were all competent, motivated, and committed to work toward the organization's noble purpose. The team leader shared the dominant culture in the team: egalitarian rather than hierarchical. During the interviews, his leadership style was consistently described as "laissez-faire" even if those specific words were not used. This worked well for the most senior members in the team, who felt fully empowered and unencumbered by unnecessary interventionism. Others appreciated the freedom to take initiatives. However, some complained about the leader's lack of guidance, his aversion to decisively settle conflicts ("He avoid conflicts"), and his insufficient confrontation vis-à-vis those who were not doing what they were supposed to do ("He never gives us a hard time!").

I shared this feedback during the individual coaching with the team leader prior to the team retreat. He became aware of the necessity to flexibly adjust his leadership style in various situations: to venture outside his 'egalitarian' cultural preference and be mindful to embrace a more 'hierarchical' directive approach at times.

Furthermore, while the team mission seemed clear to him, the TDS revealed that only 31% of the team shared his view. A sense of priorities was also missing: important projects for the organization were often set aside to respond to urgencies. He decided to reflect on the team mission and on what the long-term priorities should be. During the team retreat, while still encouraging the expression of various viewpoints, he took a more dominant role in setting the agenda for the future. He chose to not leave this completely open for discussion.

Team members were also reluctant to take the lead with peers due to their aversion to hierarchy: not only was hierarchy not their preference, but over 60% of the group ($N = 11$) were not at ease with it. During the retreat, they decided

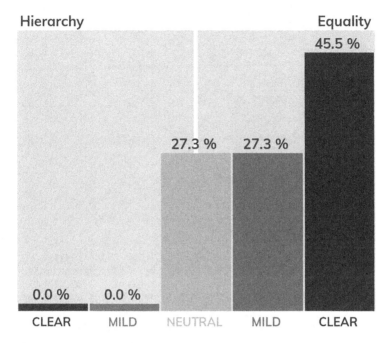

Figure 9.4 Hierarchy and equality – preferred cultural orientations

to alternate leadership and followership roles, learning to both take charge in the team and accepting that others would do the same at other times. They started to hold themselves and each other more accountable for their actions. In sum, the team became more effective by leveraging equality (democratic) and hierarchy (directive) (see Figures 9.4 and 9.5).

Universalist-particularist

On this dimension too, the team was clearly one-sided: particularist (favoring flexibility and tailored solutions) rather than universalist (favoring coherence, common rules, and processes).

To a large extent, this profile served the team well: creative team members did not feel constrained by unnecessary tight frames, ambiguity around roles allowed them to contribute outside their main areas (which proved both motivating for these individuals and helpful for the team), and suppleness permitted team members to freely contribute to interdepartmental projects.

However, by visualizing their collective profile, they could now also see the pitfalls more clearly: hiccups occurring due to the lack of clear rules (Who decides? Who supports? Who 'owns' the project?), frustration due to perceived unfairness (e.g., "some work more than others," "some are away 'in the field'

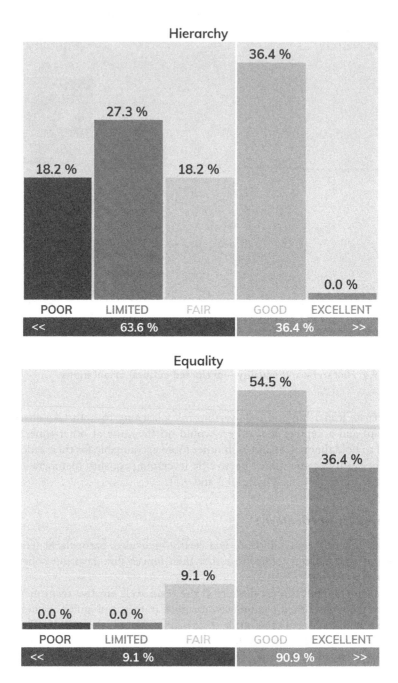

Figure 9.5 Hierarchy and equality – abilities for each possible orientation

more than others"). Most of all, team members realized that their collective reluctance for 'universalism' had led them to leave these issues unresolved. The histogram made the solution obvious to them: tap into the underused universalism! The challenge was to do so without sacrificing flexibility, by combining both polarities. The team did so by establishing new ground rules that still made room for agility (see Figures 9.6 and 9.7).

Direct-indirect

The team histogram for this cultural dimension is more heterogeneous. Generally speaking, whereas homogeneity facilitates mutual understanding among team members (all on the same 'wavelength'), it increases the risk of 'groupthink,' since members are more likely to overlook the other perspective (a probable common blind spot). Conversely, heterogeneity is also a double-edge sword: a source of misunderstanding, frustration, and conflict if left unattended, but a source of creativity when leveraged.

This team comprised both members who preferred direct communication (clarity matters most when delivering a difficult message, at the risk of offending or hurting) and indirect communication (sensitivity matters most, at the risk of misunderstanding). Furthermore, over 60% scored unfavorably on the

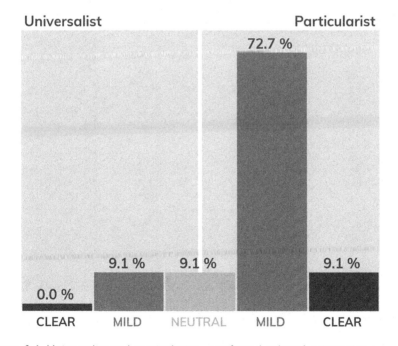

Figure 9.6 Universalist and particularist – preferred cultural orientations

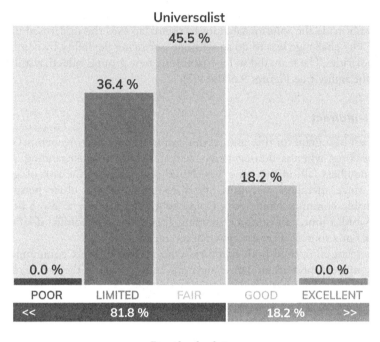

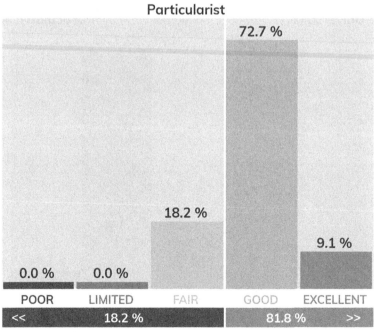

Figure 9.7 Universalist and particularist – abilities for each possible orientation

ability to communicate directly and close to 50% unfavorably for indirect communication. As you would expect, the interviews confirmed the problem. Some complained that certain members were too direct, which they perceived as aggressive. Others, upset by colleagues, would passively accept the situation without confronting their peers for fear of alienating them.

Showing these results allowed team members to reframe issues that had become personal into a cultural misunderstanding and offered them a path to bridge the gap: leveraging direct and indirect communication patterns can be achieved when you are clear on the content and sensitive in the form. The team learned to take the best of both cultural perspectives while sacrificing neither (see Figures 9.8 and 9.9).

These are just some examples of what we discussed. The COF gave team members a vocabulary to talk about culture. It offered a powerful way to raise cultural awareness, individually and collectively, and to achieve synergy by leveraging cultural diversity.

You will notice that the origins of cultural preferences don't matter here. Is it a question of nationality, generation, profession, or/and some other cultural groups they belong to? The COF assessment allows users to aggregate COF data per nationality, generation, etc. However, practically, the team just needs to deal with cultural preferences present in the team for whatever reason. In other words, the complexity inherent to multiple cultural origins is not an obstacle.

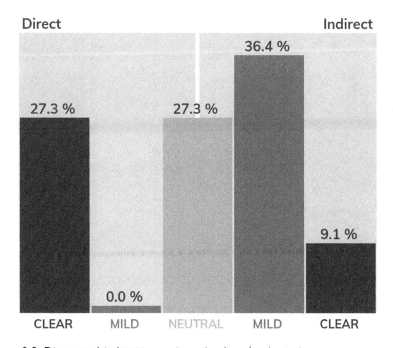

Figure 9.8 Direct and Indirect – preferred cultural orientations

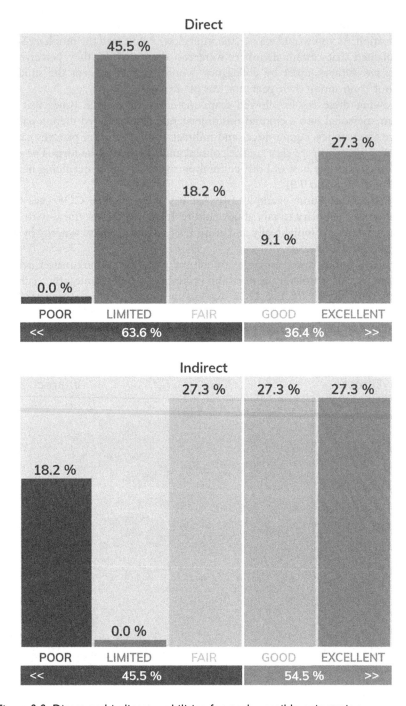

Figure 9.9 Direct and indirect – abilities for each possible orientation

Let me refer the reader to *Global Coaching* pp. 134–141 for more on this topic and in particular for examples of questions the team coach could ask to help team members analyze and act upon their COF team results.

Conclusion

All teams are intercultural. Cultural diversity may be *external* (i.e., visible differences such as ethnicity, gender, or age) or *internal* (i.e., cultural preferences regarding time management, communication, thinking, organizing, etc.). Cultural diversity is also *explicit* (e.g., different ways of communicating are manifested in the team, such as direct and indirect communication patterns) or *implicit* (e.g., the underused cultural orientations – such as universalist in our example – are still potentially available even if the team looks homogeneous and one-sided – for instance, particularist rather than universalist).

Systematically weaving a cultural perspective into team coaching represents a formidable opportunity to deploy the human potential in its rich cultural diversity, even when these cultural differences are still enfolded/latent rather than manifested. Recent research at Harvard University has shown how cultural diversity, when leveraged, promotes creativity and innovation. More research has confirmed how it then also improves team performance.

In this chapter, I have discussed how to leverage the differences in practice. I have revealed how I have been coaching intercultural teams, particularly at the executive level, in the past 25 years. I have also mentioned how global coaching makes team coaching even more powerful, particularly for dealing with complexity. I hope this chapter will encourage practitioners as well as academics to embrace this exciting field and enable executive teams to more effectively and sustainably serve their multiple stakeholders.

When we promote unity in diversity and help executive teams achieve meaningful goals, we play our part in making the world a little better.

The journey starts with our own cultural development. Our eagerness to learn from other cultures, to go beyond our own cultural limitations, and to grow throughout all of our lives will inspire our colleagues and clients to do the same.

Developing yourself

To develop yourself in this area, I invite you to examine the various books and articles in the references section. *Coaching across Cultures* and *Global Coaching* will provide you with a foundation as well as more references for further learning.

The international three-day "Leading & Coaching Across Cultures/COF certification seminars" give you a chance to learn and practice intercultural team coaching firsthand and to become part of a worldwide network of alumni.

I invite you to contact me if you want to use the COF assessment for your research project (including Postdoc, PhD, and Master) and I welcome cooperations!

Web resources

www.GlobalCoaching.pro
www.COFassessment.com
www.philrosinski.com
www.facebook.com/globalcoachingpro
www.teamcoachingzone.com
www.sietareu.org
www.coachfederation.org
www.associationforcoaching.com

Notes

1 The Coaching and Mentoring Conference, 5–8 October 1998, Amsterdam, Netherlands (by Linkage Inc.)
2 Defined as "sees the team more complexly as existing to create value with and for all its stakeholders. It focuses on who the team is there to serve and considers the future needs the stakeholders have of the team." Webinar WBECS 8 March 2018.
3 Defined as "sees the team as co-evolving in dynamic relationship with its ever-changing eco-system of interconnected teams, with which it co-creates shared value. Eco-systemic coaching focuses on the interplay between the team and other connected teams" (inter-team coaching). Webinar WBECS 8 March 2018.
4 See www.philrosinski.com/executive-team-coaching
5 I will use the masculine (instead of the combination masculine and feminine) in the rest of the chapter for the sake of readability. It is meant to include both the masculine and the feminine.
6 See also four strategies for dealing with problems in multicultural teams (Brett, Behfar, & Kern, 2006).
7 www.COFassessment.com

References

Adler, N. (2002). *International dimensions of organizational behavior* (4th ed.). Cincinnatti, OH: South-Western.

Anzieu, D., & Martin, J.Y. (1990). *La dynamique des groupes restreints* (9th ed.). Paris: Presses Universitaires de France.

Asch, S. (1956). Studies of independence and conformity. *Psychological Monographs: General and Applied, 70*(9).

Bales, R. (1950). *Interaction process analysis: A method for the study of small groups.* Cambridge, MA: Addison-Wesley.

Bell, S., Villado, A., Lukasik, M., Belau, L., & Briggs, A. (2011). Getting specific about demographic diversity variable and team performance relationships: A meta-analysis. *Journal of Management, 37*(3).

Benne, K., & Sheats, P. (1948). Functional roles of group members. *Journal of Social Issues, 4*(2), 41–49.

Berne, E. (1964). *Games people play.* New York, NY: Penguin Books.

Bowers, C., Pharmer, J., & Salas, E. (2000). When member homogeneity is needed in work teams: A meta-analysis. *Small Group Research, 31*, 305–327.

Brett, J., Behfar, K., & Kern, M. (2006, November). Managing multicultural teams. *Harvard Business Review*, 84–91.

Britton, J. (2013). *From one to many.* Hoboken, NJ: Jossey-Bass.

Carr, C., & Seto, L. (2013). An action research study on coaches' cultural awareness in the public sector. *International Journal of Evidence Based Coaching and Mentoring, 11*(2), 94–111.

Clutterbuck, D. (2007). *Coaching the team at work*. London and Boston: Nicholas Brealey International.

Dunnette, M., Campbell, J., & Jaastad, K. (1963). The effect of group participation on brain-storming effectiveness for two industrial samples. *Journal of Applied Psychology, 47*(1), 30–37.

Earley, C., & Mosakowski, E. (2000). Creating hybrid team cultures: An empirical test of transnational team functioning. *Academy of Management Journal, 43*, 26–50.

Forsyth, D. (2014). *Group dynamics* (6th ed.). Belmont, CA: Wadsworth Cengage Learning.

Gillam, C., & Oppenheim, C. (2006). Reviewing the impact of virtual teams in the information age. *Journal of Information Science, 32*(2), 160–175.

Hackman, R. (2003). Learning more by crossing levels: Evidence from airplanes, hospitals, and orchestras. *Journal of Organizational Behavior, 24*(8), 905–922.

Hall, E. (1976). *Beyond culture*. New York, NY: Anchor Books.

Hallam, G., & Campbell, D. (1994). *Manual for the Campbell-Hallam team development survey*. Minneapolis, MN: National Computer Systems.

Hambrick, D., Davison, S., Snell, S., & Snow, C. (1998). When groups consist of multiple nationalities: Towards a new understanding of the implications. *Organization Studies, 19*(2), 181–205.

Harris, T. (1969). *I'm ok – you're ok*. London: Harper & Row.

Harrison, D., & Klein, K. (2007). What's the difference? Diversity constructs as separation, variety, or disparity in organizations. *Academy of Management Review, 32*, 1199–1228.

Harrison, D., Price, K., Gavin, J., & Florey, A. (2002). Time, teams, and task performance: Changing effects of surface-and deep-level diversity on group functioning. *Academy of Management Journal, 45*(5), 1029–1045.

Harvey, J. (1974). The abilene paradox: The management of agreement. *Organizational Dynamics, 3*(1), 63–80.

Hawkins, P. (2011–2014). *Leadership team coaching* (2nd ed.). London: Kogan Page.

Hofstede, G. (2001). *Culture's consequences* (2nd ed.). Thousand Oaks, CA: Sage Publications.

Horwitz, S., & Horwitz, I. (2007). The effects of team diversity on team outcomes: A meta-analytic review of team demography. *Journal of Management, 33*(6).

Humes, M., & Reilly, A. (2008). Managing intercultural teams. *Journal of Management Education, 32*(1).

Janis, I. (1972). *Victims of groupthink: A psychological study of foreign policy decisions*. Boston, MA: Houghton Mifflin.

Jarvenpaa, S., & Leidner, D. (1998). Communication and trust in global virtual teams. *Journal of Computer-Mediated Communication, 3*(4).

Jehn, K., Northcraft, G., & Neale, M. (1999). Why differences make a difference: A field study of diversity, conflict, and performance in workgroups. *Administrative Science Quarterly, 44*(4), 741–763.

Jung, C. (1923–1971). *Psychological types*. Princeton, NJ: Princeton University Press (rev. of original English translation).

Katzenbach, J., & Smith, D. (1993, March). The discipline of teams. *Harvard Business Review*.

Kirkman, B., & Shapiro, D. (2001). The impact of team members' cultural values on productivity, cooperation, and empowerment in self-managing work teams. *Journal of Cross-Cultural Psychology, 32*, 597–617.

Klein, K. (2017, May 18). Does gender diversity on boards really boost company performance? *Knowledge@Wharton*.

Kluckhohn, F., & Strodtbeck, F. (1961). *Variations in value orientations.* Evanston, IL: Row, Peterson.

Lau, D., & Murnighan, K. (1998). Demographic diversity and faultlines: The compositional dynamics of organizational groups. *The Academy of Management Review, 23*(2), 325–340.

Leyland, P. (1998, October). The team intervention process: How it worked for Baxter Renal. *The Coaching and Mentoring Conference – Conference Proceedings,* Linkage Inc, London.

Longin, P. (1998). *Coachez votre équipe.* Paris: Dunod.

Lord, C., Ross, L., & Lepper, M. (1979). Biased assimilation and attitude polarization: The effects of prior theories on subsequently considered evidence. *Journal of Personality and Social Psychology, 37*(11), 2098–2109.

Lowe, K. (2017a). *Team coaching resources (Part 1): Five team level assessments.* Retrieved December 26, from The Team Coaching Zone www.teamcoachingzone.com/team-coaching-resources-part-1-five-team-level-assessments

Lowe, K. (2017b). *Team coaching resources (Part 2): Five books on team coaching.* Retrieved December 24, from The Team Coaching Zone www.teamcoachingzone.com/teamcoaching books

Matveev, A., & Nelson, P. (2004). Cross cultural communication competence and multi-cultural team performance. *International Journal of Cross Cultural Management, 4,* 253–270.

McLeod, P., Lobel, S., & Cox, T. (1996). Ethnic diversity and creativity in small groups. *Small Group Research, 2*(27), 248–264.

Meyer, B. (2017). Team diversity – a review of the literature. In D. E. Salas, R. Rico, & J. Passmore (Eds.), *The Wiley Blackwell handbook of the psychology of team working and collaborative processes* (pp. 151–175). Hoboken, NJ: John Wiley & Sons Ltd.

Moral, M., & Abbott, G. (2009). *The Routledge companion to tnternational business coaching.* New York, NY: Routledge.

Passmore, J. (2013). *Diversity in coaching* (2nd ed.). London: Kogan Page.

Peters, J., & Carr, C. (2013). *High performance team coaching.* Victoria, BC, Canada: FriesenPress.

Peterson, R. (2017, May 17). *Building high performance teams. The grand tour 2017.* Brussels: Global.

Rosinski, P. (2003). *Coaching across cultures.* London and Yarmouth, ME: Nicholas Brealey Publishing.

Rosinski, P. (2010). *Global coaching.* London and Boston, MA: Nicholas Brealey Publishing.

Rosinski, P. (2011). Global coaching for organizational development. *The International Journal of Coaching in Organizations, Issue 30, 8*(2), 49–66.

Rosinski, P. (2018). *Leadership & coaching global.* Combronde, France: Éditions Valeurs d'Avenir.

Salas, E., Rico, R., & Passmore, J. (2017). *The Wiley Blackwell handbook of the psychology of team working and collaborative processes.* Hoboken, NJ: John Wiley & Sons Ltd.

Seligman, M., & Csikszentmihalyi, M. (2000). Positive psychology: An introduction. *American Psychologist, 55*(1), 5–14.

Stahl, G., Maznevski, M., Voigt, A., & Jonsen, K. (2010, May). Unraveling the effects of cultural diversity in teams: A meta-analysis of research on multicultural work groups. *Journal of International Business Studies, 41*(4), 690–709.

Staples, S., & Zhao, L. (2006). The effects of cultural diversity in virtual teams versus face-to-face teams. *Group Decision and Negotiation, 15*(4), 389–406.

Steiner, I. (1972). *Group process and productivity.* New York, NY: Academic Press.

Sunstein, C., & Hastie, R. (2015). *Wiser: Getting beyond groupthink to make groups smarter.* Boston, MA: Harvard Business Review Press.

Thornton, C. (2010–2016). *Group and team coaching* (2nd ed.). New York, NY: Routledge.

Trompenaars, F. (1997). *Riding the waves of cultures* (2nd ed.). London: Nicholas Brealey Publishing.

Vandermerwe, S. (2000, October 15). How increasing value to customers improves business results. *MIT Sloan Management Review.*

Verhoeven, D., Cooper, T., Flynn, M., & Shuffler, M. (2017). Transnational team effectiveness. In D. E. Salas, R. Rico, & J. Passmore (Eds.), *The Wiley Blackwell handbook of the psychology of team work and collaborative processes* (pp. 73–101). Hoboken, NJ: John Wiley & Sons Ltd.

Webber, S., & Donahue, L. (2001). Impact of highly and less job-related diversity on work group cohesion and performance: A meta-analysis. *Journal of Management, 27,* 141–162.

Williams, K., & O'Reilly, C. (1998). Demography and diversity in organizations: A review of 40 years of research. *Research in Organizational Behavior, 20,* 77–140.

Part 3

Contemporary challenges

Chapter 10

Internally resourced coaching

David Clutterbuck and Colm Murphy

Introduction

The term internal coaching may be applied to a variety of contexts, the most common being line managers adopting a coaching style of management and accredited coaches within the organization, who have a level of training equal to (and in some cases greater than) externally resourced coaches (Frisch, 2005). The emphasis of such coaching is generally on performance improvement of individuals. However, in recent years there has been increasing attention to coaching the intact work team and to creating coaching cultures within teams, and the same movement from external resourcing to internal can be observed. In this chapter, we review literature and practice in each of these areas. Finally, we pose questions relating to the integration of internally and externally resourced coaching.

Coaching for individual performance improvement

Internally accredited coaches

Trend studies of coaching indicate increasing volumes of internally resourced coaching by managers and others, who have acquired similar qualifications to their external counterparts through an accredited coach training provider and/or one of the professional associations. For example, the Ridler report (2013) found that 79% of companies expected to increase internal coaching. The assumption that external coaches are likely to be more skilled and more effective is not supported by any substantial body of evidence we can identify. Indeed, a study by Jones, Woods and Guillaume (2016) found internal coaches were perceived as more effective than external coaches. While external coaches may encounter a wider range of clients in different organizations and contexts and may do more hours of coaching overall, this does not necessarily mean that they are better coaches. In coach assessment centers (Clutterbuck, 2010), we have been unable to find any significant correlation between number of hours of coaching and quality of coaching. Many employer organizations invest in continuous professional development, as required by professional coaching bodies, and in supervision. Surveys of externally resourced coaches suggest that the proportion receiving supervision from a qualified supervisor is relatively low. We have no data, however, comparing supervision of internal and external coaches.

Challenges of internal executive coaching

The literature (Frisch, 2005; St. John-Brooks, 2013) agrees on some of the key challenges in being an internal executive coach. These can be summarized under three broad headings.

Role clarity: Most internal coaches are balancing the demands of being a coach and of their day job within the organization. This can create time pressures and guilt in not feeling the time is being appropriately given to either role. There is also the challenge of what is said and heard while in the coaching role versus what a functional role response would normally be. This is a particular issue for HR-professionals involved in internal coaching.

Maintaining confidentiality: All executive coaches seek to balance the needs to the individual coaching client and the needs of the paying organization through careful management of information flow. Being embedded in the same organization and having multiple contacts with and around the internal client makes this even more challenging in terms of what is in and out of scope.

Accountability: Line managers may see the internal coach as someone to fix a performance-related issue or person within their team. The internal coach may therefore experience a 'drop and go' approach from line management that places accountability for a 'good' outcome on the internal coach. This is often compounded by the line manager being more senior than the internal coach is and hence beyond reproach.

External coaches, especially working with very senior executives, are less likely to be affected by power distance behavioral influences resulting from perceived status (Hofstede, 1983). However, they may be equally or more prone to the similar issue of "client envy" (Clutterbuck & MacKie, 2016), where the coach feels less successful than the coachee. Internal coaches, however, are much more likely to be attuned to the organizational culture and mores, so can better contextualize their coaching. It must be said that these comparisons have not been subjected to a rigorous evidential study and analysis – a lot more research is needed!

The line manager as coach to their own direct reports

The literature on line managers as coaches is sharply divided on whether line managers can truly be coaches or simply have a coaching style of management. On the one hand, Wageman, Nunes, Burruss, and Hackman (2008) identify coaching as one of the key qualities and activities of a line manager, and this view is supported by research by Google (Garvin, 2013).

On the other hand, studies identify significant barriers and conflicts of interest between the roles and responsibilities of a line manager and those of a coach. A study by Stephen Ferrar (2006) identified a range of behaviors and habits by line managers and their teams, which exacerbate the problem. Among these are:

- The tendency for managers and direct reports to fall into "parent-child" roles in any conversation;
- The sense that both parties may have hidden agendas (for example, on the manager's part about their plans to reorganize the team and on the employee's part about how long they intend to stay with the company);
- Conflict between the employee's desire for some things to remain confidential and the manager's accountability for the welfare and performance of the team as a whole;
- Conflict between pressure to deliver short-term task objectives and the longer-term development needs of team members;
- Groupthink. People who work together tend to adopt the same filters on the world around them and have the same blind spots. Paradoxically, the better the relationship between line manager and learner, the more likely this is to be the case; and
- Inequality in who gets coaching. Time pressures often mean that the manager concentrates coaching on particular individuals or subgroups of the team. This could be because he or she sees that they have either bigger performance problems or greater potential. If the former, people often resent being 'picked on'; if the latter, other people resent being left out. In such situations, the line manager/coach can't win!

The mediating effect of team culture

Our view of these contrasting perceptions is that they lead to simplistic thinking. For example, the current wave of re-evaluating performance management and appraisal processes (Clutterbuck, 2012; Bersin, 2007) is largely about replacing mechanical processes with learning dialogue, which is the essence of coaching. The literature on leader–member exchange (Gerstner & David, 1997) over more than 30 years demonstrates the difficulties many managers face in letting go of task focus to achieve greater people focus.

In some unpublished experiments with several organizations, including the UK subsidiary of a global retail chain, a utility, and a university administration function, one of us carried out focus groups to understand what happened when line managers went on courses to learn how to coach their teams. The narratives consistently showed that goodwill and enthusiasm rarely led to a significant and lasting change in behavior by the managers, who often gave up the coaching mid-frame after as little as a few days. We theorized that the issue was one of systems behavior. When one part of a complex system changes, the rest of the system tries to bring it back to where it was. When the line manager was the only person who understood coaching and was trying to do coaching *to* individuals within the team, it was hardly surprising that they met intentional or unintentional resistance. (It takes two to tango!)

In these experiments, teams and their managers were supported in learning about coaching theory and practice together. At their regular team meetings, they would take time to share learning and consider together how to integrate this into how they worked together. Among observations of these teams were that:

- Psychological safety is an essential foundation for the open conversations teams required to create a coaching culture;
- Everyone in the team needs to know how to coach and how to be coached (including the line manager);
- Everyone in the team takes collective responsibility for performance and for each other's learning; and
- The team collectively created and implemented team development plans that integrated individual development plans with team goals.

These experiments demonstrated at a level of face validity that line managers can be effective coaches to their teams, as long as they are able to develop a safe coaching culture and climate. In an unpublished study for another dot-com giant,[1] one of us carried out focus groups across the globe with a number of its internal teams designated as high performing (on the basis of a mixture of high reputation, high scores on employee opinion survey, reputation as a team other people wanted to work in, and consistently beating targets). A recurrent theme was the role of the leader, who created a secure coaching environment by being secure in themselves. Among the characteristics identified were:

1   They don't feel the need to control. They trust others, because if mistakes happen, the leader has big enough shoulders to share responsibility.
2   They demonstrate that they *care* – both about the team goals, but also about each of the team members as individuals. They make time for human interaction.
3   Instead of trying to manage the team, they support team members in managing themselves.
4   These leaders encourage the team to decide what they need to inform the leader about and what to take responsibility for communicating themselves.
5   They protect the team from distractions from outside.
6   They ensure that everyone understands and is aligned with the overarching team goals and trust they will find the best way of achieving them.
7   They encourage feedback from team members. They have a 'growth mindset' – focused equally on their own development and that of the team and see themselves as 'a work in progress.'

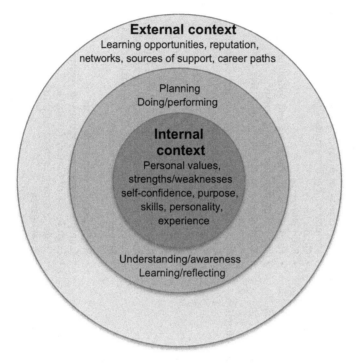

Figure 10.1 Internal context: external context

Coaching through a systemic perspective

Whether internally or externally resourced, coaching of line managers carries the dilemma that the issue brought to coaching is only a part of the picture. A survey of executive coaches by the *Harvard Business Review* (Kaufman & Coutu, 2009) found that almost all reported that the initial goals of an assignment changed as the client got to understand their own values and needs and the context around them. Indeed, all coaching is a conversation that links greater understanding of the internal context with greater understanding of the external context (see Figure 10.1). It can be cogently argued that all effective coaching is systemic in nature – to change the individual, you have to take into account the influences on them and the world around them.

At the simplest level, the dilemma for line mangers as coaches is how to work with that part of the system, which consists of just them and the direct report. To what extent is the direct report's performance contingent upon the behaviors and assumptions of the manager? Shifting the emphasis

Table 10.1 Indicators of team function/dysfunction and high/low performance

Context	Dysfunction indicators	High-performance indicators
Purpose and motivation	• Purpose too vague/people interpret it in different ways • Purpose not endorsed from above/inadequate direction from above • Little or no connection with people's strongly held values (so low energy for achieving it)/conflicts with other strongly held values • Conflict about priorities between goals • Personal agendas predominate over the collective agenda • Low individual and collective resilience	• High clarity of mission, linked with wider (often societal or environmental) purpose • Goal clarity • Role clarity • High levels of collective and individual energy • High alignment on goal priority • Willingness to put team priorities before personal priorities • Ability to review and change goals rapidly • Engagement of stakeholders with the mission • Strongly shared values • Rapid recovery from setbacks
External processes, systems, and structures	• Reputational issues • Lack of key resources • Operating within a political environment • Failure to establish clear expectations with stakeholders • Environmental/market change • Cultural influences	• Strong radar for threats and opportunities • High reputation among stakeholders • Clarity of stakeholders' needs and aspirations • Strong communications (listening and informing) • Customers and suppliers have easy access • Strong attention to quality
Relationships	• Conflict is not addressed/is denied • Lack of psychological safety • People feel undervalued/unsupported • Cliques and subgroups • Lack of willingness to share responsibility for collective performance (blame) • Communication problems (relational)	• Right people with right skills • Complementary strengths and weaknesses • High levels of honest feedback • Understanding each other's strengths and weaknesses • Positive conflict encouraged and valued • High level of support for colleagues • Psychological safety • Valuing diversity

Internal processes, systems, and structures	• Recurring quality problems • Lack of clarity about tasks and roles • Inadequate systems of review • Lack of clarity about what constitutes good (high) performance in this context • Unclear decision-making processes • Communication problems (systemic)	• Clarity of who is in the team and not • Appropriate team size • Distributed leadership • Strong decision-making processes • Working to everyone's strengths • Strong attention to quality • Rapid innovation • Role clarity
Learning processes	• 'Too busy syndrome' (no time for reflection) • Individual and collective learning insufficiently valued • Lack of sources of external perspective and/or ideas • Low learning maturity/differences in personal maturity • Resistance to change • Mistakes are repeated (not learned from)	• Team development plan for collective learning • Positive attitude towards mistakes • Learning objectives linked to evolving environment • Habit of reflection – time to step back from doing • Asking for feedback • Co-coaching/coaching mindset
Leadership	• Absentee or over-controlling leadership • Power concentrated in the leader • Lack of open conversations between leader and team • Politics	• Seeking to be ahead of change • Leader provides moral direction • Role model for learning and values • Leadership is distributed • Leader is 'secure'

from hierarchical coaching to co-coaching – as underpins new ways of looking at performance appraisal – lays the foundations for a more systemic perspective.

Coaching for team performance

The use of teams in organizations has increased rapidly due to increased complexity and globalization (Piña, Martínez, & Martínez, 2008) and as work has shifted from being organized around individual jobs to team-based structures (Kozlowski & Bell, 2003). Teams are considered to be at the center of how work gets done in modern organizations (Kozlowski & Ilgen, 2006). Teams have been called the vital link between individuals and organizations (Mathieu, Hollenbeck, van Kippenberg, & Ilgen, 2017).

A team with a coaching culture can be argued to be better equipped to take an even wider, more complex view of the dynamics of the systems behind performance and dysfunction.

The approach to coaching the team as a whole depends upon the relationship of the leader to the team. Are they outside the team, looking in? Or inside the team, doing the same task or similar tasks to the rest of the team, but 'first among equals'? Or are they partly in and partly out? The systems dynamics of each of these three positions are potentially substantially different and likely to have different implications for the nature and efficacy of the coaching. Once again, we have a surprising paucity of relevant research to illuminate these different contexts.

The ultimate objective of team coaching from outside the team, whether internally or externally resourced from an organizational perspective, is to enable the team to develop its capacity to self-coach. Tackling specific performance issues on the way is part of how the team undertakes this learning and transition. Sometimes it needs an external (to the team) coach to get the team started on this journey.

The wide literature on team performance is only partially helpful here. It tends to concentrate either on what teams must do to achieve high performance or on what makes teams dysfunctional. However, performance and dysfunction are not opposites: more accurately, we are dealing with high or low performance, which is a result of high or low functionality. The most quoted model of team dysfunction comes from Lencioni (2002), who proposes five key dysfunctions of a team: absence of trust, fear of conflict, lack of commitment, avoidance of accountability, and inattention to results. In this model, one dysfunction gives rise to another. However, there appears to be little or no evidence to support this assertion, and it is not hard to think of examples where cause and effect may operate much more randomly. It assumes that all performance-disrupting factors are internal to the team, yet this is clearly not always the case – Hackman and Wageman (2005) have demonstrated the importance of structure, size, and resources, for example. And it largely omits the moderating effect of leader behaviors and abilities. What complexities arise when, for example, a team leader is less mature, either socio-emotionally or cognitively, or both, than team members are (Laske, 2015)?

Table 10.1 below offers a perspective that integrates both function and dysfunction through the PERILL model, and Table 10.2 integrates these with the mediating effect of leadership.

Table 10.2 below illustrates ways in which these contexts interact to affect team performance (pale gray) and dysfunction (dark gray). The white boxes indicate the moderating effect of the leader's qualities and behaviors (LQB).

Salas, Shuffler, and Thayer (2015) have tried to aid practitioners to make sense and practical use of the vast and often contradictory literature on team processes by identifying six key processes that directly, or through influencing one another, have the biggest impact on the five contexts of team performance outlined above in the PERILL model. A summary of practical steps that leaders can implement with their own teams is outlined in Table 10.3.

Hackman and Wageman (2005) recommend a much narrower focus. They suggest that the team leader only focuses on three performance processes (the level of effort team members expend carrying out team tasks; the appropriateness of the performance strategies that the team use to carry out the team tasks; and the amount of knowledge and skill team members bring to bear on the task), but only to the degree that they are relevant to the team task and life cycle. They propose that a focus on effort is most meaningful at the beginning stage of a team's life cycle; a focus on performance strategy at the midpoint; and a focus on the learning and knowledge is only possible at the end point, as the anxiety of doing the task is gone and the team is now capable of such reflection.

It can be argued that one-to-one and team coaching are mutually supportive. So, for example, a line manager wishing to create a coaching culture in his or her team may benefit from intensive one-to-one coaching about how they will bring this change about. Through being coached, they may become more effective at coaching individuals within their team. With increasing confidence, the team and its leader may become ready to embark on collective coaching, either with the support of a team coach from outside the team or by developing the skills of collective self-coaching. This also increases the possibility of there being multiple sources of leadership within the team and therefore a shared/distributed leadership operating as the team develops and progresses.

Challenges of team leader coaching their team

The two most obvious challenges for any leader wanting to coach their team is whether (a) they have the trust of the entire team to create the space for honest dialogue and (b) if they have the emotional intelligence competencies (self-awareness, self-management, awareness of others and management of others) to react and appropriately deal with the guaranteed insight that they, as the leader, will be part of the issue impacting the team's performance.

Table 10.2 PERILL: the contexts of team performance and dysfunction

LQB	Purpose & Motivation	Externally facing processes	Relationships	Internally facing processes	Learning
Purpose and Motivation	LQB	Alignment of values between the team and its key stakeholders	Working enthusiastically together towards shared goals	Clarity of priorities; putting collective priorities before personal	Actively seeking ways to leverage and expand team strengths
Externally facing processes	Stakeholders unclear what you stand for	LQB	Strong collaborative relationships with stakeholders	Rapid and effective response to quality issues	Rapid product and service innovation
Relationships	People pursue their own agendas	Conflict with stakeholders; disrespect for stakeholders	LQB	High level of psychological safety leads to constant questioning of what we do	People take active responsibility for supporting each other's development
Internally facing processes	Duplication and waste of effort	Quality issues not acknowledged or addressed	People avoid "interfering" in each other's territory. Large "elephants in the room".	LQB	Culture of continuous process improvement
Learning	Learning focused on the individual not the collective	Slow to innovate	People "hoard" knowledge and expertise	Resistance to change	LQB

Table 10.3 Practical steps for leaders

Critical Consideration	Definition	Practical Steps for a Leader
Cooperation	The motivational drivers of teamwork including team orientation, psychological safety, trust, and collective efficacy	Early wins help develop collective efficacy. Individuals trust others perceived to be similar to themselves so sharing of prior experience relevant to team tasks is useful to create this.
Conflict	Perceived incompatibilities in the interests, beliefs, or views held by one or more members that can be task-based, relationship-based or process-based conflict, with some arguing relationship-based conflict most detrimental	Create norms on how team should handle conflict by using conflict management strategies such as Thomas-Kilmann Conflict Model. Good teams deal with conflict and confront it through building psychological safety and giving team members the license to speak up.
Coordination	Sequencing and timing of interdependent actions	Team roles and responsibilities should be clarified to guide expectations on coordination. Quality team charters laying out roles and responsibilities were found to impact team performance (Mathieu & Rapp, 2009). Utilizing debriefs following key deliverables to review positive and negative aspects regarding coordination.
Communication	A reciprocal process of team members' sending and receiving information that forms and reforms a team's attitudes, behaviors, and cognitions	Information sharing positively and significantly predicts team performance (Mesmer-Magnus & Dechurch, 2009). It's about the uniqueness of the information being shared as opposed to volume. Create norms so that all team members receive information when needed and that the receipt of the intended information is confirmed (McIntyre & Salas, 1995).
Coaching	Enactment of leadership behaviors to establish goals, set direction, and recognize when breakdowns are occurring. Multiple individuals may share these behaviors, both internal and external to the team	Creating environment for shared leadership within the team can facilitate effective teamwork (Carson, Tesluk, & Marrone, 2007). Critical role for leaders is diagnosing and addressing team problems at both team and individual levels.
Cognition	A shared understanding among team members that is developed as a result of team members' interactions.	Building a clear shared understanding of high-performing teams and specific team functioning. Learning about the roles of other team members.

(Murphy & Sayer, 2018)

In our experience of coaching teams, it takes a leader with a certain level of maturity and a balance of authority and vulnerability to support a process with an external coach. These requirements are multiplied if the leader intends to hold the space for honest team development on their own. However, the leader can still set up the conditions (outlined in Tables 10.2 and 10.3) and the culture that allow the team to be the best they can be.

Challenges of internal team coaches

From our experience of running team coaching postgraduate programs in the UK and Ireland, we find that internal team coaches face four key challenges. These challenges are also experienced by external team coaches and also echo the some of the challenges of internal 1 to 1 coaches.

- Confidentiality: A fundamental principle of team coaching is that team is the client. This creates a scenario were normal rules of blanket coaching confidentiality need to be revisited. The team coach needs to explicitly contract for confidentiality (Clutterbuck, 2007; Hawkins, 2017) at the team level (whatever is said does not go outside the team) while making it clear that comments from any individual team member to the team coach will be shared with the rest of the team if that is the judgment of the coach. This mitigates the team coach being told key information relevant to the success of the team that he or she then feels compelled not to share if a blanket offer of confidentiality was made to all individuals.

  These are even trickier waters for an internal team coach to navigate as they may have prior relationships with individual team members or may have heard things via the internal water cooler. Explicit contracting and re-contracting is a must throughout.
- Clarity of roles: Another area that needs explicit contracting and re-contracting involves the clarity of the role and expectations of the internal team coach and of the team. At a conscious or unconscious level, teams can set up traps for the team coach to fall into. Common role traps include

  - Being the expert, in which the team place the responsibility on the team coach to teach them as opposed to supporting the team learning through itself.
  - Being the fixer, in which the team coach is invited to fix the problem or the problem person and the team step back and observe.
  - Being the leader, in which the team don't experience the team leader as providing appropriate authority and direction but see these attributes in the team coach.

The fixer and leader roles can be particularly seductive to the team as the internal coach is 'one of us' within the organization. The team coach loses their value of being an objective visitor to the team's system if they fall into any of the above roles.

- Systemic pressures: An internal team coach may also experience the expectations of the wider organizational system to play one of the above roles. To be system aware when one is a paid-up member of the system is an ongoing challenge.

- Emergent nature of the work: Teams, team leaders, and sponsors are used to a training approach to development where content and outcomes are predictable and familiar. The internal team coach needs to face and manage his expectations, knowing that the very nature of team coaching is emergent and is about staying with the conversation more than the process.

Being inside the organization gives these challenges a particular nuance. One of the reasons for providing supervision for internal team coaches is to mitigate these challenges (St. John-Brooks, 2013).

Integrating internal and external coaching

Such scenarios allow us to step away from the either/or perspective of internally or externally resourced coaching (McNally & Lukens, 2006). Among the possibilities is bringing external and internal coaches together for joint education or supervision sessions.

Developing the internal coach pool

Another area of interest is the management of internal coach pools. Without a body of literature to investigate this, we have to rely on anecdotal evidence of the challenges faced in creating and maintaining a pool of internal coaches, who will have sufficient credibility and competence to meet some or all of the company's coaching needs. One of the fundamental issues we have been able to identify from a series of interviews with human resources professionals with oversight of coaching is the difficulty in maintaining interest in coaching long term. Part of the answer here appears to be to establish a progression, by which coaches can add to their skills portfolio and obtain higher levels of accreditation. The National Health Service Leadership Academy in the UK has revitalized coaches' enthusiasm, for example, by providing additional training and support for them to become "ethical mentors" – helping other employees to work through ethical dilemmas in ways that are not damaging to themselves or the organization. The additional skill sets include an understanding of the psychology of ethicality and tools to help people make better values-based decisions.

Other issues include the lack of coaching role models at the top of the organization; overloading of the most effective coaches, to the extent that their main job suffers; and continuity arising from having a dedicated person overseeing the quality of both internal and external coaching.

These are all pervasive challenges that need to be addressed in any strategy for achieving a coaching and mentoring culture (Clutterbuck, Megginson, & Bajer, 2016).

Conclusion

As organizations aim to adopt more of a coaching culture, in order to become more agile and better places to work and to increase both individual and collective performance, reliance on external coaching resources becomes less and less tenable. There will in the future still be a requirement for externally sourced coaching, but the emphasis has already shifted towards the development of internal resources and capacity. The skills of coaching and being coached are required at all levels in an organization and, indeed, it is arguable that they should be developed in potential employees during their education before entering the world of work.

Developing yourself

David Clutterbuck – "The PERILs of Team Coaching: Team Performance & Team Dysfunction" www.youtube.com/watch?v=JX2jr-INrSc

Scott Tannenbaum on the "Science of Teamwork" www.youtube.com/watch?v=ibBtQG5Thxc

Melissa Sayer and Colm Murphy, "Coaching teams to increase team effectiveness and diffuse organisational learning" www.teamcoachingzone.com/colm-murphy-melissa-sayer/

Note

1   Permission to name the company has not yet been granted.

References

Bersin, J. (2007). *Death of the performance appraisal*. Retrieved February 2, 2018, from http://blog.bersin.com/death-of-the-performance-appraisal-a-new-era-of-performance-management/

Carson, J. B., Tesluk, P. E., & Marrone, J. A. (2007). Shared leadership in teams: An investigation of antecedent conditions and performance. *Academy of Management Journal, 50*(5), 1217–1234.

Clutterbuck, D. (2007). *Coaching the team at work*. London: Nicholas Brealey Publishing.

Clutterbuck, D. (2010). *Are coach assessment centres helping or hindering the profession?* Retrieved February 1, 2018, from www.gptrainingconsultants.com/tools-and-resources/download/start/50/

Clutterbuck, D. (2012). *The talent wave*. London: Kogan Page.

Clutterbuck, D., & MacKie, D. (2016). Breaking taboos. *Coaching at Work, 12*(11).

Clutterbuck, D., Megginson, D., & Bajer, A. (2016). *Building and sustaining a coaching culture*. Wimbledon: CIPD.

Ferrar, P. (2006). *The paradox of manager as coach: Does being a manager inhibit effective coaching?* Thesis submitted to Oxford Brookes University. Retrieved from https://radar.brookes.ac.uk/radar/items/8b448291-6e85-4262-b646-b1ed647e189f/1/

Frisch, M. H. (2005). Extending the reach of executive coaching: The internal coach. *Human Resource Planning, 28*(1), 23–24.

Garvin, D. A. (2013). How Google sold its engineers on management. *Harvard Business Review*, 91(12), 74–82.

Gerstner, C. R., & Day, D. V. (1997). Meta-Analytic review of leader–member exchange theory: Correlates and construct issues. *Journal of Applied Psychology, 82*(6), 827–844.

Hackman, J. R., & Wageman, R. (2005). A theory of team coaching. *The Academy of Management Review, 30*(2), 269–287.

Hawkins, P. (2017). *Leadership team coaching: Developing collective transformational leadership*. London: Kogan Page Publishers.

Hofstede, G. (1983). National cultures in four dimensions: A research-based theory of cultural differences among nations. *International studies of management & organization, 13*(1/2). Cross-Cultural Management: II. Empirical Studies (Spring–Summer), 46–74.

Jones R. J., Woods, S. A. and Guillaume R. F. G. (2015). The effectiveness of workplace coaching: A meta-analysis of le arning and performance outcomes from coaching. *Journal of Occupational and Organizational Psychology, 89*, 249–277.

Kaufman, C., & Coutu, D. (2009). *The realities of executive coaching*. Cambridge, MA: Harvard Business Review Research Report.

Kozlowski, S. W. J., & Bell, B. S. (2003). Work groups and teams in organizations. In N. W. Schmitt, S. Highhouse, & I. B. Weiner (Eds.), *Handbook of psychology: Industrial and organizational psychology* (Vol. 12, 2nd ed., pp. 412–469). Oxford, NJ: John Wiley & Sons Ltd.

Kozlowski, S. W. J., & Ilgen, D. R. (2006). Enhancing the effectiveness of work groups and teams. *Psychological Science in the Public Interest*, 7(3), 77–124.

Laske, O. (2015). *Dialectical thinking for integral leaders: A primer*. Tucson, AZ: Integral Partners.

Lencioni, P. (2002). *The five dysfunctions of a team*. San Francisco, CA: Jossey-Bass.

Mathieu, J. E., Hollenbeck, J. R., van Knippenberg, D., & Ilgen, D. R. (2017). A century of work teams in the Journal of Applied Psychology. *Journal of Applied Psychology, 102*(3), 452

Mathieu, J. E., & Rapp, T. L. (2009). Laying the foundation for successful team performance trajectories: The roles of team charters and performance strategies. *Journal of Applied Psychology, 94*(1), 90–103.

McIntyre, R. M., & Salas, E. (1995). Measuring and managing for team performance: Emerging principles from complex environments. *Team Effectiveness and Decision Making in Organizations*, 9–45.

McNally, K., & Lukens, R. (2006). Leadership development: An external-internal coaching partnership. *Journal of Nursing Administration, 36*(3), 155–161.

Mesmer-Magnus, J. R., & DeChurch, L. A. (2009). Information sharing and team performance: A meta-analysis. *Journal of Applied Psychology, 94*(2), 535–546.

Murphy, C., & Sayer, M. (2018). *Standing on the shoulders of the science of team effectiveness – building rigour into your team coaching design* (submitted for publication).

Piña, M. I. D., Martínez, A. M. R., & Martínez, L. G. (2008). Teams in organizations: A review on team effectiveness. *Team Performance Management, 14*(1/2), 7–21.

Ridler & Co in partnership with EMCC UK. (2013). *Ridler Report, Trends in Use of Executive Coaching*.

Salas, E., Shuffler, M., & Thayer, A. (2015). Understanding and improving teamwork in organizations: A scientifically based practical guide. *Human Resource Management, 54*(4), 599–622.

St John-Brooks, K. (2013). *Internal coaching: The inside story*. London: Karnac Books.

Wageman, R., Nunes, D. A., Burruss, J. A., & Hackman, R. J. (2008). *Senior leadership teams: What it takes to make them great*. Boston, MA: Harvard Business School Press.

Chapter 11

Centralizing coaching provision

Brian O. Underhill

Introduction

An emerging trend in the executive coaching industry has been the centralization of executive coaching, which has taken on two forms: (1) a centralized organizational function to oversee and manage coaching throughout the enterprise, and (2) a centralization of external partners offering coaching to the enterprise. In our industry-wide coaching research study (CoachSource, 2018), organization coaching practice managers were asked about likely trends in the next 3–5 years. "Organizations centralize/streamline under fewer executive coaching vendors" was selected as fourth most likely trend out of 14 options, with 78% selecting "likely" or "highly likely."

With the rise in popularity of executive coaching, as well as other variants of coaching such as internal coaching, "leader-as-coach" training, coaching wrapped around leadership development programs and the like, organizations are increasingly burdened with the overall management of coaching activities. Previously managed in a haphazard and disparate fashion across the enterprise, firms are increasingly seeking to establish a Coaching Center of Excellence (CCoE), offering greater visibility to all assignments, greater quality control, and a more consistent experience for internal customers.

Meanwhile, this popularity combined with the rapidly expanding number of individual coaches and coaching providers in the marketplace often means larger organizations can be overseeing some 30–100 coaches and coaching providers, resulting in potentially hundreds of individual coaching engagements. Centralizing coaching under fewer partners (or even a single provider) vastly improves overall visibility for the coaching, greatly reduces the administrative workload on the organization, and yields potentially more favorable pricing and consistent experiences for recipients.

This chapter will examine the burgeoning trend of centralization of coaching provision, beginning with the history of this practice, along with a look at current and future trends in this regard. The benefits and concerns of centralization will be examined. Finally, a "coaching maturity model" will be proposed from which organizations can plot their progress and examine possible next steps.

Theory and evidence underpinning topic area

The executive coaching industry has experienced incredible growth over the past two decades (e.g., Abel & Nair, 2012; Dunlop, 2017). The International Coach Federation (ICF) estimates a total industry of 53,300 coaches in 2016, up from 47,500 in 2012 (International Coach Federation, 2012; International Coach Federation, 2016). The Conference Board declared in its 10-year anniversary study on the profession, "the story of executive coaching in organizations over the past 10 years is one of remarkable growth" (Abel, Ray, & Nair, 2016, p. 7).

Great evolution has happened since a 2004 *Harvard Business Review* article described the profession as "the Wild West of coaching" (Sherman & Freas, 2004). Over this time, there has been increased adoption of corporate-wide executive coaching programs, enhanced use of internal coaches, and further standardization of international accreditation requirements, along with many more empirical studies on the profession. Coaching has become more of a status symbol, with the early days of "coaching problem children" mostly replaced with focus on the best and the brightest – a 10% decrease in coaching for performance problems from 2013 until now (Underhill et al., 2013; CoachSource, 2018).

However, this success has now brought on a new set of challenges. Most notably, organizations are increasingly struggling with the management and oversight this burgeoning practice has offered. As an example, one PhD-qualified coaching manager from a major organization that we know found himself spending every day processing purchase orders, analyzing coach expense reports, and approving company payments (all tasks an administrator could do instead), which prevented him from doing the higher-level strategic work for which he was qualified. In a 2006 study, the management of coaching was handled at the business unit level in most cases. By 2010, 84% of organizations reported management of coaching had moved to a centralized function (Gottemoeller, 2016).

As early as the turn of the millennium, we have observed this management challenge. The first of its kind known to us was early 2000 just after Agilent Technologies spun off from Hewlett-Packard in the largest new 'start-up' initial public offering in Silicon Valley history at the time. The rapid development of Agilent's leaders became a vital priority of its CEO (Underhill, Anderson, & Silva, 2005; Underhill, Anderson, & Silva, 2006).

Executive coaching had a favorable track record at HP, but it was not linked strategically to leadership development efforts. Multiple coaches operated using differing approaches, widely varied pricing, and little oversight and coordination. Agilent instead partnered with a single vendor to design a "corporate recommended" solution, offering a prequalified worldwide coach cadre (matched to Agilent locations), a uniform experience for leaders, corporate visibility into assignments, follow-up metrics, and even a preferred discount rate (Underhill et al., 2005). Hundreds of leaders have now received coaching over the years using a pool of more than 60 coaches, coordinated by a single provider.

Additional large organizations followed suit by issuing request for proposals (RFPs, or tenders) for similar purposes: Cisco in 2001, followed by Dell in 2003 (Reyes, Yount, Underhill, & Sass, 2009; Underhill, 2011) and Microsoft in 2008 (Wallis, Underhill, & McNamara, 2010; Wallis, Underhill, & Hedly, 2012). By the turn of the decade, each year would see multiple RFPs issued by organizations of a similar vein (see the Genentech case study in this book, Chapter 19).

As early as 2003, there was evidence that organizations were beginning to place caps on the fees coaches were charging (Maher & Pomerantz, 2003). Publications and conferences focusing on the overall management of executive coaching have also been arising over the past many years as well (e.g., the Conference Board Executive Coaching conferences; Bacon, 2011; Keddy & Johnson, 2011; Riddle, Hoole, & Gullette, 2015; Underhill, Koriath, & McAnally, 2007).

Organizations are also increasingly using internal coaches, who must be coordinated and managed as well. A 2016 Conference Board study found 69% of company respondents used internal coaches (Gottemoeller, 2016). In our most recent study, 72% of organizational practice managers expect the use of internal coaches to increase over the next 3–5 years (CoachSource, 2018). Hence, the demand for better management of coaching has never been greater.

Organizational design trends

An organization's vacillation between centralization and decentralization has been long observed since the beginning of the modern age. One might think of the vast decentralized structure established by General Motors' Alfred Sloan in the 1920s. Yet, one division of an organization may discover a best-practice way to accomplish something, which could then be leveraged across the organization and coordinated in a centralized fashion. This then reduces duplicative efforts, potentially improves overall quality, and saves costs. In the Agilent example (Underhill et al., 2005), one division was making great use of executive coaching, which raised the interests of the centralized shared-service human resources function to then research how these learnings could be leveraged enterprise-wide.

Many of the benefits towards centralizing coaching provision have been provided thus far in this chapter. The primary benefit is for the organization to gain a central visibility to all coaching-related activities across the enterprise. The organization can establish and maintain a standardized coaching methodology for all leaders. Consistent screening criteria for coaches – both internal and external – can be established. Metrics concerning satisfaction and impact can be collected systemwide. The administrative management burden on the organization can be outsourced and hence reduced. All coaches systemwide can be brought together for community gatherings much more easily. An organization could potentially even benefit from preferred pricing by shifting volume to fewer providers.

However, centralization provision is not always the best solution and can carry with it potential concerns. Centralization is not well suited for all organizations. What are some of these concerns?

First, not all organizations are structurally or culturally well suited for centralization. There are organizations that are naturally incredibly decentralized – for example, a holding company (such as Berkshire Hathaway in the USA or Tata in India). The central headquarters may have a very small home office, with the vast majority of decision-making being done within the individual businesses that it owns. Should headquarters begin mandating an official approach to coaching – combined with requesting all information pertaining to coaching – this could likely be perceived as overcontrolling and may backfire.

Second, centralizing coaching down to just a few (or one) vendor(s) can also bring downsides. Should the vendor(s) provide substandard performance in any aspect of the program, the organization may be stuck in the arrangement for several years. Also, there would generally be an additional cost associated with outsourcing coach management activities that must be considered on (top of the cost of coaching). Organizations have to decide who pays this fee – the central function, or the actual businesses who are requesting coaching.

There are multiple concerns pertaining to the coaching pool in this arrangement. The organization could be limited to only the coaches affiliated with the provider(s), which might not be sufficient for provision of the program. Key coaches working with the organization prior to centralization may choose not to participate with the new vendor(s). Should these coaches be highly influential among executives, they could undermine the centralization effort. Various parts of the organization, or even key executives, may have their 'favorite coaches' who may not qualify under the new standards, causing potential conflict. Also, some vendors may pay coaches a lower percentage of the total fee, resulting in a loss of some coaches. Finally, some organizations simply prefer to have many coaches from many sources so as not to be overly reliant on any one provider's coaches.

Toward a coaching maturity model

In just the past few years, coaching conferences have begun to discuss the concept of a "coaching maturity model," that is, how advanced organizations are in the deployment of coaching. Some might do little to no coaching, and its overall management might be considered spontaneous or ad hoc. Other organizations have been purposefully evolving a robust coaching practice over the years, which may include fully centralized management, cadres of external and internal coaches, standardized package offerings, disciplined measurement regimens, etc. It is generally assumed that companies that have centralized coaching management are further along in the maturity process.

Stover (2016) has posted an early maturity model via his blog, based on his experience managing coaching for LinkedIn and as an instructor for the Coaches Training Institute. The model consists of five stages: (1) incidental (an engagement here or there, leaders find their own coaches), (2) centralized (someone is now in charge of coaching, a budget/cost center is established, the process is defined and tracked), (3) metrics-based (the increased use of coaching leads to an increased desire to measure return on investment), (4) strategic (coaching is better linked to the company strategy, coaching occurs at more levels), and (5) world class (most in the organization know what coaching should and should not be used for).

A challenge with a progressive model of this type is that some companies might be "world class" in one aspect of their coaching practice (such as coaching conversations permeating the organization), but only "incidental" in another (such as measurement). It would be difficult to then determine which phase that particular organization should place themselves. Also, as coaching practice managers come and go within an organization – along with the entire HR leadership chain – an organization's commitment to coaching practices of all types can ebb and flow. The arrival of a new CEO or chief HR officer can cause some organizations to immediately ramp up coaching activities, while others cease theirs completely. To this end, an alternative coaching maturity model addressing these concerns will be proposed later in this chapter.

Toward a "coaching culture"

Increasingly popular in the industry lexicon is the desire to create a "coaching culture" within a given organization (Abel et al., 2016, p. 18; Clutterbuck & Megginson, 2005; Hawkins, 2008; Hawkins, 2012, p. 21; Megginson & Clutterbuck, 2006; Corden, 2017). Though definitions can vary, the general concept according to practitioners we have met primarily include a component of coaching conversations permeating the organization (Hawkins, 2012). There is some evidence to indicate that a coaching culture can lead to above-average financial results compared to an organization's peers (Human Capital Institute, 2014).

A coaching culture could include leaders using coaching conversations in performance discussions, the general workforce using coaching techniques in daily discussions, internal coaches working with certain levels of leaders, external coaches working with other (usually higher) levels of leaders, a competency model and/or performance review system rooted in coaching competencies, and more (Hawkins, 2008).

A Human Capital Institute and International Coach Federation study defined the key components of a coaching culture as:

- The organization has a strong coaching culture;
- Employees value coaching;

- Senior executives value coaching;
- Coaching is a fixture in the organization with a dedicated line item in the budget;
- Managers/leaders (and/or internal coach practitioners) spend above-average time on weekly coaching activities; and
- Managers/leaders (and/or internal coach practitioners) received accredited coach training (Human Capital Institute, 2014; Abel et al., 2016).

Despite this definition, our experience is that most corporate attempts to create a coaching culture traditionally have been efforts at training the leaders (or entire workforce) in coaching skills through a 1–2 day training. This trend may be continuing, as "leader-as-coach training (teaching coaching skills to leaders)" placed second out of 14 future trends predicted by organization practice managers (CoachSource, 2018).

However, it is unlikely that this intervention alone would truly change the culture of an organization, which typically needs either a major crisis or sustained intervention by its leadership for effective culture change (Schein, 2010). Coaching culture specialist Tim Hawkes of Unlimited Potential estimates that few to no organizations have a true coaching culture (T. Hawkes, personal communication, December 10, 2015). The Human Capital Institute and ICF study found that only 13% of companies responding had a strong coaching culture (Human Capital Institute, 2014).

A comprehensive nine-step coaching culture model has been proposed by Hawkes and Haden (T. Hawkes, personal communication, April 23, 2018; van Nieuwerburgh, 2016).

In this approach, coaching-related elements are considered for each of the levels of employees in the organization (non-managers, junior/middle managers, senior managers). Each of these levels is then considered from a "knowing"/"being"/"doing" perspective. The ultimate goal is for employees to move through to the doing phase before properly fulfilling the aim of creating a coaching culture.

In a fully developed coaching culture, senior managers generally use executive coaches. They are willing to serve as ambassadors of coaching and to help

Table 11.1 The 9-step coaching culture model

	KNOWING	BEING	DOING
SENIOR MANAGERS	Use executive coaches	Ambassadors for coaching	Self-sustaining coaching system
JR/MIDDLE MANAGERS	Coach training	Internal coach pools	Internal coaching system
NON-MANAGERS	Make resources available	Improve workforce coachability	From coachee to coach

create a self-sustaining coaching system that other leaders are willing to follow. Junior or middle managers may be willing to go to coach training, internal coaching pools are built, and a formal internal coaching system is properly developed. Non-managers are also given resources to learn about coaching, are willing to be coached, and might even coach others too.

Aims and processes in topic area

To guide the balance of this chapter, I propose a comprehensive "4C Coaching Maturity Model." The intent is to build on the initial thinking by Stover (2016), while also providing additional opportunities for organizations to move up and down the maturity curve within different categories of consideration (see Figure 11.1 and Table 11.2).

The 4C Coaching Maturity Model proposes four stages of maturity: casual, conditional, centralized, and coaching culture. Each of these stages is then viewed from the perspective of five categories: marketing, menu, management, measurement, and members. This allows us to acknowledge that an organization could likely be in different stages depending on which aspect of the coaching program is considered. To this end, an organization could be "casual" in one area (i.e., ad hoc use of internal coaches), while "centralized" in a different area (i.e., full centralization of all external coaches).

The five categories are each considered from the perspective of the four stages:

> *Marketing*: How is coaching generally perceived in the organization? Perhaps no one in the organization really knows much at all about coaching (Casual), or coaching has a negative history the few times it had been used (Conditional). In Centralized organizations, coaching is generally positioned as a positive investment, where demand could possibly outstrip supply. In a Coaching Culture, coaching is highly valued throughout the organization.
>
> *Menu*: This category pertains to what coaching-related offerings exist within the organization. In a casual state, there generally are no official coaching offerings. If coaching is conducted, it is very ad hoc in nature. In our experience, we generally see organizations adding the following offerings as they mature through this category: Conditional (adds executive coaching, 'leader-as-coach' training), Centralized (adds internal coaching and coaching associated with leadership development programs), and Coaching Culture (includes all of the previous and adds other forms of coaching, such as team coaching, group coaching, peer coaching, and more). Not all organizations would necessarily provide all of these offerings, and they may not necessarily do so in the order suggested.
>
> *Management*: This category focuses on how coaching is overseen, which gets more complex as an organization matures. In Casual, very little coaching is occurring, and management is often done by the individual business who requests coaching. Otherwise there are little additional needs for

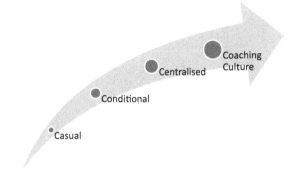

Figure 11.1 The 4C Coaching Maturity Model

coaching management. In Conditional, there may or may not be centralized management, sometimes it is controlled by a centralized unit, other
times by the individual businesses. Often the centralized unit may not
have complete visibility to all the coaching taking place in the firm and
may not necessarily care about that for now. The tracking is often done
via spreadsheets that compile information on who is being coached, by
whom, key milestones, etc.

As maturity progresses, management challenges increase, and organizations
in the Centralized category begin to oversee all assignments from one area
within the organization. This unit will have visibility to all engagements
and may require that all assignments and coach pool management route
through here. Increasingly, coaching management software is employed
(rather than at this point unwieldy Excel spreadsheets) to track all internal
and external coaching engagements. Finally, companies who have reached
the Coaching Culture level of maturity now have established a coaching
"Center of Excellence" where all aspects of coaching are overseen, not
just one-to-one engagements, but an overall center concerned with furthering all benefits of coaching throughout the enterprise.

Regarding *Measurement*, there can be great differences in how coaching is
measured, if at all. Casual assignments may not necessarily include measurement, except anecdotal reports on the success of coaching. Conditional maturity may or may not include some measurement. The leader
being coached is asked whether they improved as a result of the coaching, or perhaps their boss and/or human resources are asked about their
improvement. Centralized coaching practices tend to be more disciplined
about measurement – in the best practices we have seen they will conduct
a leader satisfaction survey after the assignment is concluded. A multi-
source evaluation of leader improvement can also be collected by quickly
surveying those working with the leader. Aggregated results of both are

Table 11.2 4C Coaching Maturity Model

Category	Casual	Conditional	Centralized	Coaching Culture
Marketing How is coaching perceived?	Coaching generally has little/no awareness in organization	Coaching seen as a 'fix it' for leaders in trouble	Coaching seen as a positive investment	Coaching – in all forms – is widely valued
Menu What coaching-related offerings exist?	No official coaching offerings.	Executive coaching 'Leader-as-coach' training	Executive coaching 'Leader-as-coach' training Internal coaching Leadership development programs with wrap-around coaching	Executive coaching 'Leader-as-coach' training Internal coaching Leadership development programs with wrap-around coaching Team coaching Group coaching Peer coaching and more
Management How is coaching overseen?	Ad hoc assignments happen in a decentralized fashion	Coaching managed by business unit HR or centrally. Some assignments/management done outside the purview of the central function Excel spreadsheets for tracking	Centralized point-of-contact Coaching management software tracks assignments and coaches	Coaching Center of Excellence established
Measurement What metrics are employed?	None	Coachee asked if they thought they improved as a result of coaching	Coaching satisfaction survey Multi-source evaluation of leader improvement	Aggregated company-wide coaching dashboards Strive for return on investment
Members Who are the coaches?	Leaders/HR find own coaches	Individual HR determines standards	Company-wide standards for coaching cadre Cadre oriented prior to beginning work Cadre meets on regular basis Company learns from observations of cadre	Continual evaluation and upgrading of all coaching practitioners Regular in-person forums at company HQ

centrally stored and analyzed. Coaching Culture mature organizations will also possess in-depth reporting dashboards on all aspects of their coaching activities. They may also strive to measure return on investment of the coaching work. Employee engagement survey results might also be analyzed to look for trends pertaining to supporting the coaching culture.

Members: This category focuses on the coaches – externals, internals, managers-as-coaches, even all employees. In a Casual state, generally external coaches are sought on an as-needed basis by the individual requester or their HR support. Sourcing can be a bit haphazard (i.e., "Does anyone happen to know a coach in Pittsburgh?") and can often rely on the same known coach(es) repeatedly. In some Conditional firms, individual HR leaders have begun to determine standards they may desire most in the coaches they work with, but they aren't necessarily shared company-wide. Centralized firms have established these standards company-wide, not just for external coaches, but for internal coaches as well. All new coaches to the firm are expected to meet these minimum criteria. The cadre of coaches may be oriented prior to working, brought together via webinar on a regular basis, and share general learnings from the cadre to the company. In Coaching Culture organizations, this looks much the same, but a few firms have invested in bringing their cadre physically together for several days of mutual learning, skill building, and further comradery (i.e., Microsoft – Wallis et al., 2010).

Tools and techniques in centralization

In centralizing coaching provision, the first step for an organization is to determine which tasks it wishes to centralize and which it would outsource to external provider(s). Some organizations actually undertake an internal coaching audit, to determine how much coaching is being done and where, and to understand who the coaches are working with in the organization. Some organizations at this point would issue a tender/request for proposal to a variety of potential coaching providers – others may already have preferred qualified providers from which to further centralize provision.

In this section, we will first define the key roles to be played by various parties to the centralization project. We will then outline various management tasks that would need to be considered for centralization. Additional considerations pertaining to the retention of existing coaches ('legacy coaches') prior to centralization will also be considered.

Role definition

In the desired future state of centralized provision, what tasks are to be performed by the organization, and which are to be performed by (an) external provider(s)?

Table 11.3 Roles: current and future state example

Activity	Responsibility	
	Today	*Future State*
Global coaching process design & quality	Organization	Organization/Provider
Internal consultation/process questions	Organization	Organization
Receive/confirm coaching requests	Organization	Organization
Nominate coaches for client selection	Organization	Provider
Track and monitor coaching activity	Organization	Provider
Distribute midpoint and final impact surveys	Organization	Provider
Generate metrics and reports	Organization	Provider
Invoicing and coach payments	Organization	Provider
Maintain coaching pool (add/remove coaches)	Organization	Organization/Provider
Coach community meetings (if applicable)	Organization	Organization/Provider

Table 11.3 serves as an example of how an organization can determine this mix in the future desired state. Of course, each organization can determine on its own which responsibilities it seeks to maintain and which it would ask its provider to oversee.

Upon determining desired future roles, further definition regarding the actual tasks to be completed is then necessary.

Management tasks

We have compiled a comprehensive list of management tasks that generally must be accomplished through the coaching management solution. This is generally assumed that an organization has retained an external provider to assist in management. This list is as follows:

Onboard Current Pool – Organization to introduce the new working arrangement to existing ('legacy') coaches. Provider to get to know existing cadre of executive coaches; input their information into a centralized resource. Establish a process to determine if some existing coaches might be screened out of the revised pool according to new organizational criteria.

Source Additional Coaches – Provider to source additional coaches in key locations where 'in-network' coaches do not currently exist. Organization to provide a list of key global sites and number of eligible potential coachees at each site to help influence where additional coaches may be needed.

New Assignment Intake – Provider (or organization) to interact with human resource business partners (HRBPs) or others regarding new coaching requests, gathering all relevant information regarding each new inquiry. Establish online coaching request form to do the same, which can be hosted by the organization or provider.

Coach Nominations – Nominate coaches from the cadre for each request. Ensure client leader eventually picks a coach or decides not to proceed. Ensure selected coach receives the 360 and other survey data as necessary to commence. Complete all required paperwork necessary to initiate assignment.

Activity Tracking – Track all coaching activities (generally with an online resource). Produce reports on an agreed-upon basis, potentially able to be viewed by division, geography, leadership level, or other desired delineation for client. Coaches track their key milestone activity online (with exact hours elapsed, if desired).

Results Metrics – Initiate appropriate results metrics as agreed upon ahead of time (for example, a Leader Satisfaction Survey to measure leader's perception of the coaching experience); an Impact Survey to measure change in leadership effectiveness. Aggregate and share results back to organization.

Coach Community – Facilitate coach community meetings virtually and/or on site to further the coach network's capabilities. Consider annual Coaching Forum to bring all worldwide coaches together at headquarters.

Coaching Marketing and Education – Arrange presentations, conference calls, and the like to further inform and educate the HRBPs and other communities to the availability and benefits of the 'preferred' corporate approach to coaching.

Billing and Expenses – Centralize and coordinate the billing procedures to ease the burden on coaching clients and the coaches. This also allows better visibility to the total spend on coaching.

Each organization may have different needs with relation to this list, which can be modified as needed.

Transferring legacy coaches to the new solution

With all that has been shared above, there are some additional considerations that must be taken into account regarding onboarding existing coaches ('legacy coaches') to the new solution. Legacy coaches often possess deep relationships with key executives throughout the organization and can unexpectedly help make or break the new solution. If not done right, this crucial phase can backfire, resulting in a loss of key coaches or potential backdoor deals between coaches and leaders, undermining the very purpose of centralization.

How an organization handles this can vary. One of our clients took a very collaborative approach, introducing the concept to the coaches, listening to their feedback, and rolling out the new solution gradually over 6 months, with constant coach gatherings to gauge the mood. However, another client simply sent out an email one day saying, "We are moving to a new coach management solution (insert some details). Effective Monday, you will work under this new solution. If not, you won't coach here anymore." Of course, the first example experienced a much greater coach retention rate (nearly 100%), but it takes more time.

First, the organization needs to determine which coaches should continue under the new arrangement. Some coaches may have not worked at the firm in many years; others are not viewed particularly positively by the organization. Which coaches should be invited to the new solution?

Second, the organization and external provider(s) should develop a change management and communications plan for inviting and onboarding the legacy coaches to the new solution. Coaches should be able to see the logic behind the change and how it will ultimately be more beneficial to them to be part of the solution. In most cases, their administrative burdens should ease under the new solution, which automatically is a great benefit.

Additionally, pay for existing coaches is an immediate concern for them. We recommend, whenever possible, that legacy coaches be paid the same as they had been previously, with any additional management fees borne by the organization, not the coach.

Finally, these coaches will also be concerned with how assignments are distributed and whether they will earn fewer engagements than they did previously. Determining a solution to this concern and communicating it to legacy coaches will be necessary.

Case study

In 2004, Dell Computer (as it was known then) issued a tender/RFP for one of the largest coaching centralization initiatives known in the industry at that time (Reyes et al., 2009). Several years prior, Dell began a process to massively enhance its focus on leadership development, recognizing that growing leaders would be key to its expansion and necessary to attract and retain the best talent. Multiple initiatives were undertaken in this regard, including the development of new leadership competencies, a 360 tool, and the expansion of coaching activities.

By 2003, however, coaching had become unruly and out of control, with varying approaches, instruments, measurements, pricing, and the like. Coaches came from all different backgrounds, without any systemwide quality standards applied. Coaching was not linked to the company talent management or leadership development approaches. Dell expected its use of coaching to actually increase, making all of these challenges greater. Two hundred executives per year would likely take advantage of coaching (600 over three years).

The decision was made to locate a single provider to oversee all aspects of coaching. This provider brought with it a consistent methodology, a cadre of screened coaches matched to Dell sites, best-practice knowledge of the coaching industry, and very favorable bulk rate pricing.

Over the years, this provider has overseen hundreds of assignments using an online coach management system, which provides regular dashboard reporting on all aspects of the program. It has coordinated a cadre of Dell-specific coaches who are oriented to the company and convene periodically. Dell has benefitted from best-practice sharing between the provider, coaches, and company. Measurable results have been achieved, all while continuing to enjoy favorable worldwide pricing.

Conclusion

Indeed, by the relative dearth of proper references pertaining to the centralization of coaching provision in this chapter, it only confirms that this is a very new area of the coaching field. Coaching has seen incredible growth, having moved well beyond the days of 'fixing problem children' into proactive, focused development on the best and brightest. Newer forms of coaching are entering organizations as we speak. The future of the profession looks bright.

Yet the 'victim of our success' is the enhanced management burden placed upon organizations to properly oversee all of this. In fact, it is not uncommon at larger organizations for a highly educated PhD (or several) to spend their full-time job(s) simply managing day-to-day activities pertaining to coaching: finding coaches, orienting them, creating nominations, tracking progress, and measuring results, as well as pushing through purchase orders and statements of work, expense reports, and even IT compliance documents. This is likely not a good use of their time!

Centralization of coaching provision eases this burden on organizations for all the reasons aforementioned, allowing those full-time employees to focus more often on higher-level strategic activities and outsourcing the day-to-day tasks to others.

Harvard Business Review stated in 2004, "Like the Wild West of yesteryear, this frontier is chaotic, largely unexplored, and fraught with risk, yet immensely promising" (Sherman & Freas, 2004). The Wild West has largely been tamed – particularly in organizations further along the coaching maturity curve – with much promise already being realized. Further centralization may help tame it even further.

Developing yourself

Recommended readings

Riddle, D. D., Hoole, E. R., & Gullette, E. C. D. (2015). *The center for creative leadership: Handbook of coaching in organizations*. San Francisco, CA: Jossey-Bass.

Underhill, B. O., Koriath, J. J., & McAnally, K. (2007). *Executive Coaching for Results: The Definitive Guide to Developing Organizational Leaders*. San Francisco, CA: Berrett-Koehler.

Web resources

Coaching Design Checklist – the last chapter of Executive Coaching for Results (Underhill et al., 2007), a downloadable checklist of everything an organization needs to consider when designing or improving their coaching program. www.coachsource.com/downloads

Coaching Maturity Model, as presented by Jeremy Stover (2016). *Stages of Maturity for Organizational Coaching Practices*. Retrieved from www.linkedin.com/pulse/stages-maturity-organizational-coaching-practices-jeremy-stover-pcc/

Various resources and statistics on the coaching industry are available from the International Coach Federation, www.coachfederation.org. (Some free, some behind paywall.)

Henley Centre for Coaching offers a vast array of materials including coaching research, webinars, podcasts, free short coaching courses and hundreds of journals in its membership centre.

The Institute of Coaching maintains a vast library of coaching research, articles, podcasts, peer-reviewed journals and more. www.instituteofcoaching.org. (Some free, some behind paywall.)

Marshall Goldsmith Library – Nearly all of Dr. Goldsmith's articles are available here at no charge. Many other resources such as videos, book information, podcasts, etc. are available at no charge. www.marshallgoldsmith.com

Jonathan Passmore Library – Nearly all of Prof Passmore's articles are available here at no cost www.jonathanpassmore.com

Peer Resources maintains an updated site covering the latest coaching literature, list of worldwide conferences, videos, training programs and much more. www.peer.ca/coaching.html (Some free, some behind paywall.)

Sample new assignment intake form. www.coachsource.com/intake

Sample coach satisfaction survey, to be administered to the leader client. www.coachsource.com/downloads

Sample "mini survey", a short multi rater survey measuring improvement in the eyes of those working with the leader client. www.coachsource.com/downloads

References

Abel, A. L., & Nair, S. (2012). *Executive coaching survey: 2012 edition*. New York, NY: The Conference Board.

Abel, A. L., Ray, R. L., & Nair, S. (2016). *Global executive coaching survey 2016: Developing leaders and leadership capabilities at all levels*. New York, NY: The Conference Board.

Bacon, T. R. (2011, January). Best practices for managing global executive coaching supplier relationships. Korn/Ferry Institute.

Clutterbuck, D., & Megginson, D. (2005). *Making coaching work: Creating a coaching culture*. London: Chartered Institute of Personnel & Development.

CoachSource. (2018). *Executive coaching for results: Industry research*. San Jose, CA: CoachSource, LLC.

Corden, S. (2017). *Coach culture: A playbook for winning in business*. Black Butte Publishing. Retrieved from www.amazon.com/Coach-Culture-Playbook-Winning-Business-ebook/dp/B07585ZLC8

Dunlop, C. W. (2017, October 5). *The success and failure of the coaching industry*. Retrieved from www.forbes.com/sites/forbescoachescouncil/2017/10/05/the-success-and-failure-of-the-coaching-industry/#91977d66765f

Gottemoeller, M. (2016). Ten years of the executive coaching survey: Four lessons learned. In A. L. Abel, R. L. Ray, & S. Nair (Eds.), *Global executive coaching survey 2016* (pp. 7–10). New York, NY: The Conference Board.

Hawkins, P. (2008). *Trade secrets: Ten steps to a coaching culture*. Retrieved from www.person neltoday.com/hr/trade-secrets-ten-steps-to-a-coaching-culture/

Hawkins, P. (2012). *Creating a coaching culture*. Berkshire: McGraw Hill Education.

Human Capital Institute. (2014). *Building a coaching culture*. Cincinnati, OH: Human Capital Institute and International Coaching Federation.

International Coach Federation. (2012). *2012 ICF global coaching study: Executive summary*. Retrieved from https://coachfederation.org/app/uploads/2017/12/2012ICFGlobalCoa chingStudy-ExecutiveSummary.pdf

International Coach Federation. (2016). *2016 ICF global coaching study: Executive summary*. Retrieved from http://researchportal.coachfederation.org/MediaStream/PartialView? documentId=2779

Keddy, J., & Johnson, C. (2011). *Managing coaching at work: Developing, evaluating, and sustaining coaching in organizations*. London: Krogan Page Publishers.

Maher, S., & Pomerantz, S. (2003). The future of executive coaching: Analysis from a market life cycle approach. *International Journal of Coaching in Organizations, 1*(2), 3–11.

Megginson, D., & Clutterbuck, D. (2006). Creating a coaching culture. *Industrial and Commercial Training, 38*(5), 232–237.

Reyes, A., Yount, A., Underhill, B., & Sass, S. (2009). Dell, Inc. In D. Giber, S. Lam, M. Goldsmith, & J. Bourke (Eds.), *Best practices in leadership development handbook* (2, pp. 336–364). San Francisco, CA: Pfeiffer.

Riddle, D. D., Hoole, E. R., & Gullette, E. C. D. (2015). *The center for creative leadership: Handbook of coaching in organizations*. San Francisco, CA: Jossey-Bass.

Schein, E. H. (2010). *Organizational culture and leadership*. San Francisco, CA: Jossey-Bass.

Sherman, S., & Freas, A. (2004, November). The wild west of executive coaching. *Harvard Business Review*.

Stover, J. (2016). *Stages of maturity for organizational coaching practices*. Retrieved from www.linkedin. com/pulse/stages-maturity-organizational-coaching-practices-jeremy-stover-pcc/

Underhill, B. (2011). The coach. Ready, steady, go! In G. Hernez-Broome & L. A. Boyce (Eds.), *Advancing executive coaching: Setting the course for successful leadership coaching* (pp. 31–46). San Francisco, CA: Jossey-Bass.

Underhill, B., Anderson, D., & Silva, R. (2005). Agilent technologies, Inc. In L. Carter, D. Ulrich, & M. Goldsmith (Eds.), *Best practices in leadership development and organization change* (pp. 1–20). San Francisco, CA: Pfeiffer.

Underhill, B., Anderson, D., & Silva, R. (2006). The Agilent Technologies story: Coaching across the enterprise. In M. Goldsmith & L. Lyons (Eds.), *Coaching for leadership: Writings on leadership from the world's greatest coaches* (2nd ed., pp. 199–209). San Francisco, CA: Pfeiffer.

Underhill, B., Koriath, J. J., & McAnally, K. (2007). *Executive coaching for results: The definitive guide to developing organizational leaders*. San Francisco, CA: Berrett-Koehler.

Underhill, B., McAnally, K., Bastian, C., Desrosiers, M., Golay, I., & Tuller, M. (2013). *Executive coaching industry research: 2013 final report*. San Jose, CA: CoachSource, LLC.

van Nieuwerburgh (2016). *Coaching in professional contexts*. Los Angeles, CA: Sage Publications Ltd.

Wallis, S., Underhill, B., & Hedly, C. (2012). Leaders building leaders: High potential development and executive coaching at Microsoft. In M. Goldsmith, L. Lyons, & S. McArthur (Eds.), *Coaching for leadership: Writings on leadership from the world's greatest coaches* (3rd ed., pp. 186–203). San Francisco, CA: Pfeiffer.

Wallis, S., Underhill, B., & McNamara, C. (2010). Microsoft corporation. In M. Goldsmith & L. Carter (Eds.), *Best practices in talent management. How the world's leading corporations manage, develop and retain top talent* (pp. 177–207). San Francisco, CA: Pfeiffer.

Chapter 12

Coaching leaders towards improved health and well-being

Tim Anstiss and Margaret Moore

Introduction

A physically and mentally healthy and happy workforce is a competitive advantage as it supports and enables optimal organizational performance (Bryson, Forth, & Stoke, 2014; Oswald, Proto, & Sgroi, 2015; Edmans, Li, & Zhang, 2014; Farmer & Stevenson, 2017). For leaders themselves, good personal health, resilience, and well-being will most likely contribute to optimal performance as a leader and the total amount of positive impact they have during their lifetime, while simultaneously modeling some of the behaviors they may wish to see more of in the workplace.

Health, well-being, and performance are interrelated in several ways. Good physical health contributes to good emotional and psychological well-being, and good psychological health contributes to good physical health. This may result in a 'virtuous circle' or 'upwards spiral' in which improvements in physical health and psychological well-being reinforce each other. Most people will be more familiar with the reverse of this dynamic, in which poor physical health can contribute to worsening mental health, and vice versa, resulting in a 'vicious cycle' and 'downward spiral' – e.g., depression increases a person's chances of heart disease and diabetes, and these conditions in turn increase a person's risk of depression.

In addition to strongly influencing levels of physical health, modifiable lifestyle factors such as physical activity and exercise, diet, sleep, stress, alcohol intake, and smoking seem to influence aspects of brain functioning and cognitive performance. Gomez-Pinilla and Hillman (2013) cite evidence from multiple scientific studies, including neuroimaging studies, which demonstrate the effectiveness of physical activity for protecting and improving cognitive health across the lifespan. For instance, Zhu et al. (2014) found better verbal memory and faster psychomotor speed at ages 43 to 55 years to be clearly associated with better cardiorespiratory fitness 25 years earlier. Higher levels of fitness may reduce the loss of brain tissue associated with aging while enhancing the functioning of higher-order brain regions involved in the control of cognition. More physical fit and active people seem able to allocate greater attentional resources toward the environment and process some types of information more quickly. At the molecular level, exercise may influence brain health and cognitive performance by stimulating the release of a brain-derived neurotrophic factor, which favorably influences both metabolism and plasticity. They find this data suggestive that good aerobic fitness may help people perform better when facing imposed challenges.

Regarding diet, Gomez-Pinilla (2008) cites evidence that certain eating patterns may well be contributing to recent increases in the prevalence of neurological, emotional, and psychiatric disorders, especially the consumption of high-calorie diets. Dietary factors have the capacity to influence processes at the cellular and molecular levels involved in the transmission and processing of information in the brain. Gomez-Pinilla and Tyagi (2013) suggest that the effects of diet and exercise on energy metabolism, the lipid composition of neuronal membranes, and other factors are crucial to the maintenance of optimal mental health and may counteract the effects of disease or injury on neurons. In a systematic review, Lourida et al. (2013) show that greater adherence to a Mediterranean diet seems to be associated with slower cognitive decline and lower risk of developing Alzheimer's disease.

Meta-analyses by Pilcher and Huffcutt (1996) and Philibert (2005) clearly indicate that people exposed to sleep loss usually experience a decline in cognitive performance and changes in mood, and Alhola and Polo-Kantola (2007) found that acute total sleep deprivation and chronic partial sleep deprivation both have a negative effect on attention and working memory, with total sleep deprivation impairing other cognitive functions as well.

In a comprehensive review of the scientific literature, Marin et al. (2011) find it unsurprising that chronic exposure to elevated levels of stress-related hormones (e.g., glucocorticoids) have an impact on cognition and the development of different psychological disorders and conditions, given that these chemicals rapidly access brain regions responsible for memory, emotions, and emotional regulation. Stress-related brain and mental health conditions include cognitive impairment, burnout, anxiety disorders (including post-traumatic stress disorder), and depressive illness, and they mention that since stress can and does influence the way a person perceives and appraises the next situation, chronic stress may put into place a chronic loop from which it is difficult to escape.

In view of all the above, it makes sense to provide support to senior leaders in their efforts to stay (or become) as physically and mentally healthy as possible. One way of doing this is to offer them health and well-being coaching by an appropriately skilled and trained professional.

Theories and evidence

Ryan and Deci (2000) suggest the existence of three basic human psychological needs or nutriments in their self-determination theory. These are the needs for autonomy, competence, and relatedness. There is a considerable body of research suggesting that when one or more of these needs are not met, individuals do not do so well, and that helping an individual better meet these needs can result in improved health, well-being, and functioning. Vansteenkiste and Sheldon (2006) have suggested that the beneficial health outcomes delivered by motivational interviewing (an effective coaching conversational style subject to over 1,000 controlled trials and 100 systematic reviews and meta-analyses) may be partially mediated by its effects on these three variables. This suggests that in coaching executives towards improved health and well-being, coaches may wish to:

1   Emphasize personal autonomy and choice when it comes to behavior and lifestyle change.
2   Build experiences of mastery and competence over time.
3   Pay close attention to important evidence-based relationship factors (Norcross, 2011) such as alliance, goal congruence, warmth, empathy, and feedback.

Self-efficacy theory (Bandura, 1977) is an important and enduring psychological theory and part of a larger theory called social cognitive theory (Bandura, 2001). Self-efficacy theory states that an individual's confidence in their ability to change (their self-efficacy) is an important determinant of their readiness to start to change and persist in the face of obstacles. Three of the main determinants of self-efficacy are previous mastery experiences, vicarious learning (watching others do the behavior), and persuasion from an authority. Coaches working with leaders to help them protect and improve their health and well-being may wish to spend some time strengthening their confidence that lifestyle and behavior change is achievable.

Another important model that informs the practice of many in the health improvement field is the transtheoretical model (Prochaska & DiClemente, 1983). As the name suggests, the model attempts to integrate several different behavior change theories. The transtheoretical model had two components: stages of change and processes of change. The model posits that the behavior change process involves people passing through the following discrete stages: pre-contemplation (not thinking about change), contemplation (thinking about but not yet decided to change), preparation (getting ready to change, but not yet started), action (starting to change), maintenance (several weeks or months into change, keeping it going), and termination (the new behavior is so engrained that the person is unlikely to ever go back to an earlier stage). In addition to these stages of change, the model described several processes of change drawn from different theories. One important process of change is relapsing, which is the process of returning to an earlier stage of change, e.g., someone who has stopped smoking or drinking for two years returning to smoking or drinking. Typically, the relapse process does not happen all at once, but may also unfold in stages – e.g., having a slip (one cigarette or one glass of wine), lapsing (smoking for a weekend, having a binge), and then relapsing (smoking or drinking regularly again). Coaches working with executives to help them protect and improve their health may wish to tailor the behavior change techniques they use according to their client's readiness to change. For instance, not rushing into goal setting and scheduling when a person is only just beginning to think about becoming more active.

Seligman's theory of well-being (2011) suggests that flourishing and well-being are made up of five distinct but related 'pillars,' which can be remembered by the acronym PERMA: positive emotions, engagement, relationships, meaning, and accomplishment. This is a slightly different way of categorizing the elements of psychological well-being provided by Ryff (Ryff, 1989), (Ryff, Keyes, & Lee, 1995), which includes self-acceptance, positive relationship with others, personal growth, purpose in life, environmental mastery, and autonomy. Both theories can help coaches focus parts of the conversation with their clients on discrete elements or pillars of psychological well-being and guide them towards experimenting with changes in one or two areas over time, including changes suggested from the psychology subdiscipline of positive psychology.

Much more is known about the functional purpose of 'negative emotions than positive emotions' (accepting that whether an emotional state is considered positive or negative depends on the context). Negatively experienced emotions such as anxiety, anger, hate, sadness, and loneliness tend to narrow the focus of attention onto one or two things, with a view to dealing with a danger or threat, or finding a way to reconnect with the lost object or people in general. Barbara Fredrickson's "broaden and build theory" (Fredrickson, 2001) throws light on the evolved function of positively experienced emotions such as joy, hope, happiness, curiosity, and acceptance. The theory states that these emotions are associated with a broadening of our attentional focus and the building of important relationships, connections, skills, and assets that can aid us in our ability to survive and thrive into the future. Coaches might use this theory to help educate clients about the importance of positive emotions for health, well-being, and performance and to encourage their clients to experiment with changes likely to bring about an improved experience of positive emotions over time.

Evidence

Theories help us think how to best bring about improved health and well-being in senior leaders, where to focus, and possible mechanisms through which coaching may help deliver good outcomes. But what actually works? What do interventional studies tell us?

One problem in this area is to do with definitions, as there is no agreed definition of health coaching. After reviewing 284 theoretical and empirical articles about health and well-being coaching, Wolever et al. (2013), described health coaching as

> a patient-centered process that is based upon behaviour change theory and is delivered by health professionals with diverse backgrounds. The actual health coaching process entails goal setting determined by the patient, encourages self-discovery in addition to content education, and incorporates mechanisms for developing accountability in health behaviours.

One of the weaknesses of this definition is that is excludes non-health professionals talking with people who are not patients. Olsen (2014) describes health coaching as "a goal-oriented, client-centered partnership that is health-focused and occurs through a process of client enlightenment and empowerment."

Perhaps it is best to think about health coaching and wellness coaching as umbrella terms involving coaching, guiding, and supporting people towards improved health, wellness, and well-being. It is also important to note that health coaching can be delivered via a range of different formats, including one-to-one conversations and in groups (Armstrong et al., 2013), as well as by telephone and online (Leveille et al., 2009; Allen et al., 2008).

Does it work? Health Education England commissioned a rapid review of 275 studies about health coaching. They concluded that there is some evidence that health coaching can support people's motivation to self-manage or to change their behaviors and their confidence in their ability to do so, and can support people to adopt healthy behaviors and lifestyle choices, with mixed evidence for effectiveness on such outcomes as cholesterol, blood pressure, blood sugar control, and weight loss. The authors point out that the task of evaluating the effectiveness of health coaching was made very difficult since the studies they reviewed described so many different intervention formats, styles, and durations, delivered by different practitioners with different levels of competence.

We find stronger evidence for the effectiveness of coaching on health and well-being outcomes when we explore some of the different approaches commonly lumped together under the health and wellness coaching banner, including cognitive-behavioral, motivational interviewing, positive psychology, humanistic, and so-called third wave behavioral approaches.

Cognitive-Behavioral Coaching focuses on helping clients improve their lives by helping them make changes to their thinking patterns, skills, and contents, as well as their behavior. Heavily informed by theory and practices from cognitive behavior therapy, there is growing evidence that cognitive behavioral approaches can help people to experience improved levels of health and well-being over time (e.g., Sudhir, 2017; Nelis et al., 2016; Onyechi et al., 2017; Castelnuovo et al., 2008; Edinger et al., 2001).

Motivational Interviewing is one of the most extensively researched approaches to helping people change their health and well-being-related behavior. Studies, systematic reviews, and meta-analyses suggest motivational interviewing can help people to become more active, eat better, lose weight, reduce their blood pressure, reduce their risk of diabetes, take their medication as prescribed, become less anxious, become less depressed, change their drinking patterns, and stop smoking (e.g., Miller, Wilbourne, & Hettema, 2003; Spencer Wheeler, 2016; Ekong & Kavookjian, 2016; Macdonald et al., 2012; Burgess et al., 2017; Al-Ganmi et al., 2016).

Positive Psychology Coaching is informed by the emerging science of positive psychology, focusing on what is right with people, positive emotional states, and optimal human development. Positive psychology–informed coaches may help clients clarify and develop their strengths, cultivate positive emotional states (for instance, noticing what went well, cultivating gratitude), savor pleasure, practice forgiveness, engage in acts of kindness, increase their contact with nature, etc. There is a growing body of evidence that coaching people and encouraging them to experiment with positive psychology interventions can help them protect and improve their health and well-being (e.g., Duckworth, Steen, & Seligman, 2005; Wood & Tarrier, 2010; Sin & Lyubomirsky, 2009; Parks & Titova, 2016).

Humanistic Coaching is informed by the insights and practices of humanistic psychologists such as Abraham Maslow and Carl Rogers. It is underpinned by the belief that human beings unfold optimally over time when provided with the right environmental conditions, including or especially social relationships, and that the counseling (coaching) relationship can help provide more of these favorable conditions and help the client grow as a human being, reach their potential, and self-actualize. For evidence that humanistic coaching can deliver improved health and well-being outcomes, see, for example, Sanders & Joseph (2016).

Unlike cognitive-behavioral approaches that commonly focus on helping people change the content of their thinking, *Third Wave Behavioral* approaches focus on helping people to change their relationship with their thoughts and the thinking process. Examples of these third wave coaching approaches, including evidence of their effectiveness, include acceptance and commitment coaching (Anstiss & Blonna, 2014) and compassionate mind coaching (Anstiss & Gilbert, 2014).

Aims and processes in topic area

Aims

Coaching a senior leader towards improved health and well-being might have one or more of the following aims:

- Helping them to reduce one or more unhealthy behaviors/behavioral risk factors – e.g., smoking, excessive drinking, drug use, unhealthy coping behaviors, driving too fast, unsafe sex, excessive snacking, etc.

- Helping them to adopt or increase one or more healthy or protective behaviors – e.g., regular aerobic activity, healthy eating, strength training, screening uptake, taking recommended medication, getting enough sleep, practicing mindfulness, changing consumption of alcohol, tobacco, coffee, and other psycho-active substances, etc.
- Helping them take steps likely to be associated with improvements in one or more of Seligman's five pillars of well-being: positive emotions, engagement, relationships, meaning, and achievement.

Of course, the exact aim or goal of the coaching will be decided by the client, possibly shaped by the preferences of any third party commissioning the coaching if the coaching is being purchased for the senior leader.

Processes

Processes convert inputs to outputs and outcomes. While we know something about the health and well-being outcomes that coaching can deliver, we know less about the processes that occur within coaching that deliver these outcomes. Process research helps us better understand these internal pathways and offers a route to delivering better outcomes by continuously improving the processes.

One coaching methodology that has paid particular attention to process is Motivational Interviewing. Bill Miller and Steve Rollnick (Miller & Rollnick, 2012) set out four processes when guiding people via conversation towards behavior change. These are engaging, focusing, evoking, and planning.

Practitioners work on the process of engagement throughout the conversation, using empathic listening, Socratic questioning, alliance building, and non-possessive warmth. They avoid jumping in with unasked-for advice, doing too much talking, ignoring what the client wants to talk about, and assuming the client is ready to change and falling into the 'rush to planning' trap which only leads to resistance.

The process of focusing involves deciding on the topic to be explored (stress, happiness, smoking, alcohol, exercise, diet, work-life balance, sleep, etc.), keeping the conversation focused on this topic for a period of time, bringing the conversation back to the topic if it wanders off (unless the new topic is obviously more important – e.g., marital crises, cancer diagnosis, etc.), and as the conversation progresses, shifting the focus from talking about why to talking about how.

The process of evoking involves drawing out from the other person their hopes and concerns, their reasons for changing, and their ideas about how to change. Socrates believed that humans had an innate knowledge or wisdom, and that the role of the philosopher was to help the person discover this for themselves. Hence the term 'Socratic questioning.' It's the same with skillful health and well-being coaching. The assumption is that this person isn't broken, nor are they in need of fixing. They are stuck. They are ambivalent about change, feeling two ways about it. In this case, the role of the health and well-being coach becomes one of evoking and drawing out that which is within the person. This taps into self-perception theory (Bem, 1972) which suggests, "I know what I think when I hear myself speak." The aim is to get the person to talk themselves into changing and staying changed.

The process of planning increases the chances that a person will make and sustain one or more behavior changes. Common mistakes in planning include doing it too early in the conversation and falling into the expert trap. Planning should really only take place once a person has decided to change. If you assume people are ready to change and rush in with goal setting, scheduling, and implementation intentions when they haven't decided for themselves if they want to change, you will probably notice 'resistance' to change and even 'false agreement' (to get you to shut up). Of course, you may wish to explore with the person how they might change, and this exploration can help develop their self-efficacy, but this is different from assuming they are ready to change. Check out if they are ready to change by asking them, "So what's next for you?" after summarizing back any change talk. Note, this is not the closed question, "Are you going to change?" The expert trap is when you assume you know what is best for the client and start telling and instructing them in how to change. It is much better to stay in 'evoke' mode and draw out from them their ideas first, using such open questions as "How do you think you will get started?" and "How often do you think you would have to do it before it became a habit?"

Other processes that practitioners use in health coaching include educating, modeling, goal setting, empathizing, visualizing, providing feedback, scheduling, and demonstrating.

Tools and techniques for health coaching

The tools and techniques used when coaching a senior leader towards improved health and well-being are similar to those coaching tools and techniques used in other areas of coaching – only the focus is different. These tools and techniques might include clarifying values, working with strengths, solution-focused scaling questions, decisional balance, looking forwards, in-session skills development and behavioral rehearsal, goal setting, personalized planning, implementation intentions, relapse prevention, signposting, digital health and apps, social support, providing feedback, encouraging self-acceptance, reframing, and sharing information.

Clarifying Values. Values are things that matter to a person and what they feel their life should be about. Helping people to clarify their values, explore the extent to which their current lifestyle is in harmony with their values, and how they might live a more value-driven life can help people change, stay changed, and experience improved health and well-being into the future.

Working with Strengths. Strengths are things that are right about people, patterns of thinking and behaving which come naturally to people and which other people tend to appreciate about them. Helping people discover and explore their strengths of character, how they are using them, and how they might use and develop them in the future can help them make progress in important life areas and experience improved quality of life and performance.

Solution-Focused Scaling Questions. Health and well-being coaching is less about finding out what is wrong with people and more about discovering what is strong with them. We help people talk about their current resources and assets, their strengths, and how they can build these over time. For instance, we might ask people to rate how confident they are that they could do something about their drinking if they decided to, on a scale of 0–10. Let's imagine they said 5. We might then ask, "Why 5 and not a lower number of 2 or 3? Why do you think you can succeed?" "And are there any other reasons.?" And then we might ask, "And what would help you become more confident, say a 6 or a 7?" And in this way we draw solutions out from them.

Decisional Balance. Many people are ambivalent about change, seeing the advantages and disadvantages of change, as well as the advantages and disadvantages of staying the same. The decisional balance technique helps the person thoroughly explore their mixed feelings about changing and in this way can help people become unstuck and move from 'contemplation' into the preparation or action stage.

Looking Forwards. Having people look forward several weeks, months, or years into the future and talk about the changes they would like to see, what they would like to have achieved, what they would like to be doing more of, and less of, can all help a client gain some clarity over what they want for themselves, what matters to them, and where they think they need to focus in order to make progress.

In-Session Skills Development and Behavioral Rehearsal. Some changes likely to be associated with improved health and well-being are easy to do and the person can just do them once they decide to – e.g., walk a mile a day, eat breakfast. Other changes may require some skills development before they can be incorporated into the person's life – e.g., becoming more assertive, cultivating self-compassion, systematic problem solving, etc.

Goal Setting. Goals help provide direction, motivation, and structure to a person's life and their health and well-being improvement efforts. Good practice involves collaborative goal setting, seating approach-type goals (rather than avoidance-type), having short-term and long-term goals in different life areas, and having goals consistent with or in line with people's values. It is also important not to rush into goal setting before the person is ready to change or has decided to change.

Personalized Plans with Implementation Intentions. Having personalized plans to reach goals increases the chances they will be achieved, as does having detailed 'implementation intentions' specifying when and where and how often the various behaviors and actions to be successful will be carried out.

Relapse Prevention. Let's be honest – a common outcome of an attempt at behavior change is failure, or a period of change followed by slipping back or relapsing to the earlier behavioral pattern. Once a person has described what they plan to do to protect and improve their health and well-being into the future (e.g., go swimming twice a week, leave work on time three out of five days, listen to a mindfulness app 10 minutes every day, etc.), then it can be helpful to ask the following questions: "What might get in the way of your plan?" and "How could you find a way around that?" In this way, you get the person to predict high-risk situations and engage in some 'anticipatory coping.'

Signposting. Raising people's awareness about other sources of information, guidance, and support for their health and well-being efforts can be helpful – e.g., website, local classes and courses, other practitioners, apps, etc.

Digital Health and Apps. There is a growing number of high-quality health and well-being apps on the market – e.g., physical activity trackers, healthy eating apps, sleep guidance, mindfulness apps, etc. Showing them to clients and talking about them can increase the chances that they may incorporate these into their personal health and well-being programs.

Social Support. Changing behavior and staying changed on your own can be hard. Enlisting social support is a helpful behavior change technique and can be explored with such questions as "Who can help you be successful?" and "What help would you like from them?"

Providing Feedback. Providing feedback might involve two different activities: you providing the person with feedback (e.g., some of the things you notice about them, their results on tests and assessment measures, how they are doing as they practice certain skills, etc.) and providing you with feedback (e.g., asking them, "How helpful did you find this conversation with me today? What was it in particular that you found helpful?").

Encouraging Self-Acceptance. One common source of poor well-being is an excessively strong inner critic or critical inner voice. This can be very judgmental, contemptuous, and damning – "You're rubbish", "No-one likes you", "There is something the matter with you", "You're such a failure", "You're a rubbish partner/father/mother", etc. Now it may be that senior leaders will be reluctant to open up about their inner critic – but rest assured, it will be there! Encouraging clients to move from labeling themselves and self-esteem (which has to be maintained and can cause problems) to self-acceptance and even self-compassion can be very helpful.

Reframing. The stoic philosophers emphasized, "it is not what happens to man which upsets him, but the view he takes of things" – an insight which forms the basis of much of the cognitive element of cognitive-behavioral coaching. Techniques to help the person change their perspective on things, identify cognitive errors and thinking traps, and develop more rational and less self-disturbing beliefs can all be very helpful.

Sharing Information. While the emphasis in health and well-being coaching should be evoking and drawing out what is within the person, sometimes the answers or ideas just aren't there. So an important technique in health and well-being coaching is sharing information with the person about, e.g., what other people find helpful, the benefits of mindfulness, the recommended amount and type of exercise in order to get particular benefits, etc.

Case study

Russ Alden (name changed to protect anonymity) is a 45-year-old global director of marketing for a software firm. His work involves frequent international travel. He is married with two children and is keen to spend more time (and quality time) with them in the future. He has gained 28 pounds in weight over the last seven years and puts this down to work-related aspects of his lifestyle, including lack of exercise, poor diet, and excessive alcohol intake. This conversation takes place at the end of his annual health check. It illustrated several important points emphasized in this chapter – but especially that of the importance of the individual coming up with the arguments in favor of change, rather than the coach.

Conclusion

Coaching senior leaders towards improved health and well-being is worthwhile in and of itself, and may also contribute towards improved leader, team, and organizational performance. The focus of the coaching conversation might be the reduction of known risk factors (e.g., smoking, excessive drinking, poor diet, etc.), the maintenance or increase of known protective factors (regular physical activity, sufficient healthy sleep, good relationships, uptake of screening, stress management, etc.) and/or activities and behaviors associated with one of more of the five pillars of well-being: positive emotions, engagement, relationships, meaning, and accomplishment.

Health and well-being coaching is poorly defined, but outcome studies do provide evidence for its helpfulness in protecting and improving health and well-being. Stronger evidence is associated with some of the specific or discrete approaches that often fall under the umbrella term 'health coaching' – such as motivational interviewing, cognitive-behavioral, humanistic, positive psychology, and third wave approaches. While we know something about the outcomes of health coaching, we don't know nearly enough about the processes that contribute to the outcomes. Four important and well-described processes taking place in the coaching conversation are engaging, focusing, evoking, and planning. While technical factors in health coaching make a difference, relationship factors are likely to explain a significant percentage of variance in health and well-being outcomes, including empathy, alliance, goal congruence, and feedback.

Table 12.1 Coaching conversation

Health coach	So, that's your test results covered. Now we have another 10–15 minutes to talk about things you might want to do to become or stay healthier into the future. But I want to emphasize, I'm not here to tell you what to do. I can certainly share with you some tips and advice, and what works for other people – but it's really up to you whether or not the time is right for you to make any changes. How does that sound?	Set the scene. Emphasize autonomy.
Russ	Sounds fine.	
Coach	Now there is a range of things people often talk with me about at the end of their health check. Some people talk about stress, some about diet and weight, some about physical activity and fitness, or sleep, or medication. We can also talk about alcohol usage, relationships, or anything else really that you would like to explore a little. Which of these topics might you want to talk about, or perhaps something I haven't mentioned. . .?	Agenda setting, emphasizing choice. Shared decision-making about what to talk about.
Russ	My weight I think. It's been going up over the last five years and I think it time I need to do something about it.	
Coach	Tell me, Russ, on a scale of 0–10, how important would you say it is to do something about your weight?	Start use of importance scaling question.
Russ	About 7 or 8.	
Coach	And why 7 or 8? You could have said 1 or 2. Why is doing something about your weight important to you?	Open question to elicit the client's arguments in favor of change.
Russ	Well, I've noticed I'm finding things a bit harder than I used to. For instance, walking long distances or taking the stairs.	
Coach	You're not as fit as you used to be.	Reflective listening.
Russ	Yes, that's right. I also want to do more with the kids at weekends. For instance, Jody has started cycling and she has asked me to ride round the park with her, and I think I'd feel a bit uncomfortable doing that at the moment.	
Coach	You're keen to be a good Dad.	Affirmation.
Russ	Definitely. And I imagine cycling would help with the weight loss too. . .	

(Continued)

Table 12.1 (Continued)

Coach	Very much. So you can see more than one benefit – quality time with your daughter and personal fitness. Why else might you want to do something about your weight?	Reflection, followed by open question.
Russ	Health. I mean, I've not got any health problems at the moment, and I would like to keep it that way.	
Coach	You want to stay as healthy as possible for as long as possible.	Reflection.
Russ	Right. I know what they say about being overweight putting you at risk of health problems, like diabetes.	
Coach	Any other reasons, Russ?	Open question.
Russ	Well, I think I would just feel better. I don't like the way I look at the moment. It would be good to get back into some of my old clothes.	
Coach	Losing weight might improve both your general well-being and your appearance.	Reflection.
Russ	Exactly.	
Coach	And Russ, let's assume you did decide to do something about your weight. How would you get started?	Not assuming readiness to change. Open question.
Russ	Well, I think I need to start eating better. I tend to just go for what's available and tasty at the end of the day, especially if I'm feeling a bit drained. And I do tend to snack during the day, when I'm not that hungry, to be honest.	
Coach	Let's imagine that you did start to make some changes to your eating habits, Russ. How confident are you that you could keep them up? Again, on a scale of 0–10, where 0 is not at all confident and 10 is very confident?	Start use of confidence scaling question.
Russ	4. . . maybe 5.	
Coach	Why 4, Russ? Why do you think you might be able to keep up a healthier diet into the future?	Open question to elicit more change talk.
Russ	Well, I've been thinking about it for a while to be honest. And I do eat better when I'm at home, so I know I can do it. I guess I've just got to break some unhealthy habits.	
Coach	What other reasons do you think you can be successful?	Open question.

Russ	Well, I've always got a lot of choices. When I'm in a hotel or restaurant there are always healthy options on the menu.	
Coach	You can make different choices each week.... Anything else?	Reflection then open question.
Russ	Well, I'm quite focused when I want to be. Especially at work. I guess I just need to transfer some of that focus to myself!	
Coach	Great ideas! You feel you can definitely do this if you put your mind to it, and you've got a lot of choices.	Affirmation.
Russ	Definitely.	
Coach	And Russ, what would build up you confidence to say a 7 or an 8?	Open question.
Russ	I think I need to plan things a bit more in advance, you know. Not just eat as I fancy...	
Coach	And how would you do that?	Open question.
Russ	I don't know. Perhaps start to put things in my diary, or have some kind of weekly plan, reminding me and including certain kinds of meals, like fish with vegetables instead of a pizza?	
Coach	Great idea. What else might help?	Open question.
Russ	Well, there's the exercise thing as well...	
Coach	And what are your thoughts about that?	Open question.
Russ	Well, there are often gyms in the hotels I stay in. I suppose I could spend some time in there. Never really been my thing though. But it's an option.	
Coach	And what would you see yourself going, if you did decide to spent – I don't know – 30 minutes in a hotel gym?	Open question.
Russ	Cycling I guess. Nothing too strenuous, just to get started...	
Coach	And that would help you get in shape for the cycling with your daughter, too. Can I share with you something other people I work with find helpful?	Asking permission to share information.
Russ	Sure.	
Coach	It's a step counter, or pedometer. Many people can download one onto their phones. And then try and get the number of steps they take each day up to, perhaps, 10,000. It seems to make a big difference to their health and well-being, and even their sleep!	Information sharing, without telling the person what to do.

(Continued)

Table 12.1 (Continued)

Russ	Good idea. I might try that as well.	
Coach	Russ, can I summarize some of the things we've talked about?	
Russ	Sure.	
Coach	So Russ, you're thinking perhaps of losing some weight. Your main reasons for this are to feel better about yourself, stay healthy, look better, and also to help you spend more quality time with your kids, and you mentioned cycling with your daughter. You would also like to get fitter. You feel you can be successful because you're quite a determined person, and you do know how to eat better – you do this at home. You feel the keys to success for you would be to start to do some weekly meal planning, and also to spend some time in hotel gyms doing some cycling on a bike, and we also talked about using a step counter to try to get your daily physical activity levels up to, perhaps, 10,000 steps each day. So, Russ, what's next for you?	Summary. Followed by the 'key question' – "So what's next for you?"
Russ	Well I'm definitely going to...	And on to personalized planning...

Developing yourself

Recommend reading

Motivational Interviewing: Helping People Change. Miller, RM, Rollnick. S. Guilford Press, NY. 2012.

Mastery in coaching. A Complete Psychological Toolkit for Advanced Coaching. Edited by Jonathan Passmore. Kogan Page. 2014.

The Wiley Blackwell Handbook of the Psychology of Positivity and Strengths-Based Approaches at Work. Oades, Steger, Fave and Passmore (Eds.), John Wiley and Sons. 2017.

The Routledge Companion to Wellbeing at Work. Cooper and Leiter (Eds.), Routledge 2017.

Useful web sites

Self Determination theory http://selfdeterminationtheory.org/

Positive Psychology www.authentichappiness.sas.upenn.edu/

Compassionate Mind https://compassionatemind.co.uk/

Self-compassion http://self-compassion.org/

Acceptance and Commitment Therapy https://contextualscience.org/act

Free resources for Acceptance and Commitment Coaching www.actmindfully.com.au/free_ resources

References

Al-Ganmi, A. H, Perry, L., Gholizadeh, L., & Alotaibi A. M. (2016, December). Cardiovascular medication adherence among patients with cardiac disease. A systematic review. *Journal of Advanced Nursing.*, *72*(12), 3001–3014.

Alhola, P., & Polo-Kantola, P. (2007). Sleep deprivation: Impact on cognitive performance. *Neuropsychiatric Disease and Treatment*, *3*(5), 553–567.

Anstiss, T. & Blonna, R. (2014). Acceptance and commitment coaching. Chapter in: *Mastery in Coaching. A complete psychological toolkit for advanced coaching.* Passmore (Ed). Kogan Page.

Anstiss, T. & Gilbert, P. (2014). Compassionate mind coaching. Chapter in: *Mastery in Coaching. A complete psychological toolkit for advanced coaching.* Passmore (Ed.). Abingdon: Kogan Page.

Bandura, A. (1977). Self-efficacy: Toward a unifying theory of behavioral change. *Psychological Review*, *84*, 191–215.

Bandura, A. (2001). Social cognitive theory: An agentic perspective. *Annual Review of Psychology*, *52*, 1–26. Palo Alto: Annual Reviews, Inc.

Bem, D. J. (1972). Self-perception theory. *Advances in Experimental Social Psychology*, *6*, 1–62.

Burgess, E., Hassmen, P., Welvaert, M., & Pumpa, K. L. (2017, April). Behavioural treatment strategies improve adherence to lifestyle intervention programmes in adults with obesity: A systematic review and meta-analysis. *Clin Obes*, *7*(2), 105–114.

Bryson, A., Forth, J., & Stoke, L. (2014). *Does worker wellbeing affect workplace performance.* Department for Business Innovation and Skills. October 2014.

Castelnuovo, Pietrabissa, G., Manzoni. et al. (2008, August). Cognitive behavioral therapy to aid weight loss in obese patients: Current perspectives. *Addiction*, *103*(8), 1381–1390.

Duckworth, A. L., Steen, T. A., & Seligman, M. (2005). Positive psychology in clinical practice. *Annual Review of Clinical Psychology, 1*(1), 629–651.

Edinger, Wohlgemuth W, Radtke et al. (2001). Cognitive behavioral therapy for treatment of chronic primary insomnia. A randomized controlled trial. *Journal of the American Medicial Association, 285*(14), 1856–1864.

Edmans, A., Li, L., & Zhang, C. (2014). *Employee satisfaction, labor market flexibility, and stock returns around the world* (February 21, 2017). European Corporate Governance Institute (ECGI) – Finance Working Paper No. 433/2014.

Ekong, G., & Kavookjian, J. (2016, June). Motivational interviewing and outcomes in adults with type 2 diabetes: A systematic review. *Patient Education and Counseling, 99*(6), 944–952.

Farmer, D., & Stevenson, D. (2017). *Thriving at work: The independent review of mental health and employers.* Retrieved January 20, 2018, from www.gov.uk/government/publications/thriving-at-work-a-review-of-mental-health-and-employers

Fredrickson, B. L. (2004). The broaden-and-build theory of positive emotions. *Philosophical Transactions of the Royal Society B: Biological Sciences, 359*(1449), 1367–1378.

Gomez-Pinilla, F. (2008). Brain foods: The effects of nutrients on brain function. *National Review of Neuroscience, 9*, 568–578.

Gomez-Pinilla, F., & Hillman, C. (2013, January). *Comprehensive Physiology, 3*(1), 403–428.

Gomez-Pinilla, F., & Tyagi, E. (2013, November). Diet and cognition: Interplay between cell metabolism and neuronal plasticity. *Current Opinion in Clinical Nutrition & Metabolic Care, 16*(6), 726–733.

Lourida, I., Soni, M., Thompson-Coon, J., Purandre, N., Lang, I., Ukoumunne, O., & Llewellyn, D. (2013). Mediterranean diet, cognitive function, and dementia. *A Systematic Review. Epidemiology, 24*(4).

Macdonald, P., Hibbs, R., Corfield, F., & Treasure, J. (2012). The use of motivational interviewing in eating disorders: A systematic review. *Psychiatry Research, 200*(1), 1–11.

Marin, M., Lord, C., Andrews, J., Juster, R., Sindi, S., Arsenault-Lapierre, G., Fiocco, A., & Lupien, S. (2011). Review: Chronic stress, cognitive functioning and mental health. *Neurobiology of Learning and Memory, 96*, 583–595.

Miller, R. M., & Rollnick. S. (2012). *Motivational interviewing: Helping people change.* New York, NY: Guilford Press.

Miller, W. R., Wilbourne, P. L., & Hettema, J. E. (2003). What works? A summary of alcohol treatment outcome research. In R. K. Hester & W. R. Miller (Eds.), *Handbook of alcoholism treatment approaches: Effective alternatives* (pp. 13–63). New York & London: Routledge, Taylor & Francis Group.

Nelis, S. M., Thom, J.M., Jones, I.R., Hindle, J.V., & Clare, L. (2016). Goal-setting to promote a healthier lifestyle in later life: Qualitative evaluation of the AgeWell trial. *Clinical Gerontology, 15* (December 2017), 1–11.

Norcross, J. C. (Ed.). (2011). *Psychotherapeutic relationships that work.* New York, NY: Oxford University Press.

Onyechi, K. C. Eseadi, C., Okere, A. U., Onuigbo, L. N., Umoke, P. C., Anvaegbunam, N. J., Otu, M. S., & Ugorii, N. J. (2017). Effects of cognitive behavioral coaching on depressive symptoms in a sample of type 2 diabetic inpatients in Nigeria. *Psychology Research and Behavior Management, 10*, 165–173.

Oswald, A. J., Proto, E., & Sgroi, D. (2015). Happiness and productivity. *Journal of Labor Economics, 33*(4). 789–822.

Parks, A. C., & Titova, L. (2016). Positive psychological interventions. Chapter 21 In A. M. Wood & J. Johnson (Eds.), *The Wiley handbook of positive clinical psychology* (pp. 305–320). Hoboken, NJ: Wiley Blackwell.

Philibert, I. (2005). Sleep loss and performance in residents and nonphysicians: A meta-analytic examination. *Sleep, 28,* 1393–1402.

Pilcher, J. J., & Huffcutt, A. I. (1996). Effects of sleep deprivation on performance: A meta-analysis. *Sleep, 19,* 318–326.

Prochaska, J., & DiClemente, C. (1983). Stages and processes of self-change in smoking: Toward an integrative model of change. *Journal of Consulting and Clinical Psychology, 5,* 390–395.

Ryan, R. M., & Deci, E. L. (2000). Self-determination theory and the facilitation of intrinsic motivation, social development, and well-being. *American Psychologist, 55,* 68–78.

Ryff, C. D. (1989). Happiness is everything, or is it? Explorations on the meaning of psychological well-being. *Journal of Personality and Social Psychology, 57,* 1069–1081.

Ryff, C. D, Keyes, C., & Lee, M. (1995). The structure of psychological well-being revisited. *Journal of Personality and Social Psychology, 69*(4), 719–727. doi:10.1037/0022–3514.69.4.719

Sanders, P., & Joseph, S. (2016). Person-centered psychology. An organismic positive approach to the problems of living and helping people flourish. Chapter 28 In A. M. Wood & J. Johnson (Eds.), *The Wiley handbook of positive clinical psychology.* Hoboken, NJ: Wiley Blackwell.

Seligman, M. (2011). *Flourish. A visionary new understanding of happiness and wellbeing.* New York, NY: Free Press.

Sin, N. L., & Lyubomirsky, S. (2009, May). Enhancing well-being and alleviating depressive symptoms with positive psychology interventions: A practice-friendly meta-analysis. *Journal of Clinical Psychology, 65*(5), 467–487.

Sudhir, P. M. (2017, September). Advances in psychological interventions for lifestyle disorders: Overview of interventions in cardiovascular disorder and type 2 diabetes mellitus. *Current Opinion in Psychiatry, 30*(5), 346–351.

Spencer, J. C., & Wheeler, S. B. (2016, July). A systematic review of Motivational Interviewing interventions in cancer patients and survivors. *Patient Education and Counseling, 99*(7), 1099–1105.

Vansteenkiste, M., & Sheldon, K. (2006). There's nothing more practice than a good theory: Integrating motivational interviewing and self-determination theory. *British Journal of Clinical Psychology, 45,* 63–82.

Wood, A. M., & Tarrier, N. (2010). Positive clinical psychology: A new vision and strategy for integrated research and practice. Clinical Psychology Review, *30*(7), 819–829.

Zhu, N., Jacobs, D., Schreiner, P., Yaffe, K., Bryan, N., Launer, L., Whitmer, R., Sidney, S., Demerath, E., Thomas, T., Bouchard, C., Reis, J., & Sternfeld, B. (2014). Cardiorespiratory fitness and cognitive function in middle age The CARDIA study. *Neurology, 82,* 1339–1346.

Chapter 13

Coaching challenging executives

Manfred F. R. Kets de Vries and Caroline Rook

Introduction

Finding the rational *homo economicus* as described in management textbooks seems to be nothing more than an exercise in futility. Most executives are not paragons of rationality. It is even a truism saying that these people don't exist. Dysfunctional behavior characterizes the actions of too many executives. And when there is rot at the top, the repercussions can be consequential. When a leader's psychological make-up is problematic, it can have a serious contagious effect. If that is the case, the organization itself is in danger of becoming a mirror image of the leader's troublesome behavior patterns (Kets de Vries & Miller, 1984). Furthermore, the resulting toxic organizational culture can make the people who work in these organizations sick (Kets de Vries, 2016). But leadership coaches who have a deep understanding of personality functioning, and are familiar with the appropriate intervention techniques of dealing with these people, can help in addressing these mental health issues in order to bring about more effective leadership practices, and ultimately more healthy organizations (Kets de Vries, 2014a).

In this chapter, we look at the mental health of senior leaders, its impact on the organization, and the role of coaching executives in the workplace. Specifically, we explore four regularly encountered toxic behavior patterns among leaders that can derail their organizations. For each personality type, we describe the conditions underlying the behavior pattern, how to recognize the pattern, how to coach individuals who exhibit this pattern, and provide a real-life case study to illustrate how coaching can bring about better ways of running their organizations.

Theory and evidence

At work, at least one in four people experience mental health issues such as depression or anxiety (Mental Health Foundation, 2017). Although a range of factors may contribute to psychological problems, senior executives in particular are at risk, due to the demands and pressures of the job. For example, factors such as the loneliness at the top, transferential issues regarding authority, and a lack of constructive feedback from peers and team members can turn what were previously very effective ways of working into very unhealthy behavioral patterns (Kets de Vries, Korotov, Florent-Treacy, & Rook, 2015). To illustrate, although a top executive such as Jack Welch, the former CEO of General Electric, can be viewed as quite narcissistic, his specific leadership style helped him to act as a very creative, gifted strategist, willing to take great risks in order to push for positive changes in his organization. We can add, however, that it would not have taken much to transform him into a destructive narcissist, if the people he worked with had blindly listened to him and had been fearful of providing him with feedback needed to keep him solidly grounded in reality (Maccoby, 2004). For people like Jack Welch, leadership coaching was helpful as a check on potentially dysfunctional behavior.

Generally speaking, leadership coaching can be a force for the good in helping executives become aware of toxic behavior patterns. Coaches can encourage executives to make efforts to change and, while doing so, to help an organization flourish (Kets de Vries, 2007). Furthermore, coaches can make executives aware of how they may resort to primitive defense mechanisms such as splitting, denial, and projection that can prevent them from making sound decisions. They can also point out irrational fears, self-defeating behavior patterns, and outdated self-perceptions that could hold them back from healthy functioning and from creating sustainable, high-performance organizations.

The psychodynamic approach

Although different approaches to coaching should be used according to the problems encountered, the psychodynamic approach aims to develop a deeper understanding of what lies beneath the surface of human and organizational functioning (Kets de Vries et al., 2015; de Haan, Culpin, & Curd, 2011). Why this approach can be so effective is that sustainable change cannot be achieved without an understanding of the invisible barriers and root causes that can block change (Kets de Vries, 2006). If the underlying factors aren't dealt with, any attempt at change will turn into a Band-Aid ritual, providing only temporary relief. The psychodynamic orientation enables the client to dive deep into deciphering what is really going on in terms of the motivational forces limiting the achievement of goals, team alignment, and high performance. Through exploring both their past and present histories, clients may realize that many of their feelings, memories, and fantasies are blocked from their immediate awareness but nevertheless influence their thinking and behavior. In creating greater awareness of these various thought processes, the expectation is that executives would no longer remain their prisoners. The insights provided through these interventions would enable them to have a greater freedom of choice (Lee, 2010) and the conditions for mind-set change that's needed for sustainable improvement (Sandler, 2011).

The goal of executive coaches is to expand their client's ability for emotional regulation. Through coaching, they can fine-tune their reflective capabilities to pre-empt primitive defenses – to prevent 'acting out.' As a caveat, what should be added is that in the case of severe personality pathologies, we have to be careful in navigating the boundaries between coaching and psychotherapy. More traditional coaching interventions may turn out to be ineffective, and even damaging, when the client suffers from a severe case of psychopathology (Berglas, 2002).

Ethical boundaries of coaching

Much of what we know about mental health is based on research in the realms of psychotherapy and psychiatry. Indeed, the way learning and development professionals label mental health issues is largely based on insights and research from psychiatry and psychotherapy and in particular the *Diagnostic and Statistical Manual of Mental Disorders* (American Psychiatric Association, 2013), which is the authoritative volume on mental disorders. Based on several decades of clinical research, this classification index defines mental disorders in order to improve their diagnoses and treatment.

Coaches can help executives address mental health issues if the coach understands common personality disorders and is able to tell whether a clinical disorder is present or whether dysfunctional personality and behavioral patterns have developed. The latter can be addressed by a coach through coaching techniques that aim to develop effective leadership. The former needs to be treated, and indeed first diagnosed, by a health professional such as a psychologist or psychiatrist.

Aims and processes

A major mandate of executive coaches is to help executives become more reflective practitioners (Kets de Vries, 2007). While working with their clients, coaches can act as a mirror to reflect their clients' ambitions, strengths, weaknesses, and avenues for positive personal development. By creating a safe transitional space and using their own unconscious as a receptive organ (Kets de Vries, 2007), otherwise 'undiscussable' (Winnicot, 1951) topics can be brought to the surface and dealt with. While doing so, executives may discover that mental and behavioral patterns that may have been effective at one stage in their life have now become counterproductive (Kohut, 1971). In the next section, we will explore in detail four types of challenging personalities: narcissistic, bipolar, psychopathic, and obsessive-compulsive.

The narcissistic leader

A healthy dose of narcissism is needed for effective leadership functioning. Without it, there will not be a foundation for self-confidence, self-expression, and assertiveness (Kets de Vries, 2016). When the narcissistic strivings of a leader become too overpowering, however, their actions can become toxic. What signifies this kind of behavior are leaders' grandiose fantasies about themselves, the exhibition of very selfish behaviors, and having a great sense of entitlement, all qualities that may compel them to pursue their personal interests at any cost.

How to recognize the condition

When referring to narcissism, we should also keep in mind that we are all narcissistic to some degree. It is an excess of narcissism, however, that can make this condition pathological. The foundation of narcissistic pathology is typically set in childhood through defective kinds of parenting (either over-, under-, or inconsistent stimulation), which contributes to the developing child's unstable sense of self. Over time, the child may turn into an insecure adult, who is constantly in search of external validation (Kets de Vries, 2016).

Narcissists know how to exploit others to reach their goals. Due to their high sense of entitlement, they think that rules are not made for them. As such, they do not feel beholden to the rules and moral boundaries that guide other people. And when they do not get what they think they deserve, they are prone to outbursts of anger. These people constantly need to seek the limelight, desperate as they are in searching for admiration, which blinds them to the need of others.

Coaching narcissistic executives

When coaching the narcissistic executive, the coach should avoid anything that might upset the executive's fragile sense of self. Any strong form of disagreement is quickly perceived as a personal attack. Therefore, before presenting the client with his or her dysfunctional behavior, a foundation of trust has to be established as a basis for a safe working alliance. What this implies is that when starting a coaching relationship, the coach should acknowledge the need of their client to be recognized and show empathy to gain his or her trust. This ground-laying work will enable the coach, at a later stage, to help narcissists really deal with their dysfunctional behavior.

The coach should be aware of the fact that narcissists also tend to have a rather binary mindset, meaning that they idealize or devaluate the other. In particular, people in positions of authority are quickly idealized – although (the coach should also keep in mind) devaluation is always around the corner. Not much is needed to have narcissists change their minds. Experienced coaches, however, can use the narcissist's tendency for idealization to gain their initial trust so as to be able to confront some of their dysfunctional behavior patterns at a later stage. Also, given the competitive nature of narcissists, their inner drive to be successful can be leveraged to motivate them to make changes in their behavior.

Apart from one-on-one coaching, the leadership coach could also engage in team coaching (Kets de Vries, 2017) as another way to help address these executives' destructive narcissistic behavior patterns. In a group setting, the narcissistic executive's dysfunctional ways of acting out would become more noticeable. This being the case, group coaching offers the opportunity of the others (not just the coach) to make suggestions for change. In such a setting, the narcissistic executive will find it more difficult to ignore the feedback. The group effect enables the other executives to challenge the narcissist's dysfunctional ways of working with others. Under the influence of peer pressure, the narcissistic executive will more likely make efforts to adapt to more acceptable behavior patterns. Of course, before such a team coaching process can occur and be effective, there should be a minimum amount of trust among the members of the team. Without this trust, it will be difficult to bring about the changes that are needed. The challenge for team members is to give narcissists critical and constructive feedback that can be tolerated in light of this person's fragile self-esteem. Similarly, the leadership coach, in his or her facilitating role, needs to be able to sense what the narcissist can tolerate and be astute to know when "to strike when the iron is cold," meaning to be very careful in judging how far he or she can go.

A case study

Simon entered a coaching engagement to prepare himself for possible succession into the CEO role in his organization. Although he was seen as the most promising candidate within the company, some of the non-executive directors remained doubtful. For example, Simon had embarked on extensive expansion plans despite cautionary feedback from his colleagues. Also, his proposal to buy a corporate private jet, despite the precarious financial situation of the organization, was also seen as a troublesome sign. Simon also seemed to be keen to regularly appear in the press and to bypass the guidelines from the corporate communications department. It was clear that he very much liked the limelight. What added to the various concerns was that some of his colleagues felt somewhat exploited when working with Simon. According to them, he was very good in using others, making him not much of a team player.

Given his tendency to slot people into the positions of either heroes or villains, Simon quickly viewed his coach as an authority figure. His willingness to do so allowed the coach space and legitimacy to bring up more delicate, constructive suggestions. Instead of explicitly targeting problematic and pathological behaviors, the coach framed most of the discussions around the attainment of the ultimate external prize: how to turn the succession to the CEO position into a reality. For example, in his dealings with Simon, the coach did not directly criticize Simon's self-serving demands, but instead reframed the situation, which helped Simon reflect on his actions. The coach commented that although a private jet was very practical for a busy executive like him (hence empathizing with him), at this point in time, this idea might not be the wisest thing to do in the context of the cost-cutting efforts that were occurring throughout the entire organization (providing context and alternative ways of framing the situation). In addition, the coach used Simon's competitive streak to instigate behavioral change. He mentioned that as Simon was in a 'race' with a number of outside candidates for the CEO position, it would more strategic and advantageous to toe the line and adapt to some of the wishes of the non-executive directors. As time passed, the coach, while being very supportive of Simon's ambitions, was able to help him change some of his more dysfunctional qualities.

The bipolar leader

Executives with mild forms of bipolar disorders oscillate between having the feeling that anything is possible to suddenly feeling that everything is hopeless. Whereas challenging or traumatic events in a person's life can lead to depression, the bipolar condition is more of a genetic issue – mostly caused by physical changes in the brain. In more severe cases, this condition needs to be treated with medication (lithium), in combination with psychotherapy (Kets de Vries, 2014a).

What's most challenging with people who suffer from this disorder are their mood swings, thus the popular name of manic-depressive disorder. These mood swings can have a very negative effect on their working and family lives. Given their behavior, people who are bipolar often suffer from a high degree of career derailment, may become estranged from family and friends (due to their disturbing behavior), have problems with promiscuity, may get themselves into financial difficulties, and may be prone to alcohol and drug abuse.

How to recognize the condition

Bipolar executives oscillate between manic and depressive states. In their manic state, they will be full of energy, can be euphoric, and can be extremely optimistic about whatever challenges they are up against. Consequently, their outlook translates into the kinds of leadership behavior patterns that can be greatly inspiring. Their energy galvanizes the others to positively transform projects and organizations. When they are in a depressive state, however, bipolar executives experience a sense of fatigue, are overly pessimistic, and tend to withdraw as they feel a sense of inner deadness.

How to coach bipolar executives

Comparable in establishing a coaching relationship with a narcissist, for executives with bipolar tendencies, the coach needs to help create awareness among these people of the ramifications of their personality make-up. Bipolars need to realize how their behavior affects their relationships with others; that although their behavior can be extremely energizing, their mood swings can also be very destructive. Furthermore, their overly optimistic outlook (when they are on the upswing) can be very visionary, but can also be unrealistic, and in the long term could set the organization up to fail.

In dealing with these people, coaches should realize that the reality-testing abilities of bipolar people are quite limited. In their eyes, the world seems either full of exciting opportunities or is completely hopeless. What's more, to help moderate their mental state, they are not eager to accept the obvious recommendation: to take medication. On the contrary, taking medication can make their life feel flat as it will contain their feelings of euphoria. But although they may be reluctant to take medication, they may be incentivized to change when the consequences of doing nothing are made explicit to them. The coach can also explore with them how, by restructuring their working life, they may acquire a greater sense of well-being. Of course, when dealing with a severe bipolar disorder, psychotherapy combined with medication is needed to stabilize the mental state of the executive.

A case study

Peter was motivated to seek coaching due to a feeling that he was falling apart, which he explained was caused by the pressures that came with his job. Until recently, in his efforts to be a successful entrepreneur, he had been very excited to create new business opportunities for his organization. Now, however, all his responsibilities were becoming too much. As things were, presently, he felt extremely frustrated, overwhelmed by the endless stream of emails and phone messages and the constant demands of the people in the business. Furthermore, what also troubled him was a persistent and ominous fear that his business might go bankrupt.

The coach realized that Peter, without being fully aware of it, subjected himself to a thought pattern called catastrophizing. Given the way his mind was functioning, he expected a disaster to happen at any moment. He also mentioned his bouts of depression, having gone through a very severe one recently. He explained it as a result of his failure to successfully acquire another company. What's more, he took this defeat as a sign that new failures were just around the corner. His fatalistic outlook created in him an enormous amount of stress and a great sense of helplessness.

To obtain more insight into the psychology of Peter, the executive coach asked him if he could talk to some of the people he was in close contact with. After gaining his permission, the coach talked to a number of different executives in the organization to get a better idea how others perceived Peter. It became quickly apparent that Peter had tendencies to micromanage as a way to create 'the illusion of control' to prevent major disasters from happening. At the same time, it was exactly this tendency to micromanage and to take all the responsibilities onto his shoulders that accentuated his level of stress.

As a first step, the leadership coach helped Peter to restructure his job by delegating more tasks and decisions. To find a better way of working gave a great sense of relief and improved his sense of well-being. Also, the coach helped him reframe some of his distorted outlooks on life, creating a greater awareness of his tendency towards cognitive distortions. In addition, the coach pushed Peter to visit a pharmacologically oriented psychiatrist to get the kinds of medication that could help him balance his mood states.

The psychopathic leader

One might also call psychopaths in organizations 'seductive operational bullies' (SOBs) (Kets de Vries, 2014b). Often, their charismatic and Machiavellian qualities help them reach senior executive positions. Given their talents at 'mimicry,' they know how to please the people that count in the organization. Quite eager to win at any cost, many of them have the dedication and business acumen that would create the appearance of success. Most often, however, their success comes at the exploitation and abuse of others. These people are infamous for taking credit for other people's work.

In organizations, psychopathic executives are very talented in making the people they work with emotionally dependent on them; they prey on the emotional vulnerabilities of others. Also, they excel at power plays. Given their seductiveness – their ability to use smoke and mirrors to create the appearance of success – they are often perceived as the ideal employee. If top management does not spot their destructive disposition early on, however, such executives may be slotted for a fast track career to the top, where it will be more difficult to contain their destructive tendencies.

How to recognize the condition

We should keep in mind that when we talk about psychopaths in organizations, we refer to less extreme forms of psychopathy – in other words, psychopaths 'lite.' Usually, when the word psychopath is used, we are referring to a more serious condition in which people are often genetically born with a lack the capacity to form any emotional bonds or do not possess any sense of social responsibility – the people that may end up in prisons. In organizations, SOBs exhibit psychopathic behaviors but are still able to function and even succeed in their environment.

SOB leaders are able thrive because it is so difficult to nail down their dysfunction, due to their exceptional skills at manipulation and impression management. Given their Machiavellian disposition, they are quick to rationalize and convince others of their unethical behavior. Emotionally deficient and lacking a moral conscience, psychopathic executives are unaware of the effect they have on others (Kets de Vries, 2016). They are blind to their own short-comings, obsessed as they are by the game of winning.

Probably, in their early development, executives with milder forms of psychopathy were not necessarily born without having a total incapacity to experience emotions. What exactly contributes to their psychopathic disposition, however, is a nature/nurture puzzle that remains unsolved. In some instances, we can hypothesize that a deactivation of emotional bonding may have developed during childhood through repeated disillusionment and physical or sexual abuse or other forms of mistreatment.

Coaching SOB executives

It is extremely difficult, if not impossible, to successfully coach an executive with psychopathic tendencies, as their emotional capacity is impaired or deactivated. Furthermore, what makes coaching psychopaths such an uphill challenge is the fact that they are exceptionally skilled in manipulating any relationship – including the one with the leadership coach. Psychopathic executives will go through great efforts 'to seduce' the coach, trying to make him or her an ally against other people in the organization – the ones who may have forced coaching onto him or her. Alternatively, the psychopathic executive will try to impress the coach to gain other advantages (Kets de Vries, 2014c). One way, however, to engage in a grounded and meaningful discussion with this kind of executive is to use a 360-degree feedback process to gather perspectives of others, which collectively form a basis for discussion. It could lead to a realistic discussion of the motivation and source of the SOB's people management style.

A case study

Arnold was seen as one of the high potentials in an organization. At the same time, the comment was made that he seemed to 'rub too many people the wrong way.' In order to ensure that he would be a candidate for a fast-track position, coaching had been suggested to help improve his leadership skills. Arnold happily accepted the coaching offer, as he saw it as an indication that he would soon be promoted. Subsequently, the coach conducted a 360-degree feedback leadership survey to help obtain information on how Arnold was perceived by others – and what steps could be taken to improve his leadership skills. Surprisingly to the coach, hardly any of Arnold's colleagues had given him feedback. When a reminder was sent to them to do so, the feedback he received was very negative. From the information given, it was clear that Arnold never owned up to his mistakes. He would shift responsibilities onto others, had no respect for confidentiality, and would quickly take credit for other people's work.

To not alienate Arnold, the coach did not directly confront him about this consistent negative feedback but asked him what he found surprising in the feedback he received; what feedback he saw as fair and what he saw as unfair; and how he might adapt some of his leadership behavior to more productively work with others.

During the coaching process, Arnold tried to convince the coach about the progress he was making. But the coach was quite uncertain if this progress was real. Was what was described as progress merely an exercise in smoke and mirrors? Eventually, despite the reservations of the coach, Arnold did manage to convince his bosses to stop the coaching engagement – that he had changed for the better. Subsequently, he was promoted into a senior position. But not surprisingly to the coach, not long after, Arnold was fired, rumors going around that he was caught in unethical behavior like accepting bribes to steer contracts to specific suppliers.

The obsessive-compulsive leader

Many executives display elements of obsessive-compulsive behavior, as control and order is part of what organizational life is all about. But in some instances, such behavior can go too far. When being perfect becomes the only acceptable standard, it can cause serious problems. Ironically, in their obsession with perfection, executives with this leadership style stifle creativity and impair the workflow of the organization.

Moreover, what makes these people difficult to work with is that obsessive-compulsive individuals often come across as stubborn, unreceptive to considering alternatives, and suspicious of others. They find it hard to build close relationships with colleagues and team members, making them not a natural for effective teamwork.

How to recognize the condition

In many instances, the perfectionism of obsessive-compulsive executives can interfere with their task completion. Often, they act indecisively; the word procrastination is not strange to them. For many of them, the term analysis-paralysis is also very appropriate, as they cannot tolerate making mistakes. But as the expression goes: people who don't make any mistakes, don't do anything. Mistakes are part and parcel of organizational life. No wonder that for these people, decision-making can become such a drawn-out, difficult process. Also, obsessive-compulsives are not very good in establishing emotional bonds. They express affection in a too-controlled manner. They can become quite uncomfortable when dealing with highly emotionally, expressive people. And as is the case of many other personality disorders, the origins of this behavior can be found in childhood. Most likely, the foundation of obsessive-compulsive behavior is created by being exposed to emotionally withholding, overprotective, or overcontrolling caretakers.

Coaching obsessive-compulsive leaders

Through the process of coaching, obsessive-compulsive executives may realize the negative effects and source of their controlling behavior. Also, they may become more aware of the kinds of secondary symptoms that accompany this condition (such as anxiety and depression).

Often, obsessive-compulsive executives don't realize the negative effect that their perfectionism has on others. They are also not aware that their seemingly cold emotional behavior alienates the people they work with. Thus, given their mental outlook, the coach could explore with these executives what 'good enough' rather than 'perfect' would look like. It's essential to allow these executives to accept different ways of working and other ways of achieving success. Also, experimenting with more effective ways of dealing with people will be an important factor in improving their leadership skills.

A case study

Rita was recently appointed as CEO of a large organization after a serious search to fill the position. Although she appeared to be the best candidate for the job, the chair of the board had a number of reservations. He was concerned that her rigid way of working and her obsession with details would make it hard for others to help her be successful in the position. He thought that an onboarding coaching arrangement would be helpful. Rita saw the offered coaching engagement as a good opportunity, in light of her anxiety of being able to deliver.

During the coaching process, the coach explored with Rita the up- and downsides of her rather perfectionistic tendencies. After a number of sessions, she acknowledged her difficulties in prioritizing and in making decisions. She recognized that she should stop tinkering with strategic proposals for board meetings. She should be satisfied in creating a 'good enough' report rather than a 'perfect' one. She had not been aware before that asking her team members to endlessly change strategic documents and project plans frustrated them immensely. Furthermore, from talking to other executives, the coach learned that Rita's workaholism created serious work-life balance issues among the people that worked for her. Upon prompting, she admitted that things at home were not great, particularly as her husband and children found her not only increasingly absent but also emotionally distant.

Gradually, throughout the coaching process, Rita learned to control herself when things did not go 100% her way. She also became better at delegation. This change in behavior gave her more space. It helped her to adopt a more reflective approach to her leadership style, which resulted in much more positive relationships with her team and the board members. Furthermore, it also made for more time for her family.

Conclusion

Executives often fail to recognize their irrational side. They may be oblivious of the negative effects that they have on others. In making this observation, it should be reiterated that irrationality is part of the human condition. All of us have moments of irrationality. Some executives may even be highly successful despite or maybe because of their mental health challenges, as their symptoms may be adaptive and reinforced by the specific organizational cultures they work in. However, in the long term, these executives could also make themselves and others around them sick due to their toxic work behavior. In such cases, as this chapter has shown, leadership coaches can be of great help to spot the danger signs and support the executive in exploring more productive rather than destructive ways of leading. In this chapter, to illustrate this point, we have examined a number of common personality disorders that can be found among executives. We have also outlined a number of intervention techniques available to coaches to tackle these issues in order to create more effective leadership and ultimately healthier organizations.

Thomas Jefferson once said, "Nothing can stop the man with the right mental attitude from achieving his goal; nothing on earth can help the man with the wrong mental attitude." Leadership coaches can do much to make the first observation become a reality.

Developing yourself

Key recommended readings

To find out more about common unhealthy personality patterns found among executives, you can read the following book, which illustrates these further with several case studies and gives suggestions on how coaches can deal with such tricky executives:

Kets de Vries, M. F. R. (2016). *You will meet a tall, dark stranger. Executive coaching challenges.* Basingstoke: Palgrave Macmillan.

To learn more about personality disorders, which can develop out of unhealthy behavioral and personality patterns, the following book gives an introduction to clinical disorders such as narcissistic personality disorder, schizoid personality disorder, histrionic personality disorder, etc. This book also examines in detail how personality disorders develop and how psychologists and psychiatrists assess personality disorders:

Millon, T., Grossman, S., Millon, C., Meagher, S., & Ramnath, R. (2004). *Personality disorders in modern life* (2nd ed.). New York, NY: John Wiley & Sons.

Web resources

If you do not have the time to read a book, this blog will give you a good overview of common unhealthy personality patterns found among executives and gives suggestions on how coaches can deal with such tricky executives:

Kets de Vries, M. F. R. (2014). *Coaching the toxic leader.* HBR Blog. Retrieved from: https://hbr.org/2014/04/coaching-the-toxic-leader

Coaches can help executives address these mental health issues if the coach understands common personality disorders and is able to tell whether a clinical disorder is present or whether dysfunctional personality and behavioral patterns have developed. The latter can be addressed by a coach through coaching techniques that aim to develop effective leadership. The former needs to be treated, and indeed first diagnosed, by a health professional such as a psychologist or psychiatrist. This blog outlines the dangers of coaching when a coach is not able to tell appropriately whether a personality disorder is at play or not:

Berglas, S. (2002). *The very real dangers of executive coaching*. HBR Blog. Retrieved from: https://hbr.org/2002/06/the-very-real-dangers-of-executive-coaching

Following on from the above point, the *DSM-5* defines and classifies mental disorders. Engaging with this *Diagnostic and Statistical Manual of Mental Disorders* that is used by health professionals will give you further insight into existing mental disorders and the latest research findings on their diagnosis and treatment:

American Psychiatric Association (2013). *Diagnostic and Statistical Manual of Mental Disorders (5th Ed.)*. Retrieved from: www.psychiatry.org/psychiatrists/ practice/dsm

If you want to explore more statistics on mental health issues in the workplace, employer case studies, and recent research on mental health, the Mental Health Foundation provides several resources on their website, such as the below e-book:

Mental Health Foundation (2017). *Managing mental health in the workplace*. [E-book] Retrieved from www.mentalhealth.org.uk/publications/managing-mental-health-workplace

References

American Psychiatric Association. (2013). *Diagnostic and statistical manual of mental disorders* (5th ed.). Retrieved from www.psychiatry.org/psychiatrists/ practice/dsm

Berglas, S. (2002). *The very real dangers of executive coaching*. Retrieved from https://hbr.org/2002/06/the-very-real-dangers-of-executive-coaching

de Haan, E., Culpin, V., & Curd, J. (2011). Executive coaching in practice: What determines helpfulness for clients of coaching? *Personnel Review, 40*, 24–44.

Kets de Vries, M. F. R. (2006). *The leader on the couch: A clinical approach to changing people and organizations*. Chichester: John Wiley & Sons.

Kets de Vries, M. F. R. (2007). *Leadership coaching and organizational transformation: Effectiveness in a world of paradoxes*. INSEAD Working Paper, 2008/71/EFE.

Kets de Vries, M. F. R. (2014a). *Coaching the toxic leader*. HBR Blog. Retrieved from https://hbr.org/2014/04/coaching-the-toxic-leader

Kets de Vries, M. F. R. (2014b). The psycho-path to disaster: Coping with SOB executives. *Organizational Dynamics, 43*(1), 17–26.

Kets de Vries, M. F. R. (2014c). Coaching the toxic leader. Four pathologies that can hobble an executive and bring misery to the workplace – and what to do about them. *Harvard Business Review, 92*(4), 100–109.

Kets de Vries, M. F. R. (2016). *You will meet a tall, dark stranger: Executive coaching challenges*. Basingstoke: Palgrave Macmillan.

Kets de Vries, M. F. R. (2017). *How to manage a narcissist*. HBR Blog. Retrieved from https://hbr.org/2017/05/how-to-manage-a-narcissist

Kets de Vries, M. F. R., Korotov, K., Florent-Treacy, E., & Rook, C. (2015). Introduction: A psychodynamic approach to leadership development. In: M. F. R. Kets de Vries, K.

Korotov, E. Florent-Treacy, & C. Rook (Eds.), *Coach and couch: The psychology of making better leaders* (2nd ed.). Basingstoke: Palgrave Macmillan.

Kets de Vries, M. F. R., & Miller, D. (1984). The neurotic organization: Diagnosing and changing counterproductive styles of management. San Francisco, CA: Jossey-Bass.

Kohut, H. (1971). *The analysis of the self.* New York, NY: International Universities Press.

Lee, G. (2010). The psychodynamic approach to coaching. In E. Cox, T. Bachkirova, & D. Clutterbuck (Eds.), *The complete handbook of coaching* (pp. 23–36). London: Sage Publications Ltd.

Maccoby, M. (2004). *Narcissistic leaders: The incredible pros, the inevitable cons.* HBR Blog. Retrieved from https://hbr.org/2004/01/narcissistic-leaders-the-incredible-pros-the-inevitable-cons?cm_sp=Article-_-Links-_-Top%20of%20Page%20Recirculation

Mental Health Foundation. (2017). *Managing mental health in the workplace.* [E-book] Retrieved from www.mentalhealth.org.uk/publications/managing-mental-health-workplace

Sandler, C. (2011). *Executive coaching: A psychodynamic approach.* Maidenhead: Open University Press.

Winnicott, D. W. (1951). *Transitional objects and transitional phenomena. Collected papers: Through paediatrics to psychoanalysis.* London: Tavistock Publications.

Chapter 14

Coaching leaders with neuroscience

Paul Brown and Kate Lanz

Introduction

In the seventeenth century, Newton and his colleagues developed experimental philosophy into what became the science of physics (Newton, 1687). Up to that time, the mysteries of the world had been attributed to an all-powerful God. But such unverifiable explanations (beliefs) gave way, through science, to understanding that there were systematic laws governing the natural world and that accurate and replicable observation could unravel them.

So science, rather than theology, became the way knowledge could be systematically acquired and systemically applied. Argument proceeded not through assertion but through demonstration. In 1660, "Believe no man's word"[1] became (the translation of) the motto of the first scientific society in the world, the Royal Society.[2]

Psychology of the twentieth century, claiming to be the science of human behavior, created a plethora of different schools of psychology. With hindsight, the competing claims of the different schools look more like sources of disputation than accumulations of scientific fact. Human psychology struggled to apply experimental method to tackle core fundamental questions, such as What is the central integrator that we call the Self? Such questions were left to the non-replicable private explorations of ideologically driven and belief-based psychotherapies.

The twenty-first century is creating a body of knowledge that offers the opportunity of a radical reappraisal for understanding human behavior. It is called applied organizational neuroscience. This chapter explores that opportunity with special reference to coaching senior leaders.

Underpinning theory and evidence

Applied neuroscience takes its scientific sources from the research laboratories of the modern neurosciences. The origins of modern neuroscience lie in the well-documented case of the 24-year-old American railway foreman Phineas Gage. In 1848, aged 25, he suffered a catastrophic head injury when a tamping iron rod that he was using to fill a blasting hole in rock with explosive black powder inadvertently caused a spark. That spark drove the tamping iron through his left cheek and out through the top of his skull, causing extensive damage to his left frontal lobe.

Despite the severity of his accident, Gage remained conscious and survived a further 12 years, but with substantial personality changes.[3] Survival after massive head injury was very rare at the time, and so Gage attracted a good deal of medical attention with an increasing focus on his personality changes. From having been a highly reliable and valued worker he became feckless, eventually immigrating to South America where he drove a stagecoach until a series of fits forced his return to the USA. There he died of an epileptic seizure at age 36. What Gage's accident did, however, was start to focus medical attention on localization in the brain – what part of the brain does what? This became of great interest in the twentieth century as electrical stimulation of the brain during neurosurgery allowed detailed mapping of the way the body is represented in the brain (Penfield, 1975).

Prior to an interest in localization, and since classical antiquity, understanding the brain had been essentially the province of exploring its structure through detailed gross anatomy post mortem and, with the nineteenth century's advances in microscopy, drawing its cellular structure. With the advent of clinically useful magnetic resonance imaging of the brain in 1980, however, it became increasingly possible to see the living brain inside the skull working in (almost) real time. Gradually, a new question arose: How is it all connected? This led to the new science of connectomics (Seung, 2012). Connectomics tackles the question of how the specialized regions of the brain interconnect to create a functioning whole that is not conflicted at the boundaries of specialist centers. As an analogy, this has interesting ramifications for organizations, where the energy wasted at the departmental boundaries and in interpersonal conflict is often huge.

A further new science that the modern neurosciences have generated is epigenetics.

In unraveling the gene, twentieth-century science showed that genes control behavior. But some 20 years ago, cell biologists began to focus on the fact that the gene can express itself in a wide variety of ways. But what factors drive this process?

The answer that emerged was 'perception.' The way any one of us 'sees' our world triggers the neurochemistry that is linked to our experience, and our unique experience alone, which immediately informs the DNA at the center of the gene which in turn instructs the RNA to create the particular proteins that will generate specific behaviors (Lipton, 2005, 2015).

Imagine arriving at the office one day, accompanied by a colleague. As you are just about to enter the office building, you suddenly see an old and valued friend who, in the circumstances of busy lives, you have not seen for three or four years. The instant reactions of pleasure on both your parts at meeting unexpectedly would have come without any conscious determination. But they would not be experienced by the colleague with you.

Your reactions would have come from how you instantly and without conscious thought *perceived* the situation. Your colleague, seeing your pleasure, might have had pleasure in your pleasure. But the friend would not have generated the same spontaneous reactions in your colleague as in you. Your perception of your friend upon meeting so unexpectedly is what created your behavior *determined by your own emotional patterning and its underlying neurochemistry*. No stranger that you had passed in arriving at the office that morning had generated such a reaction, though many might have generated reactions of polite avoidance. And had a complete stranger approached you with a smiling face and open arms as your friend did, your reactions would have been very different.

So perception tells the genes how to get the neurochemistry flowing that, among the huge repertoire of responses available to you, will produce the responses from within you that your system expresses. It is part of the purpose of this chapter to show how a coach helps a leader create a perception of him- or her-Self that shifts subordinates' perceptions in such a way that they tune to the leader's brain. This makes for a leader who others willingly follow. Then directional energies are more readily and creatively available to pursue the organization's strategic and operational goals.

Dispenza (2014) has proposed that the deliberate generating of specific perceptions is a largely unexplored tool from whose systematic use individuals might greatly benefit. He recounts his own single case experiment of avoiding extensive spinal surgery after a serious road traffic accident through imaginal rehearsal of his recovery. He also records other clinical accounts of remarkable examples of the way that the self-healing properties of the human body might be mobilized through the use of focused perception. Achieving such goals opens up new horizons for focusing organizational achievements, and what part the leader plays in releasing such power.

It is part of the task of any leader to have the clearest organizational vision (perception) of the future, however uncertain that future might be. Laloux (2014) has shown that there are remarkable beneficial changes in organizational output to be achieved through perceptual (and hence behavioral) shifts. The leader is the agent of such shifts. Coaching a leader is to raise the possibility of such shifts.

Centuries of slowly accumulating knowledge about the brain is beginning to come together very rapidly towards a new formulation of human behavior. It sees human beings as being part of the physical world of energy, *not*, as the twentieth century proposed, some specially favored, higher order psychological beings. Profit or outcome in any organization is the result of the way that human energy has been applied in pursuit of strategic and operational goals. Beginning to see human beings as energy systems raises the fundamental question of how energy is to be released and channeled.

That is the task of the leader. The coach facilitates that process. The starting point is for the leader to understand his or her own brain; for it is that brain to which all other brains in the organization preferentially wish to tune.

Aims and process

The special province of coaching a leader using applied neuroscience, therefore, is to understand that perception controls create the neurochemistry that controls behavior; that the leader can quite easily acquire a working understanding of how his or her own brain functions; and that the prime task of the leader is to get others' brains in tune.

This perspective – that it is the brain of the leader creating the conditions that invite other brains to tune to the leader's brain – is complicated by the very recent understanding that men's and women's brains function differently.

The conclusive evidence for this appeared in December 2013, when the University of Pennsylvania published the composite results of nearly a thousand fMRI brain scans (428 males, 521 females) from healthy individuals aged 8 to 22. Male brains showed high connectivity *within* each hemisphere. Female brains showed high connectivity *between* the hemispheres (Ingalhalikar et al., 2013).

A subsequent paper from the same source (Tunc et al., 2016) showed that male brains are structured to facilitate connectivity between perception and coordinated action, whereas female brains are designed to facilitate communication between analytical and intuitive processing. One possible conclusion to draw from this is that the male brain opts for either/or solutions and wants action, while the female brain opts for both/and solutions and looks for wholeness. In consequence, the male brain is good at problem solving while the female brain is good at solution seeking.

This picture of male and female brains being different is further complicated by the suggestion that the sex of the brain itself may vary along a male-female continuum, and thereby be different from the observable sociobiological sex of the individual (Moir & Jessel, 1989).

We all start out life, embryonically, as female. At around week 6 to 7, those embryos that have XY chromosomes receive a surge of male hormone that starts the process of the embryo becoming male instead of remaining female.

A male foetus may have enough male hormones to trigger the development of male sex organs, but these may not be able to produce the additional male hormones to push the brain into the male pattern. His brain will 'stay' female, so he will be born with a female brain in a male body. In the same way a female baby may be exposed in the womb to an accidental dose of male hormone . . . and end up with a male brain in a female body. . . . Most non-scientists – that is, most people – are unaware of this fundamental fact of life. If most of us do not know that our brains are made differently, it is not surprising that we have difficulty acknowledging, or understanding, each other's differences.

(Moir & Jessel, pp. 24–25)

This, then, is the starting point for using neuroscientific information in coaching leaders – a knowledge that not only are men and women different in the way they behave because their brains are differently connected, but that apparent sex – male or female – is not itself a necessarily reliable guide to the way any one person's brain actually works.

And there is still one further complication. Concepts of leadership have typically been founded on masculine models. There is as yet no working model of what an organization run on feminine (perhaps 'female-brain' would be a better descriptor) principles would look like. In the feminist world of assumed equality between men and women, it has not been acceptable to consider that there actually are differences. So the emergence of women in their own right into organizations has been at the price of teaching women organizationally how to be the best organizational men they can be.

Countering this, there is some accumulating evidence from which deductions can be made about how an organization run on female brain principles might work. Laloux's (2014) fieldwork has shown how people organized for purposes to which they are profoundly attached, generating high-trust settings, and being essentially self-regulating, can create outcomes of which they are proud. Benefits seem to follow, as the proper output of the organization, *not* as its primary purpose. Long-term shareholder value is seen in the way that individuals give of themselves and their skills, making contributions that result in profit, not simplistically being used as a means of profit.

So the brain-aware coach may start out, in coaching a leader, with a crucial conversation about the individual's business philosophy.

In the performance-driven cultures that have been especially characteristic of the past three decades of organizational endeavor in the Western world, the individual is presumed to be an agent whose energies are to be directed, from above, in pursuit of the organization's specified goals. It is a model that saw its apotheosis in the banking crisis of 2008/9. So many organizations have had their business process systems geared up around performance-driven models that such models still persist. Driving people from above is seen as the proper mechanism for engaging human energy, though with the result of an increasing irritation with HR (*Harvard Business Review*, 2015; Brown, Kingsley, & Paterson, 2015).

The new model for the twenty-first-century sustainable organization comes from the brain sciences and relies upon a working assumption of individuals as self-regulating systems. Given the right conditions of leadership, individuals will bring to the organization far more of themselves than can be demanded of them. The leader's key task, therefore, is to know how to release this energy in pursuit of the organization's strategic and operational goals. From this perspective, the primary task in leadership coaching is to help create within the leader the skill to manage his or her own brain-based emotional energy in such a way that it releases the energies of others.

Tools and techniques

Pragmatic business leaders generally love seeing knowledge turned into added value. So the starting point for coaching a leader from a brain-based knowledge point of view is three-fold.

The first is the shared recognition that coaching is designed to change the leader's brain. The second is providing accurate information about how the brain works and what is likely to change and what the intended consequences are. The third is in conducting a method of inquiry into understanding the leader's life processes that have shaped uniqueness, and in so doing develop the leader's understanding of him- or her-Self that is consistent with the first two statements.

The first of the above – a shared recognition that coaching is designed to change the client's brain – comes from the incontrovertible fact that all successfully embedded new experiences, new learning, new insights, and new behaviors *must* be accompanied by changes in the brain, for otherwise there could be no changes in behavior.

There is no way in coaching of not being explicit with the leader about this. It makes for an early and invigorating conversation when, in answer to the typical question early in a first session from the leader that says, "What are we going to be doing, then?" the answer comes, "Change your brain."

Brains do not generally like to be changed – that is to say, operate differently from whatever their preferred mode already is. The brain that got a leader to being a leader is, from the brain's point of view, the best brain to get him or her anywhere else. And in any event, change is a resource-intensive process, and brains like to be economical with their resources. Nevertheless, the purpose of coaching is to facilitate personal change and development which, if it is to be effective, must be represented in neurochemical and structural changes within the brain.

The three most important pieces of information that a coach needs to feel competent in discussing with a leader are the tripartite structure of the brain; the functioning of the amygdala coupled with emotional recognition and regulation; and the new certainty that the brain is essentially driven by its emotional rather than cognitive processes.

So the coaching conversation moves into its second phase of providing accurate information about the brain and what is likely to change and what the intended consequences are for leadership behavior. This stage necessarily arises from the coach's acceptance of assuming professional knowledge about the workings of the brain. Two discrete pieces of information are required for this.

The first is an understanding of the tripartite (sometimes called 'triune') brain and the way it works bottom-up rather than top-down. Figure 14.1. shows this.

A major shift in the modern understanding of the brain is that it is energized by the emotions rather than by thought. When the word 'emotion' is hyphenated into 'e-motion,' knowledge that has long been embedded in the word but only recently understood becomes apparent: Energy = action. Descartes's aphorism that *I think, therefore I am* gives place, in its modern neuroscientifically derived form, to *I feel, therefore I can think I am*.[4]

It is now apparent that, at any moment in time, the brain has prepared itself and the body for action well in advance of that preparedness coming into conscious awareness. So the leader's cognitive system is not primarily to discover and convey rational decisions. It is to discover what the brain has already decided or to help create the conditions under which the brain can arrive at a conclusion. From a brain-based perspective, an essential function of a leader is to be tuned into his or her own feeling system and to be able to make verbal (apparently 'rational') sense of that.

The cognitive system makes sense of what the brain already knows. The brain can organize itself for action within 85 milliseconds, but awareness of that does not arise until 250 ms. This leads to an understanding that our brains are more in charge of us than we are of our brains, and that an understanding of the emotional system that gives meaning to the stimuli of experience is a necessary part of the leader's armamentarium of knowledge. Leaders thereby make sense of their own behavior and can direct attention to what is significant in the observable decision-making of others.

However, a practical understanding of the emotions is complicated by the fact that the very extensive literature on the emotions has established no scientific agreement as to what the emotions actually *are* or what their number are. Brown and Brown (2012), using Goleman's thinking in *Emotional Intelligence* as a starting point (Goleman, 1996), have proposed a working model of the emotions, subsequently defined operationally as "activity in the brain areas that direct our attention, motivate our behaviour and determine the significance of what is going on around us" (Swart, Chisholm, & Brown, 2015). This working model proposes eight basic emotions that trigger behavior along a continuum of escape/avoidance to attachment. Figure 14.2 shows this in its currently developed form.

In practice, it is useful to have both Figures 14.1 and 14.2 reproduced to share with the client. This provides a leader with a visual reference about the science of the brain and the way that basic emotions drive behavior. It also creates a rich and focused conversation that allows the subject of the emotions, which are often disparaged in management conversations, to come into existence. And the coach becomes professionally established within a framework of knowledge that has immediate and practical application to understanding those least-understood phenomena in organizations – the vagaries of human behavior.

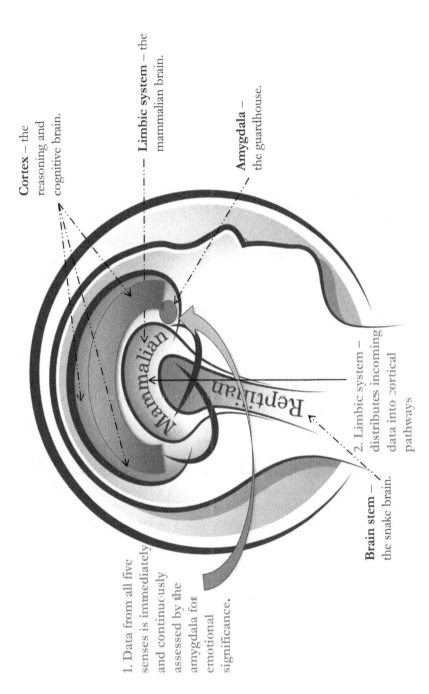

Cortex – the reasoning and cognitive brain.

Limbic system – the mammalian brain.

Amygdala – the guardhouse.

Mammalian

Reptilian

1. Data from all five senses is immediately and continuously assessed by the amygdala for emotional significance.

2. Limbic system – distributes incoming data into cortical pathways

Brain stem – the snake brain.

Figure 14.1 The tripartite brain – stem, limbic system, and cortex

8 BASIC EMO+IⴲNS

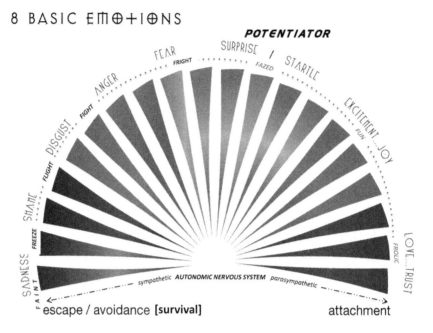

Figure 14.2 The London protocol of the emotions showing the eight basic emotions and their behavioral significance

This leads into an understanding that the leader's brain is a unique brain because of the life experience of the leader creating the consequent perceptions that s/he has. And the same is true for all the brains in the organization.

It is from this understanding that the coach can then move into the third part of the coaching conversation and engage in a systematic inquiry with the leader as to the origins of the leader's own emotional system and uniqueness. This inquiry underpins a proper pursuit of the coaching goals and the means of achieving them.

Damasio (2000) offered the idea that the basic emotions can be considered rather like the primary colors. In the way that three primary colors can create the whole of the color palette, the basic emotions create the whole of the feeling system. This usually makes immediate working sense to a leader, who can begin to see also how the palette of emotions that results in culture within his or her organization creates the behavior that it does. More importantly, perhaps, it starts to create a framework for the leader to understand how and what s/he is continuously transmitting by way of emotional messages. For the other amygdala – all of them, all of the time – in the leader's (part of the) organization are continuously monitoring and modifying the behavior of each individual in turn.

Perhaps the most productive discovery for the leader during this process is that the organization as a whole and each individual in particular can be seen as an energy system. The task of the leader, therefore, becomes one of so managing these individual energy systems (people) that they combine individual outputs into the best possible means of achieving the strategic and operational goals of the organization. As already noted in the Introduction, above, this shift from seeing individuals as primarily psychological systems to understanding them as energy systems is a major revision in this century of understanding organizational behavior.

This understanding also underpins a discussion that might be had with a leader about the difference between a mind-less organization and an organization that is continuously alert, adaptive, and resilient. Siegel has variously proposed (e.g., 2010, 2012) that we can deduce the existence of mind from the workings of a brain that is continuously managing information, energy, and relationship in a dynamic balance. What the second half of the twentieth century has done, it might be observed, is to have maximized information in organizations and ignored energy. Poorly managed energy then presents itself as stress. Much HR has also so circumscribed relationships through protocols of behavior that process-driven organizations in the present century risk becoming mind-less. This destroys the very human qualities of adaptive creativity engendered by the proper flow of information, energy, and relationship that, in a fast-changing world, is of substantial value.[5]

This means that the coach's task is first of all to engage the leader in an agreement about deliberately changing the leader's brain, and in the second place to provide the leader with the kind of information about the workings of the brain that makes both personal and organizational high-value sense to the recipient. The third part of coaching a leader from a brain-based point of view is to conduct an exploration through biographical inquiry that explores the leader's own unique developmental processes and emotional patterning. These are the underpinnings of any leadership style. Coaching brings them into integrated conscious awareness. This then sets the stage for a mutually understood agreement about what it is that will be the focus of change and how that will be achieved.

Brown and Brown (2012) have described a framework called HASIE within which to conduct such a biographical inquiry. It is a synthesis of developmental psychology and applied neuroscience with special reference to organizational experience. Expanded in a research setting by Hasanie (Brown, Hasanie, & Campion, 2018), its essential elements are as described in Figure 14.3.

It starts from the assumption that we are born into a **H**ierarchy and are dependent on others for all our needs. That dependency is played out in multifarious ways within organizational settings.

	Key Elements	Insights
Hierarchy	• Shape of the family/client's role in the family • Key authority figures over time (parents, teachers, bosses)	• Adult personality stems from the client's family experiences • Impacts how client works and relates to authority figures
Attachment	• Significant relationships in the client's early, adolescent, and adult life • Explore how these relationships have evolved over time	• Early attachment experiences shape the way the brain processes information • Insight into how the client relates to others
Siblings	• The nature of the sibling relationship – how it has evolved and current day • What is the client's position in these relationships • Extended family relationships/other close relationships that may of existed	• Insight into how the client works in teams • What is the preferred role in teams • Insight on how this role perception impact goals
Identity	• Explore the client's understand of self • What are the client's major drivers for achievement • How does the client cope with failure • How has the client integrated all their experiences into a functioning approach to life and work	• Identity is formed though experiences over the course of the client's life • Explore the actual versus desired identity • Insight into the key aspects of self (or selves) which impacts the clients approach to life and work
Emotional Tapestry	• Explore the dominant emotions in early, adolescent, and adult life • What were the patterns and themes • What are the dominant emotional drivers for the client – escape versus attachment • What are the drivers for joy and passion	• Emotions are the gateway to understanding why the client behaves the way they do • How do stress triggers impact emotional state • What are the dominant emotions at play for the client (in past and present)

Figure 14.3 The HASIE approach to conducting a biographical inquiry

HASIE Model Overview

Attachment is the second element. It explores the way an individual has learned to manage relationships and helps a leader to make sense of their own style of leadership.

Siblings, present or absent, are the third element, linked to how individuals manage themselves within team settings.

Identity is the fourth element – where and how an observable identity was acquired, nurtured, shaped, and used, together with what its current strengths and limitations might be.

Emotions are the final component, often referred to as the emotional tapestry. It is emotions transmuted into feelings that give meaning and significance to all experience.

These five elements then form the basis of considering the characteristics of any one leader with reference to the model of the brain-aware leader first described by Brown, Swart, and Meyler (2009) as the limbic leader. It is the only leadership model in print that is derived from a combination of developmental psychology and a defined understanding of the emotions. Figure 14.4 shows the six elements that define the limbic leader. It gives special emphasis on the individual's capacity to trust him- or her-Self (the first five elements) as the basis for being trusted (the sixth element).

Trust is itself the interrelationship mechanism by which others' energies will flow in the direction that the leader wishes them to flow. Mobilizing this capacity – to create in others the continuous gift of their own self-regulated

The **limbic leader** is known by having the capacity to --

Connect
> **Be courageous**
>> **Be clever enough**
>>> **Walk own talk**
>>>> **Inspire others into action**

and then ...
>>> **Be worth following**

In all of which the common denominator is trust –
in the first 5, trusting one's Self: and in the sixth,
being trusted.   © P T Brown

Figure 14.4 The qualities of the limbic leader that tune others' brains to the leader's brain; by which means individual energy flows in the direction that the leader wishes it to flow in pursuit of the strategic and operational goals of the organization

energy, deployed in pursuit of the strategic and operational goals of the organization – is the essence of using applied neuroscience in coaching a leader.

Case study

Family companies are complicated by family dynamics – the non-conscious patterns of relating that are so well entrenched in the family that they define that family's style.

Kate came into coaching as the CEO of a niche engineering company, supplying and servicing regulator valve systems in the oil and gas industry. Based in the UAE, with a husband and young son, she had taken the company over from her father in critical circumstances.

Founded by a Swedish grandfather 60 years ago, the company had been run by her father during the boom times of the oil and gas industry. He was a genial, relationship-driven man, hugely successful in creating business, not very interested in controlling it. The company had apparently thrived under his leadership, but neither he nor the company were fit to cope with crisis. The sub-prime banking crisis that started in 2007 followed by structural changes in the oil and gas industry as a result of fracking had put the company under acute financial pressure.

Both Kate and her younger brother Mike – the only boy in their family with three sisters and a mother above him – had trained as engineers. They were both in the company, on its board as family shareholders, and apparently financially secure until the crisis hit. Kate took the lead in encouraging her father to retire, became CEO, and set about finding investors to take the company through the crisis and into a next phase of growth. She found a venture capital company who took a convertible loan option, injecting life-saving capital into the business.

Two issues then arose immediately for Kate as she also learned to become a CEO. The first was that she now had to consider the venture capital (VC) people in all her decisions. They were not shareholders but, if things worked out, they would be. And if things didn't work out, the company would go under and all family assets would have to be liquidated to cope as best as possible with the loan issues.

The second, and it surprised her, was that her younger brother hugely resented that she had taken the lead position. Instead of supporting her, he became truculent.

The HASIE approach let Kate see that she had to learn new patterns of relationship with her VC partners. Coaching used a model of treating them as long-term guests, being informative and welcoming but also managing boundaries in new ways. It focused also on not using old patterns of relationship as if they were family members.

The relationship with her brother proved much more problematic. She began to understand how, as the last arriving child and only boy, he had always expected both to be looked after and indulged. Highly intelligent and analytical, he nevertheless always wanted to get his own way. Truculence had always been his own form of emotional blackmail. Kate learned both to recognize it, manage it, and create for him a strategic role that kept him at the heart of the company's recovery but without significant line authority.

Conclusion

Using knowledge about how the brain works, with an understanding that the emotions are the main drivers of behavior and that individuals are primarily energy systems, enables a coach to inquire into the origins of a leader's individuality. This brings leadership style into informed consciousness. It is then possible to address whatever the specific goals of coaching might be. This starts from an understanding that there are key elements of being a leader that are connected to trusting oneself and, in consequence, being trusted by others. This is the process by which individual energy flows outwards into corporate objectives.

In a wider context of the development of a profession, the chapter has raised the question as to how executive coaches lead themselves forward professionally. It is implicit in the above that a shared body of scientific knowledge, that has at its heart a radical shift of understanding about how human beings work, is an important next stage in the evolution of coaching as a profession (Fillery-Travis & Collins, 2017). What has been outlined here are the starting components of such a body of knowledge and practice.

Notes

1 *Nullius in verba* is its proper Latinate form.
2 The Royal Society of London for the Improvement of Natural Knowledge.
3 See https://en.wikipedia.org/wiki/Phineas_Gage for a detailed account.
4 This reformulation first emerged in a conversation in 2010 between the senior author and executive coach Brenda Hales.
5 There are considerable implications in this for the redevelopment of HR, too.

References

Brown, P. T., & Brown, V. (2012). *Neuropsychology for coaches: Understanding the basics.* Maidenhead, Berks: Open University Press and McGraw-Hill Education.

Brown, P. T., Hasanic, S., & Campion, H. (2018). Applied neuroscience in the context of coaching supervision. In J. Birch & P. Welch (Eds.), *Coaching supervision.* London: Routledge. (in press).

Brown, P. T., Kingsley, J., & Paterson, S. (2015). *The fear-free organization: Vital insights from neuroscience to transform your business culture.* London: Kogan Page.

Brown, P.T., Swart,T., & Meyler, J. (2009). Emotional intelligence and the amygdala: Towards the development of the concept of the limbic leader in executive coaching. *NeuroLeadership Journal, 2,* 67–77.

Damasio, A. (2000). *The feeling of what happens: Body, emotion and the making of consciousness.* London:Vintage Books.

Dispenza, J. (2014). *You are the placebo: Making your mind matter.* New York and London: Hay House, Inc.

Fillery-Travis, A., & Collins, R. (2017). Discipline, profession and industry: How our choices shape our future. Chapter 40 In Bachkirova, T., Spence, G. & Drake, D. (Eds.), *The SAGE handbook of coaching.* London: Sage Publications Ltd.

Goleman, D. (1996). *Emotional intelligence: Why it can matter more than IQ.* London: Bloomsbury Academic.

Harvard Business Review. (2015, July–August). Cover story: *It's time to blow up HR and build something new: Here's how.* pp. 53 *et seq.*

Ingalhalikar, M., Smith, A., Parker, D., Satterthwaite, T. D., Elliott, M., Ruparel, K., . . . (2013, December 2). *Sex differences in the structural connectome of the human brain.* Proceedings of the National Academy of Sciences. Retrieved from www.pnas.org/content/early/2013/11/27/1316909110

Laloux, F. (2014). *Reinventing organizations: A guide to creating organizations inspired by the next stage of consciousness.* Brussels: Nelson Parker.

Lipton, B. (2005, 2015). *The biology of belief* (rev. ed.). New York and London: Hay House, Inc.

Moir, A., & Jessel, D. (1989). *Brain Sex: The real differences between men and women.* New York, NY: Bantam Doubleday Publishing Group, Inc.

Newton, I. S. (1687). *Philosophæ naturalis principia mathematica.* London: The Royal Society.

Penfield, W. J. (1975). *The mystery of the mind: A critical study of consciousness and the human brain.* Princeton, NJ: Princeton University Press.

Seung, S. (2012). *Connectome: How the brain's wiring makes us who we are.* New York, NY: Houghton Mifflin Harcourt Publishing Company.

Siegel, D. (2010). *Mindsight: Transform your brain with the new science of kindness.* London: Oneworld Publications.

Siegel, D. (2012). *Pocket guide to interpersonal neurobiology: An integrative handbook of the mind.* London and New York, NY: W. W. Norton & Company.

Swart, T., Chisholm, K., & Brown, P. (2015). *Neuroscience for leadership: Harnessing the brain gain advantage.* London: Palgrave/Macmillan.

Tunc, B., Solmaz, B., Parker, D., Satterthwaite, T. D., Elliott, M. A., Calkins, M. E., . . . (2016). *Establishing a link between sex-related differences in the structural connectome and behaviour.* Philosophical Transactions of the Royal Society B 371: 2015111 Retrieved July 20, 2018, from http://dx.doi.org/10.1098/rstb.2015.0111

Chapter 15

Coaching super-vision

Damian Goldvarg and Jonathan Passmore

Introduction

As coaching has continued to grow in popularity, coaching practice, and what's considered good practice, has also been evolving, all be it at different rates in different continents. Coaching supervision is one example, and we believe it has a significant role to play as the profession of coaching continues to mature.

Coaching supervision, or as we prefer to describe it, 'super-vision,' can provide a reflective space for coach practitioners to reflect and learn from their own practice. For experienced coaches working with senior executives, it offers the opportunity for the coach to explore issues, think through dilemmas, manage emotions and personal barriers, and engage in meta-learning, drawing from individual cases and critical sessions.

The development of coaching supervision, however, has been diverse. In some continents, such as Europe and specifically in countries like the UK, France, and Germany, supervision is well understood as a developmental tool, widely practiced and well respected. In North America, there are lower levels of engagement and understanding, although all the evidence this can be expected to grow over the coming decade.

Hodge (2016) notes that there is skepticism and general ignorance about coaching supervision and how it works. As a result, many coaches do not engage in supervision, or they believe supervision is only for rookie coaches. Coaching supervision is often misinterpreted as a 'quality evaluative practice,' a 'management role,' or an 'overseeing' of task, reflecting its title of 'supervision' rather than as a collaborative developmental opportunity, which offers value to all coaches, from novices to the most experienced through a process which is about reflecting and looking in more detail; super-vision.

The word 'supervision' may have a negative connotation for other professionals, in part revealing its origins, as a mechanism of supervising the practices of others such as in nursing or clinical services. This hierarchical aspect, however, is unhelpful in coaching supervision. Passmore and Goldrick (2009) argue that separating the word 'super' and 'vision' to create 'super-vision' can help change the meaning and reinforces the idea of a meta-perspective. Super-vision offers the possibility of having a 'vision' from a distance, accessing different views as a result of that distance and in effect providing space for an overview or helicopter perspective of the work taking place in the coaching dyad.

In this chapter, we will explore in more depth the nature of coaching super-vision, clarify some misconceptions, and share some insights from theory and research. We recognize our readers being from diverse traditions; some may either have very limited knowledge of coaching super-vision or have never engaged in super-vision, and others may well have read widely around the topic, been engaged in super-vision for a decade, and even been trained as a coaching supervisor. This chapter is aimed more towards readers who may be experienced coaches, but who have less experience of coaching super-vision. Our aim is to illustrate how coaching super-vision can contribute to the growth and effectiveness of executive coaches, clients, and the wider stakeholders involved in the coaching process, with a particular focus towards coaches working at senior levels within the organization.

Definitions of coaching super-vision

The European Mentoring and Coaching Council (EMCC) defines coaching super-vision as

> the interaction that occurs when a mentor or coach bring their coaching or mentoring work experiences to a supervisor in order to be supported and to engage in reflective dialogue and collaborative learning for the development and benefit of the mentor or coach, their clients and their organizations.
>
> (EMCC, 2015)

It has been suggested that supervision in general serves three functions, which have been broadly accept by professional bodies:

1   The *Developmental* Function

    Concerned with development of skills, understanding, and capacities of the coach/mentor.

2   The *Resourcing* Function

    Providing a supportive space for the coach/mentor to process the experiences they have had when working with clients.

3   The *Qualitative* Function

    Concerned with quality, work standards, and ethical integrity
                                                      (Hawkins & Smith, 2006).

The ICF holds a similar view: "Coaching Supervision is a collaborative learning practice to continually build the capacity of the coach through reflective dialogue and benefit to his or her clients and the overall system" (ICF, 2018). The definition one of us (DG) developed and adopted to train and certify coaching supervisors defines supervision as "the collaborative reflective process to enhance the work of supervisee for the benefit of all stakeholders." For the ICF, coaching super-vision may include:

- Exploring the coach's internal process through reflective practice
- Reviewing the coaching agreement and any other psychological or physical contacts, both implicit and explicit
- Uncovering blind spots
- Ethical issues
- Ensuring the coach is 'fit for purpose' and perhaps offering accountability
- Looking at all aspects of the coach's and client's environment for opportunities for growth in the system

These definitions emphasize:

- the collaborative nature of the supervisory relationship;
- the reflective characteristic of the activity;
- the multiple stakeholders benefited by the practice (coach, client, organizations); and
- the ongoing opportunity for learning, development, and emotional support.

In reviewing the wider literature and diversity of definitions, De Filippo (2016) noted,

> while these definitions are distinct, they agree that coach super-vision is 1) a formal process; 2) is interpersonal and can be undertaken one-to-one, in groups or in peer groups; 3) involves reflection on client work and 4) has goals that include developing greater coaching competence.
>
> (De Filippo, 2016 p. 37)

Responsibilities of a coach supervisor

Five of the main coaching associations (EMCC, AC, APECS, SGCP, and WABC) include coaching super-vision as a requirement for coaches seeking accreditation. The European Mentoring and Coaching Council recommends that coaches get one hour of coaching super-vision for every 35 hours of practice with a minimum of four hours per year.

In comparison, the International Coach Federation (ICF) recognizes coaching supervision as one of the activities appropriate for continuing professional development and suggests that coaches obtain appropriate coaching supervision training in order to fully provide the service.

It is worth noting at this stage that the concept of coaching super-vision emerged from the use of supervision in counseling and other clinical settings. In both the UK and Europe, it has been brought into coaching by individuals working in these domains, who found the practice useful and adapted traditional supervision approaches for their coaching work. The growth of coaching super-vision is thus practice led, as is much of coaching, with individuals finding it useful and continuing to use it as part of their practice.

Proctor (1986), reviewing supervision in nursing and the caring professions, suggested that supervision has three functions: normative, formative, and restorative. The normative function offers direction on ethical and professional practices. The formative function refers to providing a space for learning new models, theories, and tools for use with clients. Finally, the restorative function offers the nursing practitioner a supportive environment to normalize experiences, express emotions, and find support in what can be emotionally challenging work.

According to the International Coach Federation, mentor coaching has been a core practice in the development of professional coaches; however, it is different from coaching super-vision. Coaching super-vision could be considered to focus on building capacity, using reflection as its primary tool. In contrast, the mentor coaches role focuses on helping the coach to acquire specific skills through a review and feedback process. It is thus concerned with capability (ICF website).

How should the executive coach choose a partner for the super-vision work?

The coaching super-visor, like the coach mentor, should have appropriate formal training and a recognized qualification, follow ethical standards, and be held to account by a professional body. As in coaching, the appointment process should be based on pre-determined criteria:

The EMCC has developed a model that establishes six competencies required to perform effectively as a coach super-visor (available at: https://www.

Table 15.1 Six questions to ask a prospective Coaching Super-visor

---

1 What training (qualifications) have they undertaken?
2 What experience have they of delivering supervision?
3 What is their philosophy of supervision?
4 What theories or models do they use in their work?
5 Does the supervisor have their own supervisor?
6 Is the supervisor part of a coaching professional association?

emccouncil.org/wp-content/uploads/2018/01/EMCC_-_competences_-_supervision_-_EN_v2.pdf):

1   Manages the coach super-vision contract and process
2   Facilitates development through a process of collaborative reflection
3   Promotes professional standards and compliance with ethical codes
4   Provides support, prioritizing supervisee well-being
5   Relationship awareness, working effectively with multiple layers of relationships
6   Working with groups, enabling all participants to benefit from the session

Other bodies offer different models. The ANSE (Association of National Organizations of Supervision in Europe) is the largest supervision federation with 9,000 supervisors across 24 European countries, working across disciplines including counseling, therapy, and coaching. Even though ANSE's supervision activity goes beyond coaching, its competence framework has been recognized by the European Union. According to Michel Moral, a leading French coach and supervisor (personal communication, 2018), this framework is more extensive than those currently endorsed by the EMCC, ICF and Association for Coaching.

Coaching supervision research

Coaching super-vision, as a formal practice that follows professional standards, was developed originally in the UK. As a practice, it may have been offered from the onset of coaching training in the early 1990s, but publishing and formal training began, in earnest, in the early 2000s. As noted above, many of the writers and coach super-visors have backgrounds in clinical or psychological settings. Despite this, the literature has remained fairly sparse in comparison with the wider coaching literature.

Hawkins and Schwenk conducted a review on coaching super-vision in the UK and found that 86% of coaches believed that coaches should have ongoing supervision but only 44% received it in 2006 (Hawkins & Schwenk, 2006).

A follow-up study with 428 coaches revealed that from 2006 to 2014 there has been an increase in the number who regularly receive coaching super-vision in the UK, rising from 44% to 92% (Hawkins & Turner, 2017). In comparison, the figure for the US and Canada suggests that the state of development of coach super-vision is at roughly the same point as the UK in 2006, with just under half of coaches indicating they receive coaching super-vision.

However, a larger study, with a sample of nearly 1,000 UK coaches, found significantly lower levels of engagement with coaching super-vision (Passmore, Brown, & Csigas, 2017). This too may be an over-report and reflect social desirability bias, with individuals reporting higher levels of a desirable activity.

Much depends on the sample, with more professional accredited coaches using supervision than individuals who practice less frequently or work as internal coaches inside organizations.

In the same study by Hawkins and Turner, 2017 the authors found that coaches who did receive coaching super-vision did it as part of their commitment to good practice (93%) and as part of their CPD (52%), and only a third as a requirement from the professional body that accredited them (34%). However, the lack of robust empirical research in this area prevents a definitive view as to the long-term benefits of coaching super-vision.

Bachkirova (2015) has argued that the individual's ego development is related to their development as a coach. Using a conceptual encounter research methodology, Bachkirova found that coaches might filter information intentionally or for personal reasons and act accordingly. Some examples include coaches overstepping the boundaries of their practice when working with issues that require referrals to a therapist, challenging clients for their own personal reasons, failing to recognize ethical issues, and colluding with their clients against the organization.

In a study of Australian coaches, Grant (2012) found that there was overwhelming support for coaching super-vision for providing a space for reflection, development of insights, and new perspectives and assuring the delivery of good quality coaching, especially in difficult cases. Grant found that 82% of participants received some sort of super-vision: formal, informal, or peer super-vision. He also found that 30% had a negative experience due to unskilled coach super-visors. Grant noted the main perceived barriers to coaching supervision were finding a good super-visor and the cost of the service.

Hodge (2016) conducted a study on the value of coaching super-vision as a development process for executive coaches. She interviewed six executive coaches and five coach super-visors who engaged in regular supervision sessions. She found that supervisees appreciated the relationship between supervisors and supervisees as well as the process of dialogic reflection to support them in their overall well-being and effectiveness. She concluded, "supervision provides a restorative space for offloading concerns of their personal and professional lives and appreciated the value and reassurance, affirmation, feedback, challenge and encouragement" (Hodge, p. 95). Hodge found that mutual trust, safety, and respect developed over time and were key ingredients to creating a safe place for coaches to explore their practice and clarify dilemmas and doubts in working with their clients.

Lamy and Moral (2015), in their study on maturity, compared coaches, supervisors, and the general public. To address this issue, they sought to understand whether coaching super-visors had a specific defensive style, implementing Bond's Defense Style Questionnaire with 72 items. They found that coaches and super-visors have higher levels of maturity and lower immature ego defenses than the general population, yet there was not a meaningful difference of maturity between coaches and super-visors except that super-visors have a lower level of 'idealization.'

Day and his colleagues (Day, De Haan, Blass, Sills, & Bertie, 2016), in a study of critical moments in coaching relationships, applying a critical incidents technique, found that coaching super-vision can help to manage these challenging situations effectively. Critical moments are unforeseen emotional episodes that can create tension and stress in the client-coach relationship, concluding with new insights and a learning opportunity for the client/and or coach or can effectively break the engagement. Researchers interviewed 28 experienced coaches and found that these critical moments created anxiety and self-doubt in coaches, and the outcome of the experience depended on the capacity for the coach to 'contain' the client's anxiety and provide a reflective space for learning. Some of the most common coaches' anxieties included boundary issues (contracting, triangulations); issues around satisfying outcomes (expectations from stakeholders) and advice; and issues around being more or less directive. They noted that the relational space was key to managing these critical moments effectively and that super-vision helps coaches to understand themselves better, gain reassurance and guidance, and plan.

Tkach and DiGirolamo (2017) reviewed the state of coaching super-vision. They analyzed the diverse range of definitions of coaching super-vision and concluded that even though super-vision plays a valuable role in the industry, there is no agreement regarding what role it should have. They noted, however, common themes around its contribution to practice, which included:

- managing boundaries regarding ethics and confidentiality
- generating organizational learning
- providing support for the coach
- providing quality assurance
- providing ongoing professional development for the coach

Sheppard's (2017) work focused on how coaching super-visees helped or hindered their super-vision. She interviewed 12 super-visees and 7 super-visors and found that super-visees valued the super-vision process and learned a great deal from super-vision. The main inhibitors to the process were anxiety, fear of judgment and shame, lack of urgency, and not seeing themselves as an equal partner to the super-visor. Super-visees enablers included adopting a positive mindset, co-creating the relationship, participating actively in the process, and undertaking supervision training. These factors echo wider research on learning and thus suggest super-vision's key role is as a learning space.

De Haan (2017) conducted a large-scale survey of trust, safety, and satisfaction in coaching super-vision and found from the 518 responses that "experienced coaches are considerably safer, more satisfied and more trusting of their supervisors than was found in comparable research in counseling and psychotherapy" (p. 37). This can be in part because it is not experienced as a mandatory experience and because coaches were able to choose their own supervisors. De Haan noted that when compared with studies on supervision in occupational therapy

(Martin, Kumar, Lizarondo, & Tyack, 2016), the perceived quality of the super-vision is lowered when supervisees cannot choose their supervisor. De Haan also found gender to be a factor in the super-vision relationship with women more open than men, and as a result they receive more support. Additionally, older and more experienced coaches reported higher levels of vulnerable, and higher levels of trust, in their coaching super-visors.

What does this research tell us? Joseph (2016), in his review of publications about business coaching supervision research, noted that studies lacked meth-odological rigor but provided insights into the function and benefits of super-vision. For example, he lists:

> maintaining ethical practice, negotiating complex systems and ensuring that boundaries are appropriate. There are also educational and advise giv-ing functions related to enhancing professional knowledge and under-standing . . . and developmental functions such as self-awareness and ability to reflect on their coaching practice.
>
> (p. 165)

What is clear is that there is a need for more rigorous methods and a move-ment to quantitative research to measure the perceived benefits of supervision, as well as potentially compare it with other methods for continuous profes-sional development. For example, is coach mentoring more or less effective in enhancing ethical maturity? Does this vary with the experience of the coach? Other questions which need to be considered are: Can super-vision can be damaging to individuals? How can coaching supervision be of value as part of a suite of continuous professional development tools?

Coaching supervision models

Among the best-known models is Peter Hawkins's "Seven Eyed Model" that explores three systems in the coaching super-vision practice: client-coach (super-visee), coach super-visor, and the overall system. For the first system, client-coach, there are three eyes or variables to pay attention to: the client, the interventions from the coach, and the relationship between the client and coach. For the second system, coach super-visor, the eyes include the coach and his/her reactions, challenges, and concerns, i.e., the 'who' of the coach, the relationship between super-visee and super-visor, and the super-visor (his/her reactions to the super-visee and the session). Finally, the last eye explores the overall system, i.e., what is going on with other stakeholders, their organiza-tions, and political, economic, and social influences.

A second widely used model is the Full Spectrum Coaching Super-vision model (Murdoch & Arnold, 2013). This model emphasizes "who you are, is how you super-visee," highlighting the relationship between super-visor and super-visee across eight elements within the organizational field.

Table X: Eight elements

> Supervision Tools,
> Energy Management,
> Relationship Building & Sustaining Tasks,
> Self-awareness and support,
> Psychological perspectives,
> Coaching/Counselling Boundaries,
> Contracting and ethics
> Systemic Awareness of Contexts.

(Adapted from Murdoch & Arnold, 2013, p. xxix)

Mike Munro-Turner has proposed the Three Worlds and Four Territories model (Munro-Turner, 2018). This covers the three worlds that the supervisor can attend: the coach's world (and its workplace and wider life), the coaching session (including the coach's world), and the super-vision session. Within each of these three worlds are four territories: insight (sensing what is and what could be in the world), readiness (constraints or enablers in response to the world), authentic vision (desired way of being), and skillful action (transforming vision into action). Turner's model attempts to bring the whole system to the discussion, to encourage new insights for the coach through the discussion.

Clutterbuck (2011) offers the Seven Conversations in super-vision model. This distinguishes seven conversations: the coach's reflection/preparation before the session, the client's reflection/preparation before the session, the coach's internal dialogue during the session, the spoken dialogue, the client's internal reflection during the session, the coach's reflections after the session, and the client's reflections after the session.

Hodge (2016) offers the Three Pillars model. The model aims to provide the conditions for a generative dialogue to enable new knowledge, insights, and learning. The three pillars are:

1   The supervision relationship, in which the safety of the relationship (that allows for vulnerability and feeling) is supported towards learning and growth.
2   Creating the core conditions for adult learning, i.e., establishing a reflective learning space that is voluntary, collaborative, and dialogic. The research shows that making supervision compulsory may have a negative impact on how coaches relate to supervision.
3   Promoting the value of reflective practice. Research into coaching supervision illustrates the value of participants preparing in advance for the super-vision session, as well as writing up their reflections after the sessions.

A final framework is Joseph's model (Joseph, 2017), which aims to provide a structure to assist supervisors in their self-reflection. SAFE TO PRACTICE includes the Systems in which coaching is taking place and its multiple stakeholders, the Agenda for the coaching, and Frequency and Ethical guidelines the coach applies in his/her work. TO focuses on the Theoretical Orientation (such as ontological, co-active, person-centered, systemic) the coach applies to his/her work. PRACTICE relates to Professionalism, Reflectivity, Actions, Challenge, Transparency, Insight, Support, and Empathic engagement.

The growth in models supports the idea that coaching super-vision is becoming more popular and that like coaching models, a wide range of approaches are available. Such diversity allows both the client and the super-visors to make choices about the most appropriate model for any conversation, or to change each super-vision conversation using a different lens to explore issues brought by the client and through these enable the meta-learning to take place, which we have discussed above.

Case study

In this section, we present a case study in order to demonstrate the way Hawkins's Seven Eyed Model can be used with super-visees. In this case study, the super-visor explores two issues that were discussed during the super-vision process with an executive coach working with a senior executive: emotional reactions to the coachee and challenging a client, when the client is stuck and there is a lack of progress.

Vivian started supervision after attending a mentor coaching certification program that I (Damian) facilitated. This helped her to jump into work right away since we had already established trust in our relationship. She was in her late 40s, living in Buenos Aires, Argentina. While we had met in person a few times at ICF Chapter Argentina events, the super-vision process was conducted virtually from my office in Los Angeles, California. Vivian was a successful executive external coach, with a background in HR in a multinational company for many years. She was enthusiastic, energetic, and friendly. Her clients were senior executives from different companies located throughout Argentina.

During our first session, we spent a significant amount of time on the contract and I explained coaching super-vision, including how it works and how executive coaches and senior executives benefit from the process, such as in exploring dilemmas, normalizing situations, developing clarity, and planning strategically in the complex, volatile, uncertain, and ambiguous environment in which they work. We agreed on responsibilities and focus for the process. Vivian wanted to bring to super-vision some challenges working in particular with young senior executives (millennials) and some emotional reactions she had with them. I believe that clear contracting is a good foundation for the coaching relationship as well as the mentor/coaching and coaching super-vision relationships. Many of the challenges coaches bring to super-vision are related to issues associated with lack of effective contracting. Considering this, it's also my belief that super-visors should model effective contracting.

In the subsequent sessions, we explored different clients and issues around coaching young leaders. One case was about a young successful senior executive towards whom Vivian had some conflicting feelings: she wanted to support him while also feeling impatience with his slowness and lack of commitment to the actions agreed on during coaching. He worked for a multinational company, located in Buenos Aires, and was referred by HR to support him in a new challenging position that required new skills, but the executive felt confident about his new job and level of skills and was not sure if really needed extra 'help' to ensure his success. Vivian needed to work with the client to develop trust not only with her but also with the coaching process.

Coaching super-vision is an ideal space to explore triangulation issues between the executive coach, the senior executive, and the sponsor (HR in this case). We spent time clarifying the different stakeholders and system dynamics (eye 2 and 7 from Hawkins's model), and Vivian concluded that there was not enough 'buy in' from the executive to the process. Even though the young executive said he was committed to the process, his behaviors showed something different. Vivian confronted the client and explored what he needed in order to trust her and the process. This worked well, and the client started to demonstrate more interest and commitment to the process. This dance of supporting and challenging the client is a very common issue discussed in supervision.

By exploring her own assessments and feelings of frustration toward the client (eye 4 from Hawkins's model), she realized the client reminded her of her son, who had similar characteristics: both were successful, young, and arrogant. Both felt they did not need any help from anybody. By developing awareness of her 'countertransference' (her own reactions toward the client by projecting her own issues onto the client), she was able to separate her emotional reactions to the client's behaviors and simultaneously be more supportive and better able to confront the client's lack of trust and inaction.

By challenging the client to look at his incongruences, lack of commitment, and own boycotting tendencies, the client was able to stop deceiving himself and finding excuses for not taking action and finally start making progress. The executive was able to commit to develop skills he needed for his new job, such as strategic thinking and working effectively across teams, and start implementing his coaching plan successfully.

Super-vision helped Vivian to see how the personal had intruded into the professional by unconsciously connecting the client to her son and not challenging him effectively. As a result of the awareness, she developed confidence in confronting the client (eye 2, that focuses on interventions from the coach in the Hawkins model) who, as a result, was able to progress on his goals. We also explored the dynamic of our relationship (eye 5 in the Hawkins model) and identified how as a super-visee she may also unconsciously position herself as a 'daughter' of the super-visor (even though both of us are the same age). During supervision, we also worked with the Transactional Analysis model, which helped us to see that the super-visee was having a child/adult relationship with the client, and discussed how to move to an adult/adult relationship instead. Vivian realized that one of her own challenges working with young executives was avoiding falling in the role of mother. She saw that while she enjoys this role, it is accompanied by frustration and a great deal of responsibility – and may not serve her client's growth and development.

Conclusion

This chapter has explored the developing nature of coaching super-vision and presented a range of research and models to help those who may be less familiar with the concept to better understand how it might contribute to their practice in executive coaching. More research is needed to demonstrate its importance and value. While coaching super-vision is not mandatory for all professional coaching bodies, the trend is towards greater use of super-vision in both Europe and North America, as more coaches see how it can enhance their capacity and maturity, as well as provide a space for reflection.

Developing yourself

The main professional bodies recommends that coaches who want to become super-visors pursue formal training. There are a few options, including Henley Business School, which provides training in the UK and in Europe, Africa, and Asia, the Goldvarg Consulting Group that provides a virtual global coach supervision certification, Coaching Supervision Academy, Bath Consultancy, Oxford Brooks, and Ashridge. The EMCC provides coaching supervision programs accreditation following standards of quality. The accreditation is called ESQA (European Supervision Quality Accreditation). In terms of wider reading, the following are useful texts:

Bachkirova, T., Jackson, P., & Clutterbuck, D. (2011). *Coaching and mentoring supervision*. Maidenhead: McGraw Hill.
Cochrane, H., & Newton, T. (2018). *Supervision and coaching, growth and learning in professional practice*. London: Routledge.
DE Haan, E. (2012). *Supervision in action*. Maidenhead: Oxford University Press and McGraw-Hill.
Hawkins, P., & Smith, N. (2006). *Coaching, mentoring and organizational consulting: supervision and development*. Maidenhead: Oxford University Press and McGraw-Hill.
Passmore, J (2011). *Supervision in coaching*. London: Kogan Page.
If you speak Spanish, Goldvarg, D. (2017). *Supervision de coaching para el desarrollo professional del coach*. Buenos Aires: Granica.

For more information on websites:

ICF
https://coachfederation.org/coaching-supervision-4/

EMCC
www.emccouncil.org/src/ultimo/models/Download/7.pdf
www.emccouncil.org/eu/en/accreditation/esia

Association for Coaching
www.associationforcoaching.com/

Association of Coaching Supervisors
www.associationofcoachingsupervisors.com/about-aocs/what-is-supervision/#

Association for Executive Coaching and Supervision
www.apecs.org/

The Americas' Coaching Supervision Network (ACSN) meets monthly, presenting free webinars on topics related to coaching supervision and is open to anybody interested in the topic. There is also a new Asian Coaching Supervision Network starting to offer coaching supervision demos on monthly basis. For more information on both network meetings please contact: info@goldvargconsulting.com.

Every other year there is a Coaching Supervision Conference organized by Oxford Brooks in the UK and another yearly by Lily Seto Consulting and The Goldvarg consulting Group in North America.

References

Bachkirova, T. (2015). Self-deception in coaches: An issue in principle and a challenge for supervision. *Coaching: An International Journal of Theory, Research and Practice, 8*(1), 4-19.

Bachkirova, T., Jackson, P., & Clutterbuck, D. (2011). *Coaching and mentoring supervision* Maidenhead: McGraw-Hill.

Bluckert, P. (2006). *Psychological dimensions of executive coaching.* Maidenhead: McGraw-Hill.

Clutterbuck, D. (2011). The seven conversations in supervision. In T. Bachkirova, P. Jackson, & D. Clutterbuck (Eds.), *Coaching and mentoring supervision.* Maidenhead: Oxford University Press and McGraw-Hill.

Day, A., De Haan, E., Blass, E., Sills, C., & Bertie, C. (2016). *Critical moments in the coaching relationship: Does supervision helps?* Berkhamsted, UK: Ashridge Center for Coaching, Ashridge Business School.

De Filippo. (2016). *Executive coach supervision: The dynamics and effects.* Unpublished doctoral dissertation, University of Pennsylvania.

De Haan, E. (2012). *Supervision in action.* Maidenhead: Oxford University Press and McGraw-Hill.

De Haan, E. (2017). Large-scale survey of trust and safety in coaching supervision: Some evidence we are doing it right. *International Coaching Psychology Review, 12*(1), 37–49.

EMCC (2018). *Coaching supervision.* Retrieved on May 1, 2018, from www.emccouncil.org/quality/supervision/

Grant, A. (2012). Australian coaches' views on coaching supervision: A study with implications for Australian coach education, training and practice. *International Journal of Evidence Based Coaching and Mentoring, 10*(2), 17–33.

Goldvarg, D. (2017). *Supervision de coaching para el desarrollo profesional del coach.* Buenos Aires: Granica.

Hawkins, P., & Schwenk, G. (2006). *Coaching supervision: Maximizing the potential of coaching* [electronic version]. London: CIPD Retrieved from, via www.cipd.co.uk/NR/rdonlyres/5EBC80A0-1279-4301-BFAD-37400BAA4DB4/0/coachsupervca.pdf

Hawkins, P., & Smith, N. (2006). *Coaching, mentoring and organizational consulting: Supervision and development*. Maidenhead: McGraw-Hill.

Hawkins, P., & Turner, E. (2017). The rise of coaching supervision 2006–2014. In *Coaching: An International Journal of Theory, Research and Practice, 10*(2), 102–114.

Hodge, A. (2016). The value of Coaching Supervision as a developmental process: Contributions to continued professional and personal wellbeing for executive coaches. *International Journal of Evidence Based Coaching and Mentoring, 14*(2), 87–106.

ICF. (2018). *Coaching supervision*. Retrieved May 1, 2018, from https://coachfederation.org/coaching-supervision-4

Joseph, S. (2016). A review of research into business coaching supervision. *Coaching. An International Journal of Theory, Research and Practice, 9*(2), 158–168.

Joseph, S. (2017). Safe to Practice. A new tool for business coaching supervision. Coaching. *An International Journal of Theory, Research and Practice, 10*(2), 115–124.

Lamy, F., & Moral, M. (2015). *Who is the supervisor? His(her) profile measured with the defense style questionnaire*. Papers from the Fifth EMCC Research Conference, June 23–24, 2015, Lazarski University, Warsaw, pp. 125–132.

Martin, P., Kumar, S., Lizarondo, L., & Tyack, Z. (2016). Factors influencing the perceived quality of clinical supervision of occupational therapist in a large Australian state. *Australian Occupational Therapy Journal, 63*, 338–346.

Munro-Turner, M. (2018) *3 Worlds 4 Territories: Model of Supervision*. Retrieved on 2 October 2018 from: http://www.theocm.co.uk/sites/default/files/documents/resources/3%20worlds%204%20territories%20model.pdf

Murdoch, E., & Arnold, J. (2013). *Full spectrum supervision*. St. Albans: Panoma Press Ltd.

Passmore, J. (2011). *Supervision in coaching: Understanding coaching supervision, ethics, CPD and the law*. London: Kogan Page.

Passmore, J., Brown, H., & Csigas, Z. (2017). The State of Play in European Coaching and Mentoring: Executive Report. Henley Business School / EMCC: Henley on Thames Retrieved on 2 October 2018 from https://s3-eu-west-1.amazonaws.com/assets.henley.ac.uk/defaultUploads/European-Research-Exec-Report-2017.pdf?mtime=20171129224323

Passmore, J., & McGoldrick, S. (2009). Super-vision, extra-vision or blind faith? A grounded theory study of the efficacy of coaching supervision. *International Coaching Psychology Review, 4*(2), 143–159.

Proctor, B. (1986). Supervision: A co-operative exercise in accountability. In M. Marken & M. Payne (Eds.), *Enabling and ensuring: Supervision in practice*. Leicester: Leicester National Youth Bureau and Council for Education and Training in Youth and Community Work.

Sheppard, L. (2017). How coaching supervisees help and hinder their supervision. *International Journal of Evidence Based Coaching and Mentoring*, Special Issue No 11, 111–122.

Tkach, J., & DiGirolamo, J. (2017). The state and future of Coaching Supervision. *International Coaching Psychology Review, 12*(1), 49–63.

Turner, M. (2011). The three worlds, four territories model. In T. Bachkirova, P. Jackson, & D. Clutterbuck (Eds.), *Coaching and mentoring supervision: Theory and practice*. Maidenhead: Oxford University Press.

Turner, E., & Hawkins, P. (2015). *Multi-stakeholder contracting in coaching AC, EMCC, ICF Research Report*. Retrieved from https://gallery.mailchimp.com/aa3995bc0b72d0fa7c62ce3ae/files/Research_Report_on_multi_stakeholder_contracting_for_the_AC_EMCC_and_ICF_May_2015.pdf

Part 4

Case studies

Chapter 16

Case study

IKEA

Anja Lindberg

Senior managers that ask for coaching, at IKEA and in other organizations, are generally looking for a sounding board, seeking new perspectives on current workplace challenges, time and space for reflection, and support to drive both business and their own individual performance.

Sometimes a coach is wanted for a specific task, such as:

- Providing extra focus and clarity in goal setting.
- Giving perspective.
- Developing new skills and competences.
- Motivating individuals and teams.
- Exploring strengths to carry out change.

In 2005, IKEA started using external coaches. However, as this progressed, the costs of increasing demand for external coaching led to a new approach. In 2008, IKEA decided to invest in an internal pool of coaches. Through internal coaches, IKEA has developed a coaching culture within the organization. After conducting a selection process, IKEA decided to work with us at Coachutbildning Sverige AB (Swedish coach training company). The reasons behind IKEA choosing our company are several: among them are that we have very much the same values and that it is important for both of us to work in a true partnership.

At the first training program, participants were invited to commit at least 10% of their time working with coaching. Selection was based on individuals' understanding of IKEA values and culture and were managers with strong communication skills.

IKEA chose an external provider, Coachutbildning Sverige AB, to deliver the training and support their coaches becoming ICF certified. IKEA's view is that an internal coach should hold the same qualifications as an external coach. Internal coaches should be qualified to support leaders effectively and to ensure this Coachutbildning Sverige AB provided support and the qualification training.

The training provider had close cooperation with the coaching team at IKEA during the development of the first training program. One success factor was that IKEA was very clear on what they wanted to achieve. At the same time, they were listening to ideas and incorporating the provider's experience into the program design.

Apart from adjusting the training to fit IKEA's culture and values, the program included exercises and models to meet the specific demands of IKEA. On example is 'Shop-floor-coaching': short coaching sessions based on the task the client is performing in the moment.

Coachutbildning Sverige AB also contributed to the development of IKEA's coaching policy, for example whether the client can bring up any kind of topic, and should the coaching continue even if the client wants to leave the company. At that time, IKEA choose that the clients were free to bring up any subject at all and to continue coaching even if the client was in a leaving process. Some other companies are more restrictive in their approach.

Initially, coaching could be focused on any topic. More recently, this policy has changed, with coaching focusing more on IKEA's 'Leadership Capabilities' to align the coaching process to the business. However, other topics can also be covered as part of the wider conversation.

After the training, the coaches got mentor coaching and group supervision to get support in handling different types of cases and dilemmas and to develop further.

On completion of the training, coaches join the internal coaching pool. The purposes of the pool are several. One is to help promote coaching within the company and to match clients (coachees) with available coaches in the pool. Another reason behind the set-up of a pool was to give the coaches an opportunity to share knowledge and experience. This ensures support in handling different cases and dilemmas and in developing further as coaches. Throughout the implementation phase, many focused projects were carried out. One project was done in an IKEA store in Sweden, where all managers were given coaching by internal coaches. This project was evaluated with 67% of the managers answering, "yes much" or "yes, very much" on the question of whether coaching had a positive impact on them (33% answered "yes" or "little").

Between 2008 and 2011, four groups of 12 to 16 IKEA employees were trained to become internal coaches. The profiles of these internal coaches were a mix of high-level IKEA managers and human resources professionals, from all over the world. These individuals were asked to commit to delivering 42 sessions per year per coach. The ambition was to provide individual coaching for key managers at IKEA worldwide.

Since 2011, country-based coach pools have been developed. The criteria and education of these internal coaches are exactly the same as in the global pool. At present, there are local pools in France and Spain. These coaches coach in the local language, making coaching accessible for more key leaders who are not fluent English speakers.

Since 2011, every year five to ten IKEA managers and HR professionals take part in open training programs of Coachutbildning Sverige AB. The advantage of this is that it gives the participants insights into how other organizations work with coaching. A disadvantage can be that it does not give the same opportunities of internal networking as the IKEA-specific programs does. The fact that the training is not adapted to IKEA's culture and values has not been perceived as a problem, since these individuals are already established with the culture and ways of working.

Every 18 months, the internal coaches at IKEA are given the opportunity to meet. This is to network and to further develop their coaching skills. In addition, shorter web-based workshops have been given throughout the years. Different trainers and presenters have been invited to teach new models, tools, and ways to apply coaching. The most experienced coaches have also had training from Coachutbildning Sverige AB in 'how to mentor coach,' so now they can provide mentor coaching for individuals as well as for groups within IKEA.

During the spring of 2015, IKEA did an internal study as well as an external benchmark to assess the value of coaching. The purpose was also to determine if the global pool of coaches should continue to be administrated, trained, and followed up centrally.

The main conclusions of the study were:

- The clients who have benefited from the coaching were very satisfied.
- The relationship between the clients' topics and IKEA's needs were not clear enough.
- The amount of coaches is enough to cover the demand today, but the coaches were not being used to their full capacity.
- For the coaches, it is important to have common tools and guidelines and continuous training and supervision.

During the past five years, IKEA has continued to train its coaches. These have often had the focus of combining the coaching approach with leadership. IKEA has included coaching in a number of internal leadership programs. In some programs, the participants get an internal coach to support the participants' development. The coaching approach fits very well with the leadership philosophy within IKEA. As one manager who had coach training put it,

> The big difference between using a controlling leadership and using a coaching approach is that coaching focuses on the person in front of me. Coaching contributes to growth and a more creative behavior. I have gone from being Superman to becoming a coach.

Coaching builds security and confidence, and individuals feel listened to and trusted. This trust helps support a culture where people feel it is safe to take risks and make mistakes, and where there is a focus on trying new ideas and continually learning from engagement with colleagues and customers.

IKEA continues to use external coaches, for senior managers, where independence is a key part of the assignment. The section of these external coaches is focused on their coaching and managerial experience, which ensures that the senior managers get a positive experience from coaching, as well as the business gaining from this external input.

Table 16.1 The IKEA coaching survey

Questions	Responses
1. What do the internal coaches at IKEA get from being coaches, according to them?	* It gives me energy to see how others grow and find their way. Personal development, every time I coach someone I learn something about myself and how I interact with the person A's chance to develop and deepen my coaching skills. * To be a coach is very developing as a human being. You learn a lot about people, as well as about yourself. It is challenging and gives me a good feeling when you succeed with your coaching. * It gives me energy and inspiration. * It gives me energy and different perspectives. It gives me satisfaction and I feel gratefulness in helping people. * The most important thing for me is to be part of another person's development. * Insight into other areas of IKEA, different roles and responsibilities, different ways of thinking, different ways of solving/or not solving problems.
2. What does the coaching give the clients, according to the coaches at IKEA?	* Some of my clients have reached their goals, learned more about themselves which led to better in leading themselves in their daily lives. * Clarity, new and other perspectives, more insights, building on their strength, confidence, more trust in themselves, good feeling, awareness. * Momentum and energy to act on what they want to develop/move to reach their goal. * Clarity on their goal, how to reach it and the energy/trust to get there. * New way to see themselves and the challenges they are facing. * More energy and self-confidence. * Clarity, time to reflect and to hear them self. * Clarity, insights and motivation. * Power to influence their own situation.
3. What are common topics the internal clients at IKEA bring up?	* Energy and inspiration and also clarity and guidance. * Leadership and personal development. * Coping with stress. * Next steps/new job what is right for the person. * Coming into a new role and finding their way. * Help when get stuck in different dilemmas, not knowing what direction to go, or how to deal with a specific situation. * Relationships. * Getting more effective or to reach specific goals. * Broadening themselves – confidence and belief in themselves.

Anja Lindberg, coachutbildning.se, would like to acknowledge the contributions in this case study of the IKEA Coaching Team, and in particular Karin Åkerman, responsible for the Coach Pool at IKEA.

Chapter 17

Case study

Walmart

Josh Rogers

"One more thing . . . what's going on with executive coaching?" This was the question that gave wings to a new body of work that had previously only existed at the periphery of leadership development in Walmart. In his quarterly update with the then CEO, the interim head of talent answered, "I don't know. I'll have to get back with you."

As it turns out, the actual answer to that question was "not that much and what is happening maybe shouldn't be." Despite Walmart's sizeable workforce and longstanding tradition of developing leaders, executive coaching was being used in an ad hoc manner and was seldom tied to developing the organization's top talent. After a short fact-finding mission, a small group from the Talent Management Center of Excellence (COE) found three key themes around the current state of executive coaching:

1 Anyone that was willing to pay for a coach could get a coach – regardless of need or context.
2 Coaches were selling their services directly to the lines of business without being vetted through the Talent COE or HR.
3 A small handful of legacy coaches were paid more in the previous fiscal year than the rest of all of the engagements that were recorded by the COE combined.

As a solution for taming the "Wild West" of coaching, the newly formed executive coaching practice focused on a strategy to define: who should receive coaching (and why), how someone should go about getting a coach, and who should be doing the coaching.

In an organization that had long used coaching as a last ditch effort to save careers or as a remedial fix for poor performers, we thought it wise to start our transformation work with our eCommerce division. This division was typically staffed with less tenured leaders that were unlikely to carry some of the baggage associated with coaching as those in other parts of the enterprise. While this proved to be the case, this pilot presented its own complexities with regard to both a higher turnover trending market in the San Francisco Bay Area as well as the COE's lack of credibility with the segment leaders and HR. Additionally, though this work was triggered by a conversation with the CEO, there was never a clear executive sponsor from any of the lines of business.

After gaining approval for the first pilot from HR leadership, selection protocols were constructed for coachee/client selection. Rather than the long-standing reactive approach of using coaching to address derailing leaders, the new protocols were forward looking around developing top talent officers and future officers:

- Leaders preparing for roles with significantly increased responsibility
- Leaders in transition
- Key external hires
- Talented leaders with a history of success that need support

To go along with these new selection criteria, Walmart instituted a new intake process that involved a meeting with the leader, HR, and coaching practice leader in order to triage and quality control coaching requests. This new process was not met without resistance, as managers were used to making coaching decisions themselves and HR business partners were more accustomed to handling requests from line business leaders themselves without involving talent or COEs. That said, through much storming, the intake practice took hold and began to be generally accepted by leaders and HR alike.

Through this process, though, it revealed how broken the paradigm concerning the target audience for coaching was. Many of the initial intake conversations involved phrases like "we just want to help" or "this is this leader's last chance to turn things around." Although the budget is decentralized for coaching and line leaders have final say on whether to make the investment, we did start to see a shift in coaching spend by taking a more assertive consulting approach. In fact, Walmart saved nearly half a million dollars in the first year of establishing more robust intake protocols by avoiding paying for coaching for performance issues.

Another issue the intake process uncovered was the current coaches' varied capability. It seemed that every leader had "their guy" or "this lady that works magic." As we began to vet coaches, we found that experience levels, backgrounds, and approaches were diverse, to say the least. There were life coaches, former executives, consultants, etc., all acting as executive coaches with, in some cases, minimal experience or training. (There were also some in the system that were very good!) In one particular instance, there was a coach that had done less than five full six-month engagements total, but was charging rates that rivaled the upper end of pricing in the market.

This varied capability led us to form the "Walmart Cadre" of executive coaches who were to be vetted by the COE before being paired with clients. The group was formed of coaches sourced from a small group of coaching providers and a handful of legacy coaches that were crowd sourced from HR.

The coaches entering the cadre went through a series of screening interviews to assess experience, approach, and fit. These coaches then went through an orientation process that included a series of webinars and a one-day in-person meeting where they learned about organizational culture, strategy, and coaching protocols.

Equipped with a solid roster of coaches, the coaching practice was in a place to deploy engagements as a part of a formalized program. We could now sell the benefits of coaches that were not only qualified, but that understood our business and its strategies. Additionally, these coaches could be deployed more quickly to work with leaders despite having a more rigorous intake process. While this cadre approach did not completely eliminate suggestions for using a leader's 'guy,' it did give the coaching practice a practical response to why we should not include a new coach in the system with each new engagement.

With a successful pilot and proof of concept in hand, it was now time to roll out and scale the practice for the rest of the enterprise. As expected, the broader organization went through the same storming phases as the pilot, but over time the practice took hold. However, we were able to point to a change that one of the more progressive wings of the organization had been able to make. Fast forward a few years and the head of talent is now well positioned to answer any surprise questions from the CEO about the state of coaching at Walmart.

Chapter 18

Case study

Coaching academy – the University of Birmingham, UK

Christian van Nieuwerburgh, Ryan Sharman, and Andrew Ktoris

Introduction

As the popularity of internal coaching continues to grow, we present one sector-leading coaching academy as a case study. The Coaching Academy at the University of Birmingham is an initiative that demonstrates how a successful coaching approach can be used to leverage the power of conversation to enable an institution and its people to deliver on organizational and individual priorities.

Internal coaching

The use and development of 'internal coaching pools' has been growing in popularity over the last decade. Coaching industry surveys have been reporting increases in internal coaching over the last few years. One notable example of good practice in the UK public sector is the West Midlands Coaching and Mentoring Pool. This provides access to high-quality coaches across a number of different sector bodies, providing a cost-effective solution during times of financial restraint.

Universities have been early adopters of the idea of developing internal coaches. For example, The University of Warwick, Imperial College London, and the Open University have all developed internal coaches to provide executive coaching within their institutions. The Warwick Coaching and Mentoring Scheme has been available since 2006 and was developed to encourage learning and development conversations beyond normal line management relationships. Imperial College London set up its Coaching Academy in 2009 with the intention of providing additional confidential development support for its staff. The Open University has used its internal coaching resource to support management development programs and provide one-to-one coaching for staff.

The coaching academy – the University of Birmingham

Established in 2014, the Coaching Academy comprises of 35 externally accredited executive coaches who have been trained to provide coaching within the

University of Birmingham. All coaches hold ILM (Institute of Leadership and Management) qualifications. The majority of the coaches have ILM level 5 Certificates in Coaching and Mentoring with the rest holding ILM level 7 Certificates in Executive Coaching or equivalent.

From the outset, it was intended that the Coaching Academy would be strongly aligned to the University of Birmingham's HR strategy. It is led by the assistant director of HR (People and Organizational Development) and is integral to the organizational development function of the University of Birmingham. Currently, the Coaching Academy is firmly positioned within the university's core leadership offer and delivers over 100 coaching assignments annually.

All university staff members have the opportunity to access coaching support through the Coaching Academy. On receipt of a coaching request and approval by the assistant director of HR, a coach is assigned to the coachee before a 'chemistry' meeting is scheduled. The ultimate purpose of the chemistry meeting is to confirm there is sufficient rapport between the coach and coachee to work together on the coaching assignment. Providing the coach and coachee agree to proceed, a three-way contacting meeting is arranged between the coach, coachee, and the coachee's line manager. The purpose of this meeting is to agree on coaching objectives as well as obtain input and feedback from the line manager. One-to-one coaching sessions commence between the coach and coachee before the process ends with a final three-way coaching outcomes meeting. At this meeting, the coach will facilitate a conversation between the coachee and their manager in order to review the extent to which coaching objectives have been realized.

To support the delivery of successful coaching outcomes throughout the coaching process detailed above, the Coaching Academy provides a robust coach support framework for all its members. This includes coaching practice sessions for Coaching Academy members, one-to-one and group supervision arrangements provided by external supervisors, and a choice of Continuous Professional Development (CPD) events to attend throughout the year. Further, coaches are offered an opportunity to attend the annual Coaching Academy conference, join 'buddy' group support groups, and access dedicated coaching resources through a physical and online library.

Key successes

The vision for the Coaching Academy is "to be a highly valued and respected provider of one-to-one executive level coaching for University colleagues at senior levels and be highly respected across higher education as 'best in class.'" Evaluation outcomes indicate the university is well on its way to realizing this ambition. In 2017–2018, all clients reported they were 100% satisfied with the coaching they had received through the Coaching Academy and would recommend the service to a colleague.

Usage of the Coaching Academy continues to grow. Between 2016 and 2018, 200 coaching assignments have been completed. This internal coaching demand can be attributed in part to strong internal communication and to having the support of a senior leader. The success of the Coaching Academy has positioned coaching as a development intervention to support existing formal programs. It is now viewed less as a remedial performance management intervention and more as a way of moving from good to excellent practice. This is supported through significant investment in growing the internal capacity and capability of University of Birmingham coaches. The Coaching Academy has had a positive effect on the 'bottom line,' with a 30% reduction on spending on external coaches in the last 12 months.

Implications for practice

Based on the experiences and learning of the Coaching Academy at the University of Birmingham, the following implications may be helpful to consider when developing an internal coaching resource. These factors have been important for the success of the coaching pool:

- Gaining the support and sponsorship of senior leaders in the organization
- Identifying robust administrative arrangements for delivering the coaching service
- Developing clear and transparent recruitment processes for internal coaches
- Ensuring that coaching assignments focused on the alignment of the goals of the coachee and the organization
- Investing in internal communications that highlighted the benefits of coaching
- Attending to the needs of internal coaches by providing access to coaching supervision and ongoing continuing professional development
- Clarifying policies and procedures for maintaining confidentiality and managing ethical boundaries

Chapter 19

Case study

Genentech

Chris Pollino and Kimcee McAnally

"The call" came in Spring 2009. It was our CEO asking the head of Human Resources, "What is our ROI on executive coaching?" That triggered "the email" from the head of HR to the Executive Talent group looking for the answer. After a two-week flurry of emails, phone calls, analysis, and what has been called "the scramble" by the Executive Talent Development team – the best information available was positive anecdotal comments. The reality was we did not have much concrete information or know exactly how much coaching was happening in the company or how much we were spending. While the executive coaching program was well respected, solid facts were not easily available – and certainly no ROI data.

The Genentech coaching practice had been in place since 2005. We had well-established processes. Twenty-four talented coaches in the network supported the San Francisco campus headquarters and United States commercial operations. We had a positive reputation of being good partners to the business. Our coaching was appropriately focused on leaders' development. All managers were able to learn about coaching via our coaching intranet site where they could view each coach's bio and complete a request form online. However, coaches worked fairly autonomously, fees varied widely, and there was little visibility to how coaching was being delivered.

That same year, Genentech became a member of the Roche Group. Genentech is a 40-year old biotechnology company that discovers, develops, manufactures, and commercializes medicines to treat patients with serious or life-threatening medical conditions. Roche (headquartered in Basel, Switzerland) has operations in more than 100 countries. It was expected the team would be an integral part of merging the two companies and that domestic programs that had been primarily United States focused would soon be asked to become global operations.

The Executive Talent Development team began wondering if there was a better way to free up internal resources, while providing greater visibility and efficiency to the coaching program. While the current program had a quality network of local coaches and established practices, it was time-consuming for internal resources and challenging to track or report on. Also, the team wanted to have a better answer should the CEO or head of HR inquire again. So began the next evolution of coaching at Genentech.

This led to some strategic soul searching, and the decision was made to find a coaching partner who would have the systems, management, and global bandwidth to support a broader coaching practice. The Executive Talent Development team could then focus more on high-level strategy than day-to-day management of individual coaching engagements.

Of importance was a strong desire to retain the experienced external coaching pool that understood the Genentech culture, while locating a provider who would be flexible in adopting Genentech's current processes. The team also wanted to find an external source with industry expertise who could improve efficiency, create a foundation for anticipated future global coaching needs, and be a thought partner with industry research and knowledge.

In early 2012, Genentech conducted a rigorous RFP process, after which the decision was made to select CoachSource as Genentech's partner to provide management services. Over the next few months, the teams worked together to determine roles and transition responsibilities. There were several change management challenges to address, including getting buy-in from the head of HR, convincing existing coaches to stay in the network, and transitioning the processes to the evolved program. The final rollout involved extensive communication to the company, executives, coaches, and functional HR teams.

The Executive Talent Development team continues to be responsible for the overall quality and process design and serves as internal consultants to the business. Our external partner is responsible for day-to-day management of coaching requests, matching coaches for assignments, tracking/reporting coaching activity, and distributing surveys to measure coaching impact and client satisfaction. Together we partner to maintain the coach network and organize meetings with the coaches.

While the coaching program is primarily for directors and above, it has also supported high potentials, middle managers, and individual contributors. The current program supports a variety of coaching service options including 360 feedback, coaching engagements (three months, six months, custom), and acting as part of leadership development programs. In the past five years, the coaching program has supported more than 1,500 Genentech leaders.

A recognized highlight for the coach community is the frequent interactions with other coaches during our 'Coach Community Meetings.' These meetings occur three times a year and involve sharing what is happening in the company, ways external coaches can support new initiatives during coaching, and an opportunity for coaches to share their observations. The result is a cohesive coach community who are better able to support Genentech coaching clients.

Five years later, in addition to retaining the legacy coaches, the Genentech Executive Talent Development team is able to spend more time on strategy and work on global team initiatives. Genentech is able to leverage advanced coaching technologies, track coaching engagements, gather information tied to the business impact, and have a scalable solution with company growth.

And if that ROI call comes in today? Genentech has access to just-in-time data based on a customized coaching survey that analyzes the value of coaching, impact on ROI factors (e.g., revenue, cost savings, productivity, retention), and estimated bottom-line impacts. That same call could be answered the same day with up-to-date accurate data!

Glossary

AC Association for Coaching
www.associationforcoaching.com
AICP Associazione Italiana Coach Professionisti
www.associazionecoach.com/
APECS Association for Professional Executive Coaching and Supervision
www.apecs.org
APS Australian Psychological Society
www.psychology.org.au/About-Us/What-we-do/ethics-and-practice-
    standards/APS-Code-of-Ethics
BPS British Psychological Society
www.bps.org.uk/news-and-policy/bps-code-ethics-and-conduct
COMENSA Coaches and Mentors of South Africa
www.comensa.org.za/Information/CodeOfEthic
EMCC European Mentoring and Coaching Council
www.emccouncil.org
IAC International Association of Coaching
https://certifiedcoach.org/wp-content/uploads/CodeEthics_English.pdf
ICF International Coach Federation
www.coachfederation.org/code-of-ethics
UNM Mentoring Institute, University of New Mexico
https://mentor.unm.edu/
WABC Worldwide Association of Business Coaches
www.wabccoaches.com/includes/popups/code_of_ethics_2nd_edition_
    december_17_2007.html

Index

Note: *Italicized* page numbers indicate a figure on the corresponding page. Page numbers in **bold** indicate a table on the corresponding page.

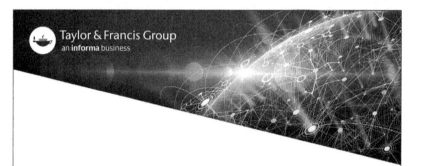

Printed in the United States
by Baker & Taylor Publisher Services